HIGHER
EDUCATION
LEADERSHIP &
MANAGEMENT
SOCIETY, INC

Administrator Evaluation:
Concepts, Methods, Cases in Higher Education
Charles H. Farmer

Published in May 1979
Higher Education Leadership and Management Society, Inc.
Richmond, Virginia

General Editors, John A. Shtogren and W. James Potter
Designer, Philip Meggs
Editorial Consultant, Karen Kevorkian

Library of Congress Catalogue Card Number 79-65285
Printed by The Dietz Press, Inc., Richmond, Virginia
Typography by Coghill Composition Company, Richmond, Virginia

Administrator Evaluation: Concepts, Methods, Cases in Higher Education

By Charles H. Farmer

General Editors:
John A. Shtogren and W. James Potter

Contents

From the Author

As institutions of higher education have become more and more complex and multifaceted, the demand for information on the efficiency of their processes and effectiveness of their products has increased. This call for accountability has given rise to a growing need for explicit and formal evaluation activities of faculty and, more recently, administrators. Traditionally, formal evaluation has had a downward flow. The university evaluates its schools and divisions which evaluate their departments which evaluate their faculty who grade their students. In the past decade a reciprocal upward trend began with students rating their faculty's teaching ability. This upward trend is continuing as procedures for involving faculty and staff in evaluating department chairpersons, deans, and other administrators are being discussed, developed, and implemented.

Although institutions have been slow to participate in administrator evaluation, the large number of interested individuals has led professional associations to consider the issue. The American Association of University Administrators (AAUA) recently exhibited an interest in identifying problems and perspectives on the evaluation of administrative performance in colleges and universities. In the 1976-77 academic year, AAUA offered regional seminars which enabled administrators and faculty to discuss a variety of issues relating to administrator evaluation. The content of the seminars was reflected in the titles of the presentations: The Need for Evaluation, Elements of Evaluation, Specific University Models (Public and Independent), Attributes and Attitudes—What Should be Evaluated?, Strategies for Implementing an Evaluation System, Perils and Pitfalls: Limitations of Evaluation Systems, and The Implications of Evaluation.

Other professional associations have shown similar interest. In February 1977, a three-day conference called "Running Higher Education" was co-sponsored by the Council for the Advancement of Small Colleges

(CASC) and the American Association for Higher Education (AAHE). This conference brought together key figures who were able to speak from their own experiences about current practices of evaluation and development of administrators in higher education.

As a result of participating in these conferences, the contributors to this volume decided there was a need to give more attention to questions concerning administrator evaluation such as: "Why have a formal system for administrator evaluation?," "What techniques and procedures are available and in what situations do they work best?," and, "How can faculty and administrators go about designing a system that would work in their institution?" The information in this volume describes our explorations of these questions. It is not an exhaustive exploration for we feel that even though we have gained many insights, we are still exploring.

This book is organized in four sections and twelve chapters. Charles H. Farmer contributed five of the chapters and the supplementary material in the final section. In Section I, "Issues and Perspectives," his first three chapters address three fundamental questions: "Why Evaluate Administrators?," "How Can Administrators Be Evaluated?," and "Who Should Evaluate Administrators?"

In Section II, "Approaches to Administrator Evaluation," four basic techniques and procedures are presented. In Chapter Four Charles H. Farmer presents the rationale for using rating scales to evaluate administration with an emphasis on the importance of individualizing rating scales. Principles of administrative behavior included in this chapter should be considered when developing such forms.

In Chapter Five, Neal R. Berte and Edward H. O'Neil postulate, as do many humanistic psychologists, that self-actualization in individuals is basic to motivation. Administrator evaluation thus becomes a means for personal and professional improvement in the broadest sense, facilitated by a growth contract. If such contracts are to be used for administrator evaluation, the administrator under review must consider it important to his or her development, and a mentor should be available with the necessary expertise to formulate, refine, and monitor the administrator's improvement plan.

An ad hoc committee model to evaluate academic administrators is given by G. Lester Anderson in Chapter Six. Central to Anderson's model is an evaluation committee which, as the name implies, exists only for the evaluation of an individual administrator. Anderson suggests that the committee's procedures and authority should be determined by negotiation and debate at each institution. In discussing the committee's composition, he clarifies the proper roles of each constituent group and states the case for formal faculty input. The dicta and caveats Anderson gives are axioms for the preservation of human rights and academic values for all administrator evaluation models. The chapter includes a comprehensive list of criteria that will be useful regardless of the approach.

Philip C. Winstead discusses management by objectives (MBO) in Chapter Seven and stresses the importance of individual evaluation within the context of overall institutional performance. The results-oriented concept of MBO strives to measure the efficacy of outcomes against stated criteria based upon specific goals and objectives. Individual performance appraisal is an integral part of the MBO process and comprehensive institutional planning. Winstead defines a useful acronym, S.W.O.T. (strengths, weaknesses, opportunities, and threats), which can be used to structure self-analysis of individuals and organizational units.

In Section III, "Practices of Administrator Evaluation," case studies describe the experiences of three institutions and a state-wide system with administrator evaluation. In Chapter Eight, Charles H. Farmer describes the University of Tulsa's attempt to use rating scales to evaluate top-level administrators and provides an analysis, with the benefit of hindsight, of what should have been done differently.

In Chapter Nine, Dan T. Bedsole describes the Career Development Program for administrators at Austin College. The program is part of an overall staff development program initiated in 1972 and uses techniques similar to the growth contracting approach presented earlier by Berte and O'Neil. Individual administrators prepare five-year plans based on their background, present role, aspirations, and concerns. Long-range and short-range goals are specified in the plan. Each year the administrator works with a colleague who serves as a Career Development Advisor to review progress and revise the plan to reflect new conditions and additional growth opportunities.

An historical overview of the development of presidential evaluation in the State University of New York system is presented in Chapter Ten by Murray H. Block. Because the dominant characteristics of successful presidents are time-dependent, Block cautions against one-dimensional evaluation criteria. A unique feature of the SUNY program is the initial document, "Guidelines for the Review Process for the Chancellor and Presidents," which was developed by a committee of presidents serving in the system. Comments from these presidents and their evaluators provide much insight for institutions contemplating administrator evaluation programs. Quotes from constituent groups indicate both their satisfaction and frustration with the process.

Philip C. Winstead returns in Chapter Eleven to describe Furman University's activities related to MBO and administrator evaluation. Furman is six years into a program which incorporates quarterly performance appraisals for administrators within its overall management process.

Section IV, "Planning a Program of Administrator Evaluation," reviews the insights from previous chapters and looks to the future. In Chapter Twelve, Charles H. Farmer offers recommendations concerning the desirable elements of an administrator evaluation system and suggests steps for getting underway. Caveats and cautions are also discussed so that a reader will gain a realistic view of what can work under various constraints.

In addition, current administrator evaluation programs are briefly described in the Appendix along with the name of a contact person for additional information. Selected sources for further reading are presented in an annotated bibliography.

There are many people besides the contributors to thank for making this book possible. First is Harold L. Hodgkinson who convinced us that gurus in administrator evaluation were not really the "unknowing leading the unsuspecting" and who provided encouragement throughout the duration of the writing. Special thanks go to Mary Lynn Crow who suggested that a book was needed and supported the project from its inception. G. Lester Anderson and Merton W. Ertell contributed valuable assistance and review. The editors Jim Potter and John Shtogren helped to shape coherent thoughts out of the early patternless morass. Coordinators of dozens of administrator evaluation programs gave their time and knowledge. Katherine Frame and Elizabeth Norton in the Office of Institutional Research at the University of Tulsa helped revise and type the manuscript a seemingly infinite number of times.

What began as an attempt to review faculty evaluation of administrators became a search for an understanding of how administrators should be evaluated. We hope that you will find the results of this search helpful for building your own administrator evaluation program.

Charles H. Farmer
Tulsa, Oklahoma
May 1979

Introduction

One of the curious and interesting things about academic life is watching new fields arise before your very eyes. Ten years ago the evaluation of faculty members was still considered by most in higher education to be a risky and immature business. There was little literature and there were few practical handbooks available to help an individual or an institution accomplish their objectives. Today of course, faculty evaluation is well established in most American colleges and universities, and we are now ready to move to a new area of endeavor—the evaluation and assessment of administrators. This book makes a major contribution to the field. It is clear from reading this material that, unknown to most of us, a new field has emerged and has already developed a fairly mature base of techniques and evaluative criteria.

All of the historical evolution of evaluation in other fields is here. The first notion is that ours is a unique field and therefore cannot possibly be assessed in terms of people's performance (faculty were saying that a decade ago, administrators are saying it now). Second is the debate over formative vs. summative kinds of evaluations—the former designed to improve performance, the latter designed to make judgements as to who stays and who goes. The third is the issue of who should have a role in the decision-making process regarding the evaluations. And the fourth has to do with how the results of the evaluation are implemented, either in terms of changing personnel or in terms of trying to improve the performance of those who remain.

This book is a complete digest of where the field of administrative assessment is today. There is a solid bibliography, excellent case materials in institutions that have actually put such programs in place, some theoretical and technical discussions of the nature of the evaluative process, and even some notions as to where the field might go from here. I strongly recommend the material to every member of the faculty and administrative community in higher education. It would seem to me to be worth the price of purchase for anyone who deals seriously with the issues of teaching and learning at the college and university level. I think Mr. Farmer and his colleagues are very much to be congratulated on what is a real contribution to the literature of higher education.

The next step of course might be to look at the evaluation of administrators in other fields who are responsible for education programs—the education directorates in the military, those who run teaching programs in hospitals, the administration of proprietary institutions that have an educational mission, and virtually all of those in any field whose responsibility is the management of an educational endeavor. We know now that this includes churches, old people's homes, the media, health and social agencies, as well as governmental ones. I hope that Mr. Farmer will now pick up this as a next task, given the success he has achieved with the present volume.

Harold L. Hodgkinson
Professional Institute of the
American Management Associations

WHY

Why evaluate administrators?

HOW

How can administrators be evaluated?

WHO

Who should evaluate administrators?

Section I
Issues and Perspectives

Administrator evaluation should not be thought of as merely a tool, a paper and pencil form, used for grading administrators. Although administrator evaluation uses tools, it is best thought of as a broad process involving clarifying role expectations and gathering, analyzing, and weighting information on an administrator's performance. But before the process can be set in motion, three fundamental questions must be raised and answered to provide the proper foundation. Those three questions are: (1) *Why* evaluate administrators? (2) *How* can administrators be evaluated? (3) *Who* should evaluate administrators? Charles H. Farmer answers these three questions in the three chapters in Section I. His discussions suggest answers and alternatives, but it is up to each individual reader to arrive at his or her own conclusions.

In Chapter One, arguments for and against administrator evaluation are reviewed, and the need for specifying the desired functions is stressed.

In Chapter Two, specific criteria and norms are discussed and four approaches or modes are introduced.

In Chapter Three, the question of who should be involved in administrator evaluation is explored. Different levels of personnel are examined for their appropriateness as data sources, judges, and decision-makers.

WHY

Why Evaluate Administrators?

A. Arguments Against
   1. The Diversity Argument
      a. Program Diversity
      b. Leadership Role Diversity
      c. Evaluation Participant Diversity
   2. The Lack-of-Technique Argument
   3. The Political Argument
B. Reasons For
   1. Formative Functions
   2. Summative Functions
   3. Institutional Functions

HOW

How can administrators be evaluated?

WHO

Who should evaluate administrators?

Chapter One
Why Evaluate Administrators?

Charles H. Farmer

The number of college administrators increased from one for every five faculty members to almost one for every four during the mid-1970s (Semas, 1977). Demands for more student services, fund raising, increased enrollment, and fiscal and academic accountability have contributed to the increased ratio of administrators to faculty. Now more than ever, faculty, funding agencies, and the public are asking hard questions about the effectiveness of all administrators and even the necessity of some. A short time ago Robert W. MacVittie (1975) noted, "There has been growing evidence of interest throughout the United States in the more formal evaluation of college and university presidential leadership." That statement is even truer today, and it is not limited to presidential leadership. All levels of administration are now being scrutinized.

There is little disagreement that administrators are and always have been accountable for their performance. As Dexter L. Hanley (1975) said, ". . . you have no choice as to whether you will be evaluated. Willy-nilly, you will be, and so will every administrator. It seems to me to be a part of wisdom to have a say in how and when the evaluation takes place." In higher education then it is not an issue to evaluate or not to evaluate administrators; informal evaluation is being done everywhere. The real issue is to determine the particulars of *why* formal evaluation should be performed in a particular institution. Once this issue is examined in the local setting, and once the reasons are made clear, then the question of *how* shall it be performed becomes of practical importance. But first caveats deserve proper attention.

There are many good reasons for undertaking administrator evaluation. Some institutions believe that evaluation can be an effective way to improve individual administrative performance. Some collect information on administrative functions as part of a comprehensive institutional self-study project. Others are motivated simply by a sense of self-preservation in this era of data-based accountability.

In surveying such reasons, one might be overwhelmed by the reasons why administrator evaluation should be done and wonder why it is not being done on every campus. Who could refute these reasons? The answer is there are many strong voices exclaiming, "Why not, indeed!" Their arguments generally fall into one of three categories: The Diversity Argument, The Lack-of-Technique Argument, and The Political Argument. Each argument is characterized below and is followed by a brief *Yes . . . but* reply. The other chapters in this volume constitute a more substantial rebuttal to these often heard reasons for not evaluating administrators.

Why Not Evaluate Administrators?

The Diversity Argument. Diversity is an attribute in academic settings. Differences in attitudes, beliefs, and points of view are fostered. However, the diversity which strengthens the teaching-learning process is often cited as an inherent weakness for assessing professional competence of the administrators in charge. The following dialogue between a dean and department chairpersons captures the flavor of the diversity argument:

> **Dean:** *The President has just told me I'm going to have to evaluate all you department chairfolks annually so I can systematically determine your pay raises. And the President says he wants us to come up with one uniform system so we can be fair to everyone.*
>
> **Humanities Chairperson:** *Fair?!?!? How can there be one evaluation system which is equally fair to each of us?*
>
> **All Chairpeople:** *(In unison) Impossible!*
>
> **Science Chairperson:** *I manage twenty-five faculty and co-sponsor four major grant projects with two other departments which bring in over a million dollars a year. Also, I personally have to order $200,000 worth of lab equipment each year.*
>
> **Arts Chairperson:** *I only have five faculty and no grants but let me tell you about the time it takes to give those five people the ego support they need to function . . . well, it looks to outsiders like I'm not doing anything.*
>
> **Humanities Chairperson:** *I lead sixty-two full and part-time faculty. And our turnover is so high I'm constantly recruiting, interviewing, reviewing vitas, and dealing with the personnel committee. How can one system evaluate us all? We don't do the same things.*

Program diversity in colleges and universities makes it difficult to answer the question, "Who is in charge?" Usually programs in business and industry are well-structured according to established goals and lines of authority, but in higher education the lines of real responsibility for success or failure are seldom clearly drawn.

Leadership role diversity is another barrier to a simple evaluation system. Effective leaders come in very different shapes and sizes depending on the role they must play. Consider just three legitimate roles:

- The Benevolent-Machiavellian is an administrator who pursues functional goals across departmental lines that have little to do with formal policies or goals of the units involved.
- The Network Negotiator serves as a middleman between polarized constituencies and fragmented sub-units.
- The Project Director operates on a specific task basis with clear products and deadlines.

How can these administrators be evaluated by one system? How do you mix apples, oranges, pears, and pomegranates without making an inedible fruit salad?

Evaluation participant diversity may be one of the most formidable barriers to a valid administrator evaluation system. Consider a unit where members have the following diverse beliefs about evaluation:

- Administrators who believe evaluation can help them grow
- Administrators who believe evaluation is something done to someone else by somebody else
- Administrators who perform effectively and therefore believe that the evaluation is fair
- Administrators who do not perform effectively and therefore believe that evaluation is unfair
- Faculty who have an ax to grind and do so
- Faculty who need to be obsequious and are so
- Faculty who are convinced the evaluation results will never be used
- Administrators who are convinced the evaluation results will be used against them

How could people with such different points of view participate in administrator evaluation and produce uniform, useful information?

Yes, diversity is a problem, but diversity is a fact of academic life—not a reason to abandon systematic examination. Administrator evaluation can meet this challenge by (1) recognizing that different administrative positions need different criteria for evaluating performance, (2) developing strategies to collect data relevant to specific positions, and (3) analyzing data so that inappropriate comparisons of administrators are avoided.

The Lack-of-Technique Argument. Because of the failure of some institutions to successfully implement just and equitable techniques, others are hesitant to begin and rightly so. They hear about the damage a slip-shod evaluation system has done and want no part of it.

> **Administrator:** *Go ahead and evaluate me. Why not use a rating form so you can reduce me down to a number. But just remember my job is to put out fires so I don't really have a neat job description. And remember my so-called peers don't work close enough to evaluate me in any meaningful sense. And don't forget my boss has no idea what I do. So go ahead anyhow and evaluate me, but you won't have me to kick around for very long!*

Evaluation which is superficial will not illuminate an administrator's special worth. No wonder many administrators view evaluation as diminishing their autonomy, security, and self-esteem and attempt to squash it.

Yes, the state of the art of administrator evaluation is still evolving, but the lack-of-technique argument is more emotional than real. Granted it is unlikely that there will ever be a panacea or magic formula that not only works but also makes everyone feel good about evaluation. However, there are some techniques that have been tried and when used with realistic expectations can be very effective. The techniques offered throughout this volume can be reliable and valid, but more importantly humane.

The Political Argument. A third category of reasons to avoid administrator evaluation holds that it is a political process where a good report is more a matter of appeasing constituencies than competent leadership.

> **Administrator:** *Why bother to get an elaborate system of evaluation going? If you don't like me, you'll only pay attention to complaints and ignore data in my favor. If you do like me, you'll forgive a slip or two. You already have your subjective impressions, and evaluation won't change them.*

A common belief is that the academic administrator may be more like a small town mayor than a corporate executive (Sprunger and Bergquist, 1978). Paul Dressel (1976) identified the political nature of administration as one of the major problems associated with administrator evaluation. "Administrators at every level deal with several different constituencies, and the communications addressed to one are often carefully contrived to appeal to that particular group."

The larger the university, the more constituencies exist. Each constituency has its view of the way things should be managed. While pleasing one group, another is likely to be offended. Frequently it is impossible to satisfy more than one constituency at a given time. So during an evaluation, each constituency may be tempted to react to how well the administrator satisfied its special needs—not to how good an administrator he or she really is. Evaluators often substitute hate and halo for thoughtful, objective analysis.

Yes, politics pose problems, especially in a time of retrenchment, but using clear criteria and gathering descriptive data eliminates a great deal of subjective latitude. Instead of the evaluators seeing their role as judgmental, for voting the rascals out, they should describe their view of administrative performance on structured narrative items similar to the following adapted from Alan K. Gaynor (1974):

- To what extent does this administrator have the ability to work with his constituencies, to provide channels through which demands can be articulated, and to provide structures and processes for aggregating conflicting demands?
- Do you feel that this administrator has a sense of what your

academic unit and the university should become in the next five years?

- To what extent does this administrator know the key trustees, administrators, faculty, staff, students, and alumni, how they are organized, what turns them on (and off), how they are likely to react in specific situations, and what they can do for the institution (or against it)?

Furthermore, precautions to insure privacy should be taken with evaluation, especially when it is tied to the reward system. The political aspect of evaluation will be reduced if it is clearly an opportunity for personal growth and development rather than a time of public trial and punishment.

Why Evaluate Administrators?

Genova *et al.* (1976) believe that the primary function of administrator evaluation is to form a basis for establishing and attaining institutional goals. Beneath the rubric of the primary purpose, Genova and his associates listed nine subordinate functions. In addition to their nine, Sprunger and Bergquist (1978) identified an additional three. The twelve functions cluster into three categories: formative, summative, and institutional. Although perhaps not as discrete as their descriptions imply, the three categories help establish primary and secondary reasons for beginning the process.

Formative functions emphasize improving performance by providing diagnostic information to individuals and groups so that remedies can be found for weaknesses as needed. Such reasons include:

- To serve as a basis for administrative development—especially if it incorporates observation, diagnosis, and training
- To help administrators compare their perceptions of their performance with those of superiors, colleagues, and faculty
- To provide a vehicle for team-building
- To determine the factors which influence administrative effectiveness by analyzing evaluation data

Summative functions are more after-the-fact than formative and relate to "bottom line" decision-making. The evaluation provides information for personnel selection, where administrators are in a sense rank-ordered, and for rating unit effectiveness. Such reasons include:

- To determine retention, promotion, and salary decisions
- To formulate and measure an administrator's specific program objective

Institutional functions in administrator evaluation have a broader focus than providing information for improving or ranking administrators. Whether reasons are internal or external to the institution, evaluation data has an impact beyond a single or group of administrators. Such reasons include:

- To explicitly define desired administrative roles and relationships
- To assess the strengths and weaknesses of the administrative staff in order to assign them to appropriate tasks
- To provide information on the degree of congruence between institutional policy and administrative action
- To extend participation in decision-making by permitting staff input in the personnel process
- To serve as a model and inducement for other evaluation processes
- To increase the awareness of administrative efforts and achievements of external audiences, such as legislators and funding agencies

The categories and related functions can be useful for organizing motives for engaging in administrator evaluation. However, rarely will an institution begin with only a single reason in mind, or even a single category of reasons. When beginning to develop a system of administrator evaluation, it is important to realize that there are often multiple and interlocking reasons for such an undertaking. Still it is important to identify each reason separately because each requires particular techniques and requires the involvement of different types of people.

Summary

There are three major arguments for not engaging in administrator evaluation. Some critics maintain that there is too much diversity in the programs, roles, and personalities of administrators and faculty to be able to make sense out of evaluation data. Others complain of a lack of adequate techniques. And some say that the politics of institutions are an insurmountable barrier to objective administrator evaluation.

For each argument against there is a reply which takes the position that administrator evaluation can provide many constructive benefits if institutions are willing to work past the surface problems.

Reasons for doing administrator evaluation can be categorized in three functional areas: summative, formative, and institutional. Whatever the reasons may be, they should be clearly identified and understood by everyone involved. Since form follows function, an ambiguous function for evaluation will result in a morass of procedures serving no purpose.

Bibliography

Dressel, Paul L. *Handbook of Academic Evaluation: Assessing Institutional Effectiveness, Student Progress, and Professional Performance for Decision Making in Higher Education.* San Francisco: Jossey-Bass, 1976.

Gaynor, Alan K. "Preparing the Organization for Effective Response." In Jack A. Culbertson, Curtis Henson, and Ruel Morrison (Eds.), *Performance Objectives for School Principals: Concepts and Instruments.* Berkeley: McCutchan, 1974.

Genova, William J.; Madoff, Marjorie K.; Chin, Robert; and Thomas, George B. *Mutual*

Benefit Evaluation of Faculty and Administrators in Higher Education. Cambridge, Mass.: Ballinger, 1976.
Hanley, S.J., Dexter L. "Evaluating a President." *AGB Reports* (March-April 1975): 42-47.
MacVittie, Robert W. "Trustees and the Evaluation of the Chief Executive Officer." New York State Regents Annual Meeting, March 13, 1975, New York, New York.
Semas, Philip W. "NEA Takes Another Look at College Organizing." *The Chronicle of Higher Education* (July 11, 1977): 7.
Sprunger, Benjamin E. and Bergquist, William H. *Handbook for College Administrator*. Washington, D.C.: Council for the Advancement of Small Colleges, 1978.

Charles H. Farmer is Director of Institutional Research, Executive Assistant to the Vice President for Academic Affairs, and Professor of Mathematics, University of Tulsa.

WHY

Why evaluate administrators?

HOW

How Can Administrators Be Evaluated?

A. Criteria
B. Norms
C. Modes
   1. Rating Scale
   2. Growth Contract
   3. Ad Hoc Committee
   4. Management by Objectives

WHO

Who should evaluate administrators?

Chapter Two
How Can Administrators Be Evaluated?

Charles H. Farmer

A slipshod approach to administrator evaluation with unclear purposes and crude procedures will punish rather than recognize and reward individual efforts. Poor evaluation may drive a person back to the faculty ranks or send him or her packing to another institution faster than low pay and a heavy workload.

In this chapter, the process of developing an administrator evaluation system will move beyond the clarification of functions to (1) describing the elements or criteria of administrative behavior and performance which can be assessed, (2) determining the reference points or norms against which behaviors and performance can be measured, and (3) introducing four modes of evaluation.

What Should be Evaluated?—Criteria and Skills

After the purposes (formative, summative, institutional, or some combination) for undertaking administrator evaluation are clarified, the next step is to decide which aspects of administrator performance should be assessed. There are a number of core attributes and skills which relate to some degree to every administrator from presidents and deans to chairpersons and directors. In Chapter Six, G. Lester Anderson describes in detail numerous criteria which can be grouped into eight categories:

- Education and Experience—job preparation
- Productivity and Efficiency—tangible outcomes
- Performance Criteria—leadership, management, personal performance
- Personal Qualities—personality, values, presence
- Educational Statesmanship—commitment to the intellectual life, academic freedom, scholarship
- Political and Fiscal Astuteness—managing conflict and scarce resources
- Administrative Style—use of authority

- Unique Criteria—special qualities which after all others make or break an administrator

While still broad categories, Anderson's classifications help to identify the dimensions of assessment for any administrator.

In his book *The Unconscious Conspiracy or Why Leaders Can't Lead,* Warren Bennis (1976) looked beyond broad categories of criteria and identified the skills needed for administrative effectiveness. He cited eight specific skills of prime importance for academic leaders:

- Peer skills—the ability to establish and maintain a network of contacts with equals
- Leadership skills—the ability to deal with subordinates and the kinds of complications that are created by power, authority, and dependence
- Conflict resolution skills—the ability to mediate conflict, to handle disturbances under psychological stress
- Information processing skills—the ability to build networks, extract and validate information, and disseminate information effectively
- Skills in unstructured decision-making—the ability to find problems and solutions when alternative information and objectives are ambiguous
- Resource allocation skills—the ability to decide among alternative uses of time and other scarce organizational resources
- Entrepreneurial skills—the ability to take sensible risks and implement innovations
- Skills of introspection—the ability to understand the position of a leader and his or her impact on the organization

Bennis' list of skills span several of Anderson's categories but primarily shows what an effective administrator "should be able to do" in the areas of Performance Criteria, Political and Fiscal Astuteness, and Administrative Style.

At this point, it may seem reasonable to further articulate and complete Bennis' list of skills and abilities in each of Anderson's criterion categories and move on to deciding how information can best be gathered to determine if administrators have what it takes to lead and manage their institutions. However, such a giant step forward may well cause a crucial point in administrator evaluation to be overlooked—effective administrators do not need high marks in all of Anderson's categories or possess all of the skills listed by Bennis. The caveat relative to criteria being raised at this point underscores the necessity of tailoring specific measures to particular administrators in particular roles. *In other words, administrative effectiveness is situationally determined and a valid evaluation system must be individualized to take this fact into account.*

Leadership developers such as Paul Hersey and Kenneth H. Blanchard (1977) and Fred E. Fiedler (1967) have shown that effectiveness is a matter of utilizing the right skills with the right people at the right time. The nature of the task (specific to amorphous) and the nature of the people involved (neophytes to old hands, friendly and not so friendly) dictate the skills and abilities an administrator must have.

James J. Cribbin's (1972) productive leadership patterns shown in Table 1 illustrate the seemingly contradictory, yet nevertheless effective ways administrators can carry out their roles. Effective administrators can exercise authority in different ways—directive, collaborative, or collegial. Under each general approach the climate may be "shape up or ship out" or egalitarian, decisions may be made by the administrator or by group consensus, communication may be downward—"NOW HEAR THIS!"—or free flowing, and so forth.

The conclusion that should emerge from the foregoing comments on the multifaceted nature of administrator effectiveness is that provisions must be made to tailor criteria to specific administrators. As shown in Chapter Four, even rating scales used for across-the-board administrator evaluation can be responsive to the situational needs for administrator skills. A more comprehensive approach proposed by Carol Zion (1978) calls for a clear rationale and role definition for each administrative position including skills and abilities which are essential for fulfilling that specific role. Thus, by comparing an individual's current capabilities against job requirements, individualized administrative development plans can be formulated and a foundation laid for subsequent evaluation.

What Bench Marks Should be Used?—Norms

Criteria deal with the question, "What areas of performance should be evaluated?". Norms refer to the question, "How good does performance have to be?" The end product of administrator evaluation is a value judgment about an individual's current ability to function in his or her role. *Good, Poor, Adequate, Needs to Improve,* or *Excellent* are words which commonly crop up, but more importantly such adjectives need to be linked to specific bench marks to become meaningful—good, poor, excellent, *as compared to what?*

Charles F. Fisher (1977) noted six types of norms which could be used to assess attributes in various criterion categories:

- His or her predecessors in the position
- All other individuals currently in similar positions
- A "platonic ideal" performance
- One's past performance
- One's own performance goals
- The performance expectations others have of him or her

Each of the six types of norms can be useful for making comparisons and arriving at judgments about the current and desired level of an administrator's performance. However, because of the strong element of diversity in administrator roles and the skills and abilities needed for

Table 1

MANAGERIAL VARIABLE	NON-PRODUCTIVE LEADERSHIP PATTERNS				PRODUCTIVE LEADERSHIP PATTERNS		
	Autocratic	**Accommodative**	**Paternalistic**	**Bureaucratic**	**Directive**	**Collaborative**	**Collegial**
RIGHT TO LEAD (BASIS OF LEADERSHIP)	Coercive Power	Ability to Avoid "Waves"	Personal Loyalty of Subordinates	Position Power	Competence and Forcefulness of Personality	Acceptance by the Group	Recognition by Peers
MANAGEMENT BEHAVIOR	Domineering	Undemanding	Protective	Ritualistic	Dominant and Directive	Consultative	Catalytic
LEADERSHIP TONE	Despotic	Live and Let Live	Avuncular	Protocol Sensitive	Exacting But Fair	Supportive	First Among Equals
ROLE OF THE LEADER	Driver	Figure Head	Shepherd (Emotional Supporter)	Overseer	Energizer—Compeller	Stimulator, Team Builder	Integrator
CLIMATE CREATED	Fear—Hate	Apathy	Harmony at All Costs	"Don't Volunteer"	Shape-Up or Ship-Out	Cooperative	Egalitarian
ACHIEVEMENT ORIENTATION	Obedience	Compromise	Please the Father Figure	Conformity	Meet the High Expectations of the Leader	Cooperate to Achieve Group Goals	Work for Team Success
DECISION PROCESS	Dictatorial Imposition	Expedience	Papa Knows Best	Official Policies and Procedures	Adjudication by Leader	Group Consensus	Relevant Expertise
CONTROL METHOD	Threats, Punishments	Non-Interference	Conditional Love	Official Rules and Regulations	Close Supervision	Group Norms	Self-Control
LEADER-SUBORDINATE RELATIONSHIP	Hostile	Indifferent	Smotheringly Friendly (Parent-Child)	Politely Deferential	Psychologically Distant	Psychologically Close	Mutually Respectful
ROLE OF SUBORDINATES	Knuckle Under	Do Enough to Prevent Top Echelon Backlash	Do Gladly What the Leader Wants Done	Follow Official Edicts	Follow the Model and Carry Out the Commands of the Leader	Contribute to Group Objectives	Share the Leadership
SUBORDINATE REACTION	Resentment—Sabotage	Contempt for the Leader	Anything for the Old Man	"Keep Your Nose Clean"	Pride in the Outfit but Annoyance with the Leader	Involvement with the Group's Success	Personal Responsibility for Team Success
COMMUNICATION FLOW	Downward—Insistent	Intermittent—Tension Releasing	Downward—Reassuring	Downward—Impersonal	Downward "Now Hear This"	Free-Flowing	Authentic and Multi Directional
MOTIVATION PROCESS	Force and Flogging	Inconsistent Incentives	Emotional Manipulation	Official Rewards and Punishments	Challenge—Reward—Clobber	Participation	Self-Motivation
MORALE INDICATOR	Compliance, Subservience	Absence of Trouble	Good Social Relations	Lack of Grievances	Taut Ship (Efficiency)	Satisfying Group Interaction	Achievement, Innovation
SUBORDINATE NEEDS SATISFIED	Survival	Pseudo Independence	Dependency	Security	Competence, Pride, Growth	Affiliation-Ego	Ego, Self-Fulfillment
CONFLICT RESOLUTION METHOD	Suppression	Agree-to-Disagree	Conflict "Oiled Over"	Legalistic Appeals System	Decision by Leader	Integration of Views	Open Confrontation
SOURCE OF INNOVATION AND IMPROVEMENT	One Best Way—The Leader's	Innovation Ignored—Contentment with the Good Enough	Leader—Pleasing Innovations Only	Tradition and Precedent	"Stretching" Caused by Leader	Group Stimulation and Reward of Suggestions	Idea Clash and Evaluation

effectiveness, the first three norms have severe limitations. First, comparisons made with predecessors often do not reflect the changing circumstances which require a different leadership pattern. Second, the idea of "similar positions" is deceiving, especially in the case of department chairpersons; the title may be the same, but department size, faculty rank, internal conflict, and enrollment patterns are just a few of the variables that will impact on what individual chairpersons must be able to do. Third, a "platonic ideal" for administrators remains a matter of speculation. Reliable research data on administrator effectiveness do not exist which would allow a general prescription for bridging the gap between "what is" and "what should be."

The latter three norms can be used while acknowledging individual performance, emphasizing development, and recognizing the political environment in which administrators carry out their roles. Using one's past performance as a gauge puts the focus on continuing to employ strengths and to minimize weaknesses; using one's own performance goals calls for the integration of personal and institutional ends and promotes commitment and motivation for achievement; using the performance expectations of others insures that an administrator's actions are responsive to the various constituencies he or she is pledged to serve.

Four Approaches to Administrator Evaluation

The following section contains an introduction to the four major modes: the Rating Scale approach, the Growth Contract approach, the Ad Hoc Committee approach, and the Management By Objectives approach. Each of these four modes will be fully discussed and exemplified in Section II, "Approaches to Administrator Evaluation." In Section IV, "Planning a Program of Administrator Evaluation," guidelines will be presented for selecting one or a combination of the four modes depending on the originally determined functions—formative, summative, or institutional: the form of the evaluation should follow its function.

Rating Scale. The rating scale approach uses paper and pencil tests which may be computer scored to provide quantitative indexes of performance. The major strengths of this approach are its ease of distribution, the conciseness of data, and the anonymity of respondents. If one has faith in the accuracy of the resulting numbers, comparisons between administrators and over time can be easily made. However, B. A. Bergman and A. I. Siegel (1972) warned that the data gathered by rating scales can be significantly biased by (1) friendship, (2) quick guessing, (3) appearance, (4) prejudices, (5) halo effects, (6) errors of central tendency, and (7) leniency. These factors serve as a caution that rating scale data should, whenever possible, be supplemented by information gathered by other means. This approach will be discussed in detail in Chapter Four.

Growth Contract. The primary purpose of administrative growth contracting is improvement, a formative function (Gross, 1977). This approach has been shown to be a viable way to stimulate professional and even personal growth, maximize managerial effectiveness, and minimize the leadership problems associated with academic longevity—on-the-job retirement. Institutions which use growth contracting are usually small since it requires a great deal of time to create a contract, gather data, analyze trends, synthesize patterns, and provide feedback to each administrator evaluated. But when the time and energy are available, this approach can be used to clearly define administrative roles, serve as a context to understand patterns of performance, and as an objective basis for decisions about retention, promotion, and salary. This approach will be discussed in Chapter Five.

Ad Hoc Committee. The familiar search committee procedure is refined and extended by the ad hoc committee approach. The committee is formulated with a specific charge, usually to gather data, analyze it, and make a recommendation pursuant to a decision on an administrator. The committee assembles a portfolio which displays data in all relevant categories of performance. The administrator under review is usually given the opportunity to assist in the specification of the categories. This approach will be explicated in Chapter Six.

Management By Objectives. The management by objectives (MBO) approach focuses on examining administrator performance in terms of stated criteria or objectives. It is most easily applied in organizations where managerial duties are relatively well defined. MBO begins when the supervisor and subordinate agree on the major duties for which the subordinate is to be held accountable. Next specific objectives and levels of performance are distilled from the list of duties. Then data are gathered on the administrator's performance and judgments are made by comparing the extent and quality of performance on the stated objectives. This approach will be more fully discussed in Chapter Seven.

Summary

The how of administrator evaluation centers on three main concerns: criteria, norms, and modes. Criteria specify the areas of performance to be examined by the evaluation. Norms specify the reference points against which performance will be judged as acceptable or not.

Four main modes were introduced. The rating scale approach is easy to administer and allows anonymity, but it is often criticized for its superficiality and susceptability to bias. The growth contract approach focuses on the evaluator and administrator formulating an agreement which can stimulate and direct improvement; it requires a relatively high amount of openness and trust. The ad hoc committee approach calls for the formation of an assessment committee to gather a portfolio of data on the administrator being evaluated. This approach requires a good deal of time and expertise to conduct properly. Finally, the management by objectives approach focuses on examining administrator performance in terms of stated objectives. In this approach, the selection of appropriate objectives is crucial since examination of performance is often limited to them.

Bibliography

Bennis, Warren G. *The Unconscious Conspiracy: Why Leaders Can't Lead.* New York: AMACOM, 1976.

Bergman, B.A. and Siegel, A.I. *Training Evaluation and Student Achievement Measure.* Lowry Air Force Base, Colorado: United States Air Force Technical Training Division, 1972.

Cribbin, James J. *Effective Managerial Leadership.* New York: AMACOM, 1972.

Fiedler, Fred E. *A Theory of Leadership Effectiveness.* New York: McGraw-Hill, 1967.

Fisher, Charles F. "The Evaluation and Development of College and University Administrators. Part One: Evaluation of Administrators" ERIC *Research Currents* (March 1977): 2.

Gross, Richard F. "Facilitating Administrator Development Through Growth Contracts." Council for the Advancement of Small Colleges/American Association for Higher Education's Conference on Evaluation and Development of Administrators, February 4, 1977, Airlie House, Virginia.

Hersey, Paul and Blanchard, Kenneth H. *Management of Organizational Behavior: Utilizing Human Resources.* Englewood Cliffs, New Jersey: Prentice-Hall, 1977.

Zion, Carol L. "Role Definition: A Focus for Administrative Growth and Evaluation." *Journal of the College and University Personnel Association 22* (Summer 1977): 5-12.

Charles H. Farmer is Director of Institutional Research, Executive Assistant to the Vice President for Academic Affairs, and Professor of Mathematics, University of Tulsa.

WHY

Why evaluate administrators?

HOW

How can administrators be evaluated?

WHO

Who Should Evaluate Administrators?

A. Personnel
   1. Faculty
   2. Self-Reports
   3. Administrative Peers
   4. Trustees
   5. Students
   6. Alumni
   7. Secretaries

B. Purpose
   1. Data Source
   2. Judge
   3. Decision-Maker

Chapter Three
Who Should Evaluate Administrators?

Charles H. Farmer

Many administrators prefer to be evaluated in confidence by their supervisor. Given the threatening nature of evaluation and the tentative state of the art, this preference is understandable. However, to make a reasoned decision about who should be permitted or required to evaluate administrators and who should not, the possible effects and contributions of each type of person should be understood.

The *who* question is actually two questions. First, who can be useful data sources in the evaluation of administrators? Second, who are appropriate evaluators, *i.e.* judges and weighters of the data collected?

Who Should Provide Data?

The contributions of the following sources of evaluation data will be considered: faculty, self, peers, trustees, students, alumni, and secretaries.

Should Faculty be Used as a Data Source? In all institutions of higher education, faculty are bound to administrators by the same concerns and issues. Hazard Adams (1976) expressed this bond in the form of antinomies or contradictions between principles which seem equally reasonable:

- Antinomy the First: The faculty is the university; the faculty are employees of the university.
- Antinomy the Second: The administration is the master of the faculty; the administration is the servant of the faculty.

In their behavior, faculty and administrators acknowledge both sides of both antinomies. Moreover, most realize that *both* halves of each antinomy together are true; each separately is false. Because of this inextricable and paradoxical relationship between administrator and faculty, let us first consider the case for faculty input in administrator evaluation.

Tyrus Hillway (1973), a pioneer in instrument design, saw a number of analogies between student evaluation of faculty and faculty evaluation of administrators which held an implied relationship—that teachers are to administrators as students are to teachers. Based on the logic of his analogy he predicted administrator evaluation by faculty would be easily accepted:

> If teachers can be aided by securing systematically the ratings of their students it follows logically that administrators also may be helped by obtaining ratings from persons with whom they deal most directly—the academic faculty. . . . Since teacher rating scales have become widely accepted . . . there seems little reason to doubt the eventual acceptance in higher education of rating scales for academic administrators.

Hillway's assumptions are logical but seem to overlook an opposing and equally forceful point of view that argues against the position that administrators are responsible to faculty. "This is simply contrary to law, tradition, practice, and reality," asserted Lewis Mayhew (1971). Mayhew's supporting examples showed the impracticality of faculty interference in administrative spheres because of their inability to reach consensus on management issues and their insufficient grasp of institutional needs. Mayhew cited several examples of this faculty shortcoming including a reference to Stephens College where budgeting for plant maintenance and equipment replacement had long been a management practice: "Had the college not been doing this, it would several times have been virtually bankrupt when forced to restore hot water systems or provide essential new classroom space." He noted, however, that the faculty members probably would have concluded that the monies budgeted for maintenance and replacement of equipment might be better assigned to their salaries.

The opposition of having formal faculty input for administrator evaluation was supported, albeit implicitly, by William C. McInnes (1971) as president of Fairfield University: "The administrator has a right to be held properly accountable only to those designated by the governing board." McInnes noted that leaders must be "responsive" and must "enjoy their confidence in a substantial way" but should neither be strictly nor formally accountable to any public other than the board of trustees or others designated by the board.

Opposition to faculty involvement in administrator evaluation is based in no small part on assumptions about the nature of power and authority. Educational institutions have traditionally been managed through a hierarchical distribution of power. Although in some ways power flows from the bottom to the top of the organizational chart, control is usually exercised by power flowing down from the top. In the case of faculty, this power is ordinarily felt through the process of re-appointment, promotion, tenure, and salary determinations. Any attempt to redistribute this power is customarily neutralized, since as Carl Rogers (1977) aptly stated, ". . . almost without exception management retains the 'right' to hire and fire."

If a belief in the hierarchical distribution of power is strongly held, faculty involvement will be seen to have little value and even be inappropriate. However, there are different views which are more in tune with the re-distribution of power and authority occurring in the last decade. In contrast to the hierarchical distribution of power, the diffusion-of-power model for academic authority means, according to Adams (1976), that "no one has the complete power to do any given thing." A similar model for colleges and universities having high mutual influence among hierarchical groups has been characterized by Genova *et al.* (1976) as a hybrid, combining three types of organizational authority patterns: "They are part 'bureaucratic,' characterized by a vertical authority hierarchy. . . . They are part 'collegial,' where authority is shared among individuals irrespective of position. . . . And, they are part 'political,' where various forms of authority are exercised by various interest groups. . . ."

If one believes in the shared control inherent in these models which ostensibly characterize governance and authority in higher education, then it follows that faculty input is needed for administrator evaluation. A final statement in support of faculty involvement, perhaps the most powerful, can be presented succinctly: to require student evaluation of faculty and to deny faculty evaluation of administrators would be intolerably hypocritical.

Faculty input can serve many valuable functions including:

- Letting administrators know where they stand with various faculty groups
- Clarifying what faculty expectations are of particular administrators
- Strengthening the faculty-administrator working relationship by communicating expectations

Every administrator who works with faculty is in a position to benefit from faculty views: department chairperson, director, collegiate dean, graduate dean, vice president for academic affairs, and the president. However, the type of faculty input will differ by administrative position following a frequency of contact rule of thumb. For example, a graduate dean would be evaluated by faculty who teach graduate courses and the director of counseling by those faculty most involved in helping students plan their undergraduate careers.

While the faculty is an important source of information to use when evaluating administrators, it can be a dangerous source to rely on if its limitations are not taken into account. Their incomplete grasp of institutional needs and vested interests does not indicate their involvement in administrator evaluation is entirely out of place, but it does demonstrate that they cannot be the sole appraisers. Their assessment must be tempered by other sources.

Should Self-Reports be Used?

O wad some Power the giftie gie us
To see oursels as ithers see us?
It wad frae monie a blunder free us
An' foolish notion.

—Robert Burns

Self-reports are a valuable input into administrator evaluation if they are descriptive and illuminate the context, such as the administrator's personal and professional goals, assumptions, barriers, and opportunities. However, when administrators (like all humans) begin to formally rate or judge their own performance in documented reports which will be scrutinized, those reports have a tendency to reflect the excesses of romantic poetry.

Judgmental self-reports will be of dubious validity for evaluations aimed at arriving at promotion or retention decisions. But if the administrator seeks to identify conditions known only to him or her that caused an effort to fail or the specifics which contributed to its success, than a self-report is a valuable input. Whenever possible, supporting material and evidence should be included in self-reports to alleviate suspicions of personal bias.

A judgment of one's self-worth is a critical part of the self-improvement process. Comparing a self-report with the perceptions of others is a good first step in a diagnostic process of examining strengths and weaknesses. Dissonance is a powerful catalyst to change. An administrator who finds unsettling discrepancies between his or her view of priorities and performance and that of the faculty or peers may work with them to clarify the problem and find ways to remedy the situation. Used in this way, self-evaluation parallels the growth contracting approach described in Chapter Five and Chapter Nine.

Should Administrative Peers be Evaluators? One obvious advantage of including other administrators as evaluators is frequency of contact as compared to faculty. Many assistant professors, for example, have very little contact with any administrator other than their department chairperson. Also peer administrators share a common frame of reference and have first hand knowledge of the constraints which control administrative performance.

Unfortunately, many administrators have no peers. The president is an obvious case. Moreover, the academic vice president is usually the "number two man" on campus. Even if all vice-presidential level positions were considered equal, most colleges and universities have specialists in the non-academic slots that know little of traditional academic matters. Collegiate deans also have their own fiefdoms and seldom interact with other deans on policy issues within their own college. Analogously, department heads from different disciplines may have little exposure to other interdepartmental workings.

Fellow administrators one step up and one step down in the reporting line, however, can bring valuable perspectives to the evaluation. The intimacy of working closely may give the best perception of all as to what a specific administrator is doing well or ill. Furthermore, as Sprunger and Bergquist (1978) noted, sharing of evaluation data among peers is a powerful team-building technique to strengthen group effectiveness.

Is Trustee Input Needed? Some trustee input is needed in all cases, as only trustees know board priorities, perspectives, and problems. Because the trustees usually hold all of the corporate power of colleges and universities, it has final say as to the form their input will take. The trustees should assume the responsibility and authority for presidential evaluation just as they do for presidential appointments. As in other internal academic matters, however, it would be logical to delegate to the president the authority and responsibility for the evaluation of other administrators.

Should Students be Involved? Most students will have little knowledge or interest about administrative tasks, unless these tasks facilitate or retard the instructional process as perceived by the students. While students have only a limited historical perspective, their transient nature gives them the unique advantage of not being in the midst of a long series of shifting events, and perhaps they will better be able to consider the administrative impact of current events. There do not appear to be strong reasons, however, for the inclusion or exclusion of students from administrator evaluation.

Is Alumni Input Useful? Even if alumni are more mature and have gained perspectives that current students lack, alumni will not know many members of the current administration. There may be some advantage, however, in requesting input from the alumni association concerning their external relations with appropriate administrators.

Should Secretaries Evaluate the Chief? Probably the most meaningful secretarial input for administrator evaluation is his or her interpretation of the administrator's day-to-day tasks. Participating in the evaluation may give a secretary an "everything I've always known you should do differently but was always afraid to say" opportunity. From an interview with an administrator's secretary, it may be possible to ascertain: (1) how the administrator allocates time, (2) how the office can be managed more effectively, and (3) what he or she can do more of to help out the boss. Such participation can raise a secretary from being a "hired hand" to an integral part of the administrative team.

Judgment and Decisions

The process of making judgments is inherent in all evaluation processes. The word judgment in this discussion refers to the successive accumulation, collation, and weighting of information from data sources until a qualitative impression of an administrator's performance is made. This impression is arrived at after a period of assessment and takes the form of a conclusion. The conclusion can lead to a decision (hire, fire, promote, increase pay, etc.), but it is not a decision itself.

In formative evaluation, the administrator gathers data on his or her performance and sifts and analyzes it until he or she arrives at a conclusion about the areas and extent of needed improvement. This judgment is a conclusion based on the accumulation of diagnostic data. In summative evaluation, the administrator's supervisor or a committee gathers comparative data and arrives at a conclusion concerning the value of his or her performance. In institutional evaluation, the judgment is usually made by a task force or administrator responsible for the study or by an external evaluation team reflecting on the accountability of an administrative unit.

Who Should Make the Decision? The decision is something often confused with the judgment. In evaluation many individuals and committees can formulate judgments and make recommendations based on those judgments, but usually one person makes the decision.

In formative evaluation, it is the administrator being evaluated who must make the decision to improve his or her performance, and if so, in what areas and to what extent.

In summative evaluation, the decision is an established procedure unique to each college and university. Typically the administrator's immediate supervisor is empowered to decide on an administrator's pay changes, promotion, contract renewal, or assignment. However, in many instances the decision can rest at a higher level of administration—sometimes even with the board of regents or the state legislature.

In institutional evaluation, the decision usually rests at the point of accountability. In special projects it is the person who appointed the team or task force who will decide the value of its continuance. In matters of accreditation or funding, it is an external agency which will approve the program or the funds.

Summary

Faculty, self, administrative peers, trustees, students, alumni, and secretarial staff are all possible sources of information in administrator evaluation. Since judgment is an important part of the evaluation process, appropriate people to make judgments in formative, summative, and institutional processes were discussed. Finally, appropriate decision-makers were identified for each of the three purposes of administrator evaluation.

Bibliography

Adams, Hazard. *The Academic Tribes*. New York: Liveright, 1976.

Genova, William J.; Madoff, Marjorie K.; Chin, Robert; and Thomas, George B. *Mutual Benefit Evaluation of Faculty and Administrators in Higher Education.* Cambridge, Mass.: Ballinger, 1976.

Hillway, Tyrus. "Evaluating College and University Administration." *Intellect* (April 1973): 427.

Mayhew, Lewis B. "Thoughts on a Statement of Rights for College Administrators." *Journal of Higher Education* (May 1971): 384.

McInnes, William C. "A Statement of Rights for College Administrators." *Journal of Higher Education* (May 1971): 380.

Rogers, Carl R. *On Personal Power.* New York: Delacorte, 1977.

Charles H. Farmer is Director of Institutional Research, Executive Assistant to the Vice President for Academic Affairs, and Professor of Mathematics, University of Tulsa.

Section II
Approaches to Administrator Evaluation

All too often administrator evaluation is equated with the kind of questionnaires commonly used in student evaluation of teaching. In Chapter Four Charles H. Farmer outlines the variables and position characteristics that are usually found in rating scales for the president, dean, chairperson, and all staff forms. The best rating scales are tailored to each administrator. He warns against an overreliance on rating scales and encourages supplementing them with information gathered by other means.

In Chapter Five Neal R. Berte and Edward H. O'Neil introduce a growth contracting approach for administrator evaluation and development. Individual administrators work with a colleague consultant to construct a plan for improvement, including specific goals and activities, and monitor progress. This personalized self-renewal technique can raise the performance level of individuals and the total staff.

An ad hoc committee model for administrator evaluation is offered by G. Lester Anderson in Chapter Six. Members of the administrator's constituencies assemble a portfolio of information representing performance appraisals from various segments of the institution. Although a thorough approach, ambiguity and complexity are still very much present.

Management by objectives incorporates performance appraisal as described by Philip C. Winstead in Chapter Seven. Administrator evaluation is closely linked to the overall mission and goals of the institution and therefore requires sophisticated and lengthy analysis and planning activities in advance. With concrete objectives performance can rise above opinion and emotion to a more rational and productive plane.

Chapter Four
Rating Scales for Evaluating Administrators

Charles H. Farmer

Like other evaluation techniques or devices, rating scales have their own strengths and weaknesses, peculiar controversies, and special instructions for optional use. Of the four evaluation modes described in this section (rating scale, growth contract, assessment committee, and management by objectives), it appears to be the least complicated to use, but it may be the most abused because of the expertise required for its development and the caution required for its proper utilitization. The greatest potential for rating scales is within the design of the other three modes. This chapter is not meant for the psychometrician seeking new ways to deal with the intricacies of test construction. Rather it is written for the administrator or faculty member who perhaps is on an evaluation committee considering the use of standardized instruments for assessing administrator performance.

Rating instruments are also referred to as forms, scales, questionnaires or opinionnaires and may be classified as either closed-form (wherein the respondent has only a limited number of pre-selected options to choose between) or open-form (wherein the respondent may provide information with less structure and direction). Like multiple-choice exams, the closed-forms are harder to design but easier to score, and open-forms, like essay exams, are easier to design but more difficult and time-consuming to analyze. Rating scales (closed-form instruments), about which this chapter is written, are somewhat deceptive in that they are harder to develop than they look and at their best should be based on research as well as a good deal of common sense.

Content Variables and Common Themes

W. H. Cowley (1969) discovered four common characteristics of good leaders: speed of decision, finality of judgment, superior intellectual ability, and a bigger reservoir of energy than their followers. He further stated that most good administrator/leaders are artists. They possess skills necessary to perform the most difficult of all arts—running their institutions democratically and persuasively. Given the artistic nature of leadership, assessing its effectiveness is something less than a straightforward task, especially when using a seemingly definitive instrument such as a rating scale. Question content poses a major difficulty in the design process. Simply put, the nature of the queries determines what kind of data you get from respondents. Although question content must be varied in order to evaluate diverse administrative positions, the following five variables adapted from William B. Castetter and Richard S. Heisler (1971) seem germane for any administrative post:

Variable A: Unit Objectives. To what unit of the institution is the administrative position assigned? Unit objectives have a natural bearing on administrative performance in that many positions grow out of the objectives of the unit to which the position is allocated. Thus administrator evaluation must involve an assessment of each administrator in terms of contributions both to the purposes of the position and to those of the larger structure of which the position is a part.

Variable B: Position Goals. What expectations has the institution for the administrative position? The evaluator must know why the position exists, how it is connected to unit objectives, its major responsibilities, and its relationship to other positions.

Variable C: The Individual Administrator. To what extent does the administrator possess the social, technical, and conceptual skills to perform effectively in the position? Without this knowledge, it is difficult for the evaluator to understand reasons for success or failure or to direct future development.

Variable D: Management and Operational Processes. How effective is the administrator in applying those management and operational processes which are essential to achieve the goals of the position?

Variable E: Institutional Milieu. Does the functional environment in which the work is performed facilitate or hinder the realization of goals.

The most common ingredient of ongoing administrator evaluation programs appears to be that rating scales have questions related to these five variables.

Sprunger and Bergquist (1978) identified seven themes which recur in most administrator evaluation rating scales. Their themes together with brief descriptions of the activities, outcomes, traits, and quality of personal relationships are as follows:

1. *Knowledge and Capacity:* exercises control of the skills and knowledge needed for the tasks associated with the position. Knows both the technical and practical aspects of higher education and modern management; traits describing breadth of intellectual and cultural interests and physical and mental vigor are also subsumed under this theme.
2. *Dependability:* responds to the job by accepting responsibility for

assignments and showing initiative; schedule effectiveness; integrity; proper dress and hygiene.

3. *Adaptability:* deals effectively with unusual administrative pressures; plans effectively and imaginatively; copes effectively with ambiguity.
4. *Interpersonal Relationships:* is effective in conflict management and verbal and nonverbal communication; works for consensus among constituency groups.
5. *Commitment to Professional Growth:* commitment to personal development in acquiring new knowledge and skills; recognizes and instills enthusiasm for the development of abilities and capacities of others.
6. *Resource and Personnel Management:* says "no" effectively; maintains efficiency by delegating responsibility with commensurate authority; practices effective budgeting procedures; maintains clearly defined standards of performance; has an "open door" policy.
7. *Institutional Loyalty:* commitment to rewarding service; participation in town and gown activities; inspires enthusiasm for institutional goals.

Position Characteristics and Performance Areas

Among the administrator evaluation forms from thirty-five universities, colleges, and community colleges reviewed by the Office of Institutional Research at the University of Tulsa, certain characteristics and performance areas were included more frequently for some positions than for others. The following is a summary of the most common characteristics specific to various administrative posts.

President. Invariably the president's communicative abilities are referenced as his or her "leadership" abilities. The other categories most often considered are management or administrative skills, fairness in the treatment of individuals in academic units, and vision and advocacy of institutional goals.

Dean. Leadership is most often included, frequently designated as instructional, professional, and personal leadership. Next in importance seems to be the dean's capacity to affect good relationships among the departments, between departments and the college unit, and between college and central administration. These items frequently refer to communication skills and advocacy. Finally, these forms stress administrative style and organizational competence.

Department Chairperson. The main priority here seems to be communication, first from the department outward and then within the department. Second in priority is administrative ability, including office management. Third, most department chairpersons' evaluations include fairness, staff development, and assistance to new staff. Finally, several instruments refer to a chairperson's role in strengthening instruction which is distinct from (and stressed more than) curriculum development.

All Staff. Far and away, the priority on the all-staff instruments is staff relationships—relations with faculty, assistance to staff in improving performance, and fairness. Next in order of frequency are professionalism, attitudes, and productivity. These forms stress leadership (vision, planning, etc.) more than managerial competence. The general forms, surprisingly, include more references to budgeting, utilization of facilities, etc., than do the specialized forms.

Questionnaire items usually address both the qualities and the activities associated with administrators—those which "conventional wisdom" regards as important and useful. Constructing a list of activities that academic leaders actually engage in may be easy. But including only items which respondents have the opportunity to observe and the expertise to evaluate is not so easy. The many groups with whom administrators must deal, such as faculty, other administrators, trustees, legislators, and funding agencies all have different views of the qualities and methods needed to facilitate the activities of the university or college. All of these views must be considered in administrator evaluation programs that purport to be comprehensive; however, none of the rating scales reviewed contain questions that deal with all constituency relationships.

Advantages, Disadvantages, Difficulties

As in student assessment of faculty, rating scales provide the ability to rapidly and systematically classify information from a variety of sources. Other advantages include structured input, ease of maintaining anonymity and confidentiality of evaluators, and the ability to obtain a longitudinal perspective by using comments on the same qualities year after year.

There is a tendency for committees engaged in administrator evaluation to regard the task of instrument design with a sigh of relief. Here is something they can grasp; the time for talk is over; now they can worry about concrete issues—those with practical solutions involving scoring devices, scale responsiveness, and technical format. If there is a moment of truth in administrator evaluation, this must surely be the moment.

Committees should not be lulled by this false sense of security. There are serious problems in using a printed form to measure the performance of an administrator in a complex system. Disadvantages of rating scales adapted from criticisms of traditional appraisal systems discussed by Castetter and Heisler (1971) include the following:

- Most scales do not incorporate institutional expectations for specific administrators nor do they evaluate performance in terms of the administrator's contribution to institutional goals.
- Most rating scales are not tailored to the precise position to be evaluated.

- Items on the rating scales are not checked for validity and are focused on the individual's personality rather than on what he or she is expected to do or on results achieved.
- Most evaluators display biases and are not qualified to assess personalities.
- Administrators under review are fragmented on paper into personality parts which, when added together, do not reflect the whole person.
- The ratings and raters are subject to organizational influence.
- The results are not utilized to assist in administrative development or to provide post-evaluation counseling.

If such technical difficulties are not sufficient to shake committee members out of the sense of security that often emerges as an instrument begins to take shape, taking a few steps back to gain perspective on the state of the art of higher education administration may add another note of reality. Alvin C. Eurich (Lahti, 1970), President of the Academy for Educational Development, has stated: "The failure to participate in the management revolution that has swept American business and industry is haunting higher education today." A variation of this view also comes from John Caffrey (Lahti, 1970), Director of the Commission on Administrative Affairs of the American Council on Education: "Until the 19th Century, the college administrator was simply a principal officer of the faculty. But this is not the year 1800 and the complexity of today's management problems and of the systems devised to solve them has created a new profession, one of the few important ones, by the way, for which little or no formal training is available." The point here is to be wary of believing that a definitive instrument can measure that which is so ill-defined.

One example of current leadership studies will serve to highlight what needs to be done in higher education before confidence can be increased in assessing administrator performance. Fred E. Fiedler (1976) has not only looked at leadership situations but at the individual's behavior in those situations and whether he or she was functioning well or badly. Fiedler posits three major components which primarily determine control and influence in a situation and leader success: (1) *Leader-member relations*—the degree to which the group supports the leader; (2) *Task structure*—the degree to which the task clearly spells out goals, procedures, and specific guidelines; and (3) *Position power*—the degree to which the position gives the leader the authority to reward or punish subordinates. Leadership effectiveness therefore depends upon the leader, the constituencies being led, and on the milieu in which the leader must operate. Perspectives on leadership as sophisticated as Fiedler's must be applied to administrators at all levels in higher education and then incorporated into rating scales and other evaluation modes. Until that time evaluators are, without undue exaggeration, attempting to assess the amorphous.

New Directions

Since distinctive qualities exist for individual administrative positions, it is desirable to design a different instrument or form for each one. Many colleges and universities have tried to develop a single rating scale for use in evaluating all administrators. Not surprisingly, such standard forms have been criticized by those doing the rating and those being rated as not being attentive to specific positions. The need is for distinct evaluation forms for posts ranging from department chairperson to president. This tailoring of instruments is necessary because administrative role definitions differ widely from unit to unit and from one institution to the next.

The Departmental Evaluation of Chairperson Activities system (DECA) developed by Donald P. Hoyt and his associates at Kansas State University attempts this tailoring of opinionnaires at the departmental level. Instead of assuming that there is a magic list of administrative techniques which describe all "good" department heads, the DECA system utilizes an "activity-oriented" definition of effectiveness. Administrative effectiveness is assessed by faculty perception of how successfully the chairperson fulfilled fifteen departmental responsibilities of varying importance during the past year. A unique feature of the DECA system is the identification of dissonance between the chairperson and the faculty as to the importance of each activity. Also, it measures dissonance among faculty as to the importance of each activity as well as the chairperson's performance.

As shown in Form 1 and Form 2 in the Appendix the DECA system gathers data from two perspectives. The chairperson uses Form 1 to rate the relative importance of fifteen activities as each pertains to his or her role. Thus, the process takes into consideration individual differences among both chairpersons and departments. Individual faculty use Form 2 to give a rating on the same fifteen activities as does the chairperson and also to rate how effectively the chairperson has been performing each activity. In addition, faculty rate how frequently the chairperson engages in thirty specific behaviors.

Chairperson and faculty data are computer scored and a three-page *DECA Report* and a *DECA Interpretive Guide* are returned to the chairperson. Form 3 displays the data for a fictitious chairperson, J.J. Doe, Department of Advanced Studies, University College. As explained in the *Interpretive Guide,* Page 1 will help Doe answer two questions:

1. To what degree is there consensus regarding the role of the chairperson/head?
2. How effectively do faculty members believe the chairperson/head is in performing specific roles or types of roles?

Page 2 shows Doe how frequently the faculty think he or she engages in thirty specific behaviors and rates the scores as "favorable" or "unfavorable" as compared to other chairpersons. A Diagnostic Summary on page 3 allows Doe to identify specific strengths and weaknesses, as perceived by the faculty, and to begin a personal development plan.

As stressed earlier, no rating scale, however well-constructed or thoroughly analyzed, should be expected to comprehensively and validly assess administrative performance. It is instructive to note that although the DECA system is better than most existing opinionnaires for summative evaluation, the authors recommend against using the reported data as the sole measure of administrative effectiveness. The Center for Faculty Evaluation and Development at Kansas State University will provide information for using DECA on other campuses.[1]

The critical incident method originally described by John C. Flanagan (1949) is another way to insure that a rating scale relates to a particular administrator at a particular time and place. Flanagan defines a critical requirement as one which was responsible for outstandingly effective or definitely unsatisfactory performance regarding an important part of the administrative position in question. Flanagan further points out that neither outstanding ability nor unsatisfactory ability can exist independently of a series of observed behaviors. In Flanagan's article there are five specific conditions that must be satisfied to establish critical requirements:

1. It is essential that actual observations be made of the on-the-job activity and the product of such activity.
2. The aims and objectives of the activity must be known to the observer. Unless this condition is fulfilled it will be impossible for the observer or judge to identify success or failure. For example, a foreman might be rated as very successful if the objective of his activity were taken as getting along well with the workmen under him. At the same time he might be rated as very unsatisfactory if the objective is to produce materials.
3. The basis for the specific judgments to be made by the observer must be clearly defined. The data can be objective only if all observers are following the same rules. All observers must have the same criteria for judging satisfactoriness. The definition must clearly state whether or not a minor imperfection will be regarded as an evidence of failure or whether a product must be completely unusable to be classified as unsatisfactory.
4. The observer must be qualified to make judgments regarding the activity observed. Typically the supervisor on the job is in a much better position to make judgments as to whether or not behavior is outstanding or unsatisfactory, than is the job analyst or psychologist. On the other hand the supervisor on the job is ordinarily quite lacking in the training essential to make an inference as to the particular mental trait which caused the behavior to be successful or unsuccessful.

5. The last necessary condition is that the situation be such that reporting is accurate. The principal problems here are those of memory and communication. It is also important that the observer's attention be directed to the essential aspects of the behavior being observed.

The Evaluation of the Academic Dean used at Findlay College, designed by President Glen R. Rasmussen (1978) when he was dean of the college, is a behaviorally anchored type of rating scale.[2] Rasmussen constructed the instrument by implicitly using the critical incident approach. A "critical incident" is any job behavior considered to represent successful or unsuccessful performance. The collection of these specific examples is the first step in the design of behaviorally anchored scales.

Individual examples of effective and ineffective performance should then be grouped by factor analysis into general categories by means of a pilot study. One resulting category might be "Planning and Management," and all related functions or personal traits would then be placed under this heading. Once the items are grouped and perhaps reworded to improve clarity and remove ambiguities, items or incidents have to be scaled along performance dimension continua. The completed rating scale consists of a number of performance scales with the critical incidents "anchoring" the points along each continuum.

Rasmussen sees the dean spending much of the time working with faculty and identifies four major functions where he or she must:

- Act as an evaluator, for example, by helping faculty evaluate their teaching, recommending salary increases and promotions, and allocating scarce funds among competing programs
- Act as a gadfly, by prodding faculty to research, write, and publish, stimulating change, and trying to reduce parochialism
- Act as a mediator, both between opposing forces within the institution and between external and internal groups
- Act as a conservator, maintaining the primary thrust of the institution and resisting fads or hasty innovations

To evaluate the dean's performance in these areas, a rating scale should provide six types of information:

1. The dean's self-evaluation of how well he or she meets his or her *own* performance goals
2. The faculty's evaluation of how well the dean is meeting these goals
3. The mean faculty evaluation of how well the dean meets the average performance goals the faculty hold for him or her
4. Individual faculty member's evaluation of how well the dean meets the performance goals held by the faculty member
5. The president's evaluation of how well the dean meets the dean's own performance goals

6. The president's evaluation of how well the dean meets the president's goals for him or her

To collect such information Rasmussen developed a twenty-two item rating scale shown in Form 4 in the Appendix. Evaluators' responses are given in four parts:

1. A statement concerning the academic dean's function
2. A continuum built on this statement
3. The evaluator's estimate of where the "ideal" dean in this institution would be on this continuum
4. The evaluator's estimate of the dean's actual performance on this continuum

The rating scale is completed by the dean, faculty, and president.

The schematic and algebraic descriptors depict the variables a dean can use to analyze the rating scale data.

Questionnaire Schematic

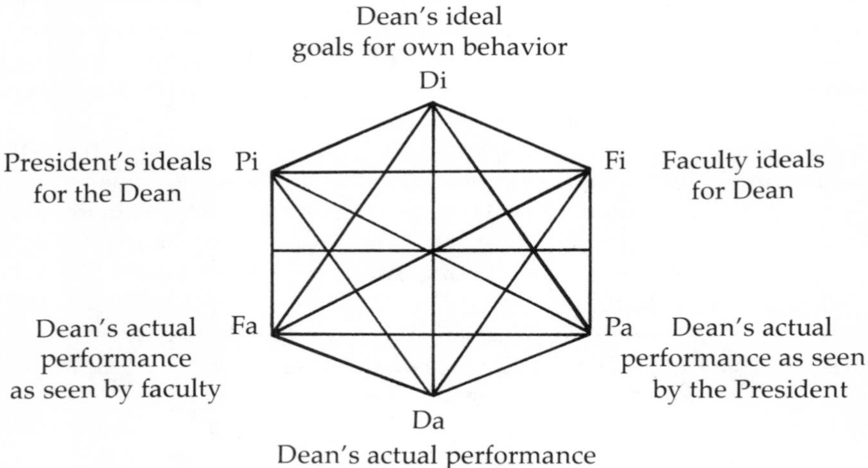

D = Dean F = Faculty P = President
i = Ideal performance for the Dean
a = Actual performance of the Dean
N = Number of responses

Di-Da For each of the twenty-two items the discrepancy between the dean's ideal goals for his performance and his actual performance as he sees it will indicate how well the dean feels he is meeting his own professional goals. If we sum the discrepancy on the twenty-two items and administer the questionnaire every two or three years we have some measure of the dean's perception of his professional progress.

$Di \pm \Sigma Fa/N$ How well is the dean meeting his ideal goals as judged by the faculty? For each of the twenty-two items we establish his mean performance on that item by adding all the faculty "a" responses and dividing by the number of faculty. The discrepancy between this number and the dean's response to the "i" part of that item provides us with an evaluation on each questionnaire item.

$\Sigma Fi/N \pm \Sigma Fa/N$ This measure will tell us how the faculty see the dean as meeting the goals the faculty as a whole hold for him. For each of the twenty-two items we sum the faculty's response to the "i" item and divide by the number of responses. The discrepancy between these two mean responses indicates how closely the dean's performance as they see it matches the goals the faculty collectively hold for him. When we sum this discrepancy for all twenty-two items we have a measure of the faculty's general level of satisfaction regarding the dean's performance.

$\Sigma Fi \pm Fa$ How does each member of the faculty perceive the dean's behavior relative to the goals that each faculty member holds for him? The sum of the "i" + "a" discrepancy for the twenty-two items indicates the individual faculty member's evaluation. If we use this same measure, add the totals of all faculty, and divide by the number of faculty, we can determine how the faculty as a whole see the dean as meeting their individual goals for him. When this is done every two or three years, the dean can determine whether his performance is getting better or poorer marks.

$Di \pm \Sigma Fi/N$ This measure will tell us how the faculty's goals for the dean differ from his own goals. A large discrepancy on an individual item probably indicates a need for more effective communication. If there is a large discrepancy on most of the items, it probably indicates a poor match between the dean and the faculty.

$Di \pm Pi$ How well do the dean's own goals coincide with the president's goals for him? If there is a large discrepancy on any of the items, the dean and the president should certainly discuss the matter.

$Pi \pm Pa$ This is simply the president's evaluation of the academic dean. It will certainly be of interest and value to the dean.

$Pi \pm \Sigma Fi/N$ This indicates how closely the president's goals for the dean match the faculty's goals for him. The dean's

	position becomes more difficult as this discrepancy increases.
$Pi \pm \Sigma Fa/N$	This measure indicates how closely the dean's performance, as seen by the faculty, meets the president's goals for him.

For each of the twenty-two items and for all of the items together, a number of additional analyses are possible. Some of the most useful would be:

$Di \pm Pa$	The discrepancy between the dean's goals and the president's perception of his actual behavior.
$\Sigma Fi/N \pm Pa$	The discrepancy between the faculty's goals for the dean and his performance as seen by the president.
$\Sigma Fi/N \pm Da$	The discrepancy between the faculty's goals for the dean and the dean's performance as he sees it.

Although perhaps formidable at first glance, every dean who has used the instrument "felt they gained a great deal of information from it" (Rasmussen, 1978). It is interesting to note that although faculty tend to be overtly critical of deans, the instrument shows that their ideals for the dean are usually more moderate than the dean's own ideals.[3]

Conclusion

The directions taken by the Departmental Evaluation of Chairperson Activities and the Evaluation of the Academic Dean can greatly improve the quality of rating scales as they become more individualized to the precise administrative position being evaluated. In addition to these advances in instrument design, thoughtful consideration must continue regarding the art of college and university administration. Earl Pullias (1972, 1973, 1973) defined thirty important principles as shown in Table 1 which can be used to gain a clearer perspective on administrative performance. Reflection on principles such as these will help to develop sensitive evaluation instruments.

In a paper on the importance of recognizing the organizational context in which an individual administrator works, Ben W. McClellen (1977) summarizes the criteria portion of the design process of rating scales when he says, ". . . the criteria must be specific to: one person, a fixed period of time, the institutional environment, the institutional mission, the person's administrative role." Because of the complexity of the criteria necessary to measure the organizational context, rating scales may be most useful as supplements to other methods of administrator evaluation whether the function is formative, summative, or institutional.

Table 1
Principles of College Administration

1. In any decision-making process, those who will be affected by the decision should be informed and, if possible, consulted.
2. The faculty, the student body, and the staff—the campus community—should be the first to hear about important decisions and developments.
3. The people who are consulted when a decision is being sought (faculty, students, alumni, etc.) should be helped to understand the way in which their advice or counsel will be used.
4. When responsibility is delegated as it should and must be in any organization—corresponding authority should be delegated within a reasonable limit.
5. As a general rule, the responsible person nearest to the involved situation should make the decision.
6. Consistent effort should be made to enable all of the college or university to understand the principle that there must be a relationship between responsibility and competence—that an individual can be given responsibility only in an area where he has established competence.
7. The practice of basic courtesy is essential in dealing with members of the academic community.
8. Favoritism, or what appears to be favoritism, is especially harmful to morale.
9. Grievance procedures in the academic community should be available and clearly understood.
10. Perhaps most important of all, the purposes and major processes of the institution should be kept for all segments of the academic community—board, students, faculty, alumni, patrons, staff in the various publics of the college or university.
11. The employer-employee relationship is not appropriate for an academic community and should be avoided.
12. Diversity and variety among staff, faculty, board, and students should be accepted and respected.
13. Every aspect of the institution, as much as possible, should bear its own weight, financially and psychologically.
14. The practice of responding chiefly to complaints—of being caught in the trap of "greasing the sqeaky wheel" psychology—should be avoided as much as is practicable.
15. A balance between change and stability, between innovation and tradition, should be sought constantly.
16. The office of the administrator—president, dean, department chairman, etc.—should be valued, protected, and enriched without overemphasis on the person who occupies the office.
17. A process for, and habit of, dealing swiftly and firmly with behavior

which is clearly outside mutually established standards of the academic community is essential for an administrator.

18. The youths of college and university age are to be respected, but not feared; and their originality or significance neither should be overvalued nor undervalued.
19. An inner corps of broadly representative, but loyal, advisors who, within council, are free and able to voice their sincere opinions is very valuable to an administrator.
20. When a decision is in process, the administrator should take care not to dominate the discussion by talking too much.
21. All possible freedom should be allowed for those working within the community of scholars, but the administrator should accept the responsibility for helping the community to set mutually agreed-upon limits.
22. The institution should have clear and achievable goals toward which it is moving perceptibly.
23. The administrator should avoid both the appearance and the reality of being indecisive.
24. The administrator's work is a cross-country run, not a 100-yard dash.
25. The power of the administrator's office should be used with care.
26. The administrator should strive to anticipate, as much as possible, the need for change and development.
27. The business of an institution can be carried on most effectively in small groups as a rule.
28. The administrator should not be influenced unduly by campus gossip and propaganda.
29. Special effort should be made to help every person who is a part of the institution to be sensitively aware of the crucial importance of money, since nothing is more certain to destroy a college or university than inefficient or careless financial management.
30. When an administrator assumes a new position, he would be wise to take ample time to study the situation carefully before undertaking major changes.

APPENDIX

Form 1

CHAIRPERSON INFORMATION FORM

for use with the DECA Survey Form

Name ____ (1-20)
(Last) (Initials)

Department ____ (21-39) (40-43)

Institution ____

Number of faculty asked to respond______________________________ (44-46)

Approximately what percentage of the faculty in this department is tenured?
(1) Over 80% (2) 60-79% (3) 40-59% (4) Under 40% ____ (47)

Are members of the department housed:
(1) In a single building? (2) In more than one building? ____ (48)

How many formal department faculty meetings were called in the past 12 months?
(1) None (2) 1 or 2 (3) 3-5 (4) 6-9 (5) 10 or more ____ (49)

How many years have you served as chairperson/head of this department?
(1) This is my first year. (2) 1-2 years (3) 3-5 years (4) 6 or more years ____ (50)

What are the terms of your appointment?
(1) I was appointed by the dean and serve at his/her pleasure (2) I was elected by the faculty for a specific term (3) I was elected by the faculty but not for a specific term ____ (51)

- **The list below describes responsibilities which some department chairpersons/heads pursue. Circle the number which describes your judgment of how important each of these is in your role as chairperson/head:**

1 — Not Important 2 — Only So-So 3 — Fairly Important
4 — Quite Important 5 — Essential

CHAIRPERSON/HEAD RESPONSIBILITIES

	RATING	
1. Guides the development of sound procedures for assessing faculty performance	1 2 3 4 5	(52)
2. Recognizes and rewards faculty in accordance with their contributions to the department's program	1 2 3 4 5	(53)
3. Guides development of sound organizational plan to accomplish departmental program	1 2 3 4 5	(54)
4. Arranges effective and equitable allocation of faculty responsibilities such as committee assignments, teaching loads, etc.	1 2 3 4 5	(55)
5. Takes lead in recruitment of promising faculty	1 2 3 4 5	(56)
6. Fosters good teaching in the department	1 2 3 4 5	(57)
7. Stimulates research and scholarly activity in the department	1 2 3 4 5	(58)
8. Guides curriculum development	1 2 3 4 5	(59)
9. Maintains faculty morale by reducing, resolving, or preventing conflicts	1 2 3 4 5	(60)
10. Fosters development of each faculty member's special talents or interests	1 2 3 4 5	(61)
11. Understands and communicates expectations of the campus administration to the faculty	1 2 3 4 5	(62)
12. Effectively communicates the department's needs (personnel, space, monetary) to the dean	1 2 3 4 5	(63)
13. Facilitates obtaining grants and contracts from extramural sources	1 2 3 4 5	(64)
14. Improves the department's image and reputation in the total campus community	1 2 3 4 5	(65)
15. Encourages an appropriate balance among specializations within the department	1 2 3 4 5	(66)

Form 2

SURVEY FORM--FACULTY REACTIONS TO CHAIRPERSON ACTIVITIES

Department ______________________ Institution ______________________

• The list below describes 15 responsibilities which some department chairpersons/heads pursue. In Column 1, circle the number corresponding to your judgment of how important each of these should be for your chairperson/head using the following code:

1 — Not Important
2 — Only So-So
3 — Fairly Important
4 — Quite Important
5 — Essential

• Use Column 2 to describe how effectively you feel your department chairperson/head fulfilled each responsibility during the past 12 months. Omit any item if you feel you cannot make a valid judgment; otherwise circle the number best corresponding to your estimate:

1 — Poor
2 — Only So-So
3 — In Between
4 — Good
5 — Outstanding

IMPORTANCE COLUMN 1	CHAIRPERSON/HEAD RESPONSIBILITIES	PERFORMANCE COLUMN 2
1. 1 2 3 4 5	Guides the development of sound procedures for assessing faculty performance	16. 1 2 3 4 5
2. 1 2 3 4 5	Recognizes and rewards faculty in accordance with their contributions to department's program	17. 1 2 3 4 5
3. 1 2 3 4 5	Guides development of sound organizational plan to accomplish departmental program	18. 1 2 3 4 5
4. 1 2 3 4 5	Arranges effective and equitable allocation of faculty responsibilities such as committee assignments, teaching loads, etc.	19. 1 2 3 4 5
5. 1 2 3 4 5	Takes lead in recruitment of promising faculty	20. 1 2 3 4 5
6. 1 2 3 4 5	Fosters good teaching in the department	21. 1 2 3 4 5
7. 1 2 3 4 5	Stimulates research and scholarly activity in the department	22. 1 2 3 4 5
8. 1 2 3 4 5	Guides curriculum development	23. 1 2 3 4 5
9. 1 2 3 4 5	Maintains faculty morale by reducing, resolving or preventing conflicts	24. 1 2 3 4 5
10. 1 2 3 4 5	Fosters development of each faculty member's special talents or interests	25. 1 2 3 4 5
11. 1 2 3 4 5	Understands and communicates expectations of the campus administration to the faculty	26. 1 2 3 4 5
12. 1 2 3 4 5	Effectively communicates the department's needs (personnel, space, monetary) to the dean	27. 1 2 3 4 5
13. 1 2 3 4 5	Facilitates obtaining grants and contracts from extramural sources	28. 1 2 3 4 5
14. 1 2 3 4 5	Improves the department's image and reputation in the total campus community	29. 1 2 3 4 5
15. 1 2 3 4 5	Encourages an appropriate balance among academic specializations within the department	30. 1 2 3 4 5

• Indicate how frequently each of the following 30 statements is descriptive of your department chairperson/head by circling the number corresponding to your judgment:

1 — Hardly Ever (not at all descriptive)
2 — Less than Half the Time
3 — About Half the Time
4 — More than Half the Time
5 — Almost Always (very descriptive)

The department chairperson/head:

Statement	Rating
31. Makes own attitudes clear to the faculty	1 2 3 4 5
32. Tries out new ideas with the faculty	1 2 3 4 5
33. Works without a plan	1 2 3 4 5
34. Maintains definite standards of performance	1 2 3 4 5
35. Makes sure his/her part in the department is understood by all members	1 2 3 4 5
36. Lets faculty members know what's expected of them	1 2 3 4 5
37. Sees to it that faculty members are working up to capacity	1 2 3 4 5
38. Sees to it that the work of faculty members is coordinated	1 2 3 4 5
39. Does little things that make it pleasant to be a member of the faculty	1 2 3 4 5
40. Is easy to understand	1 2 3 4 5
41. Keeps to him/herself	1 2 3 4 5
42. Looks out for the personal welfare of individual faculty members	1 2 3 4 5
43. Refuses to explain actions	1 2 3 4 5
44. Acts without consulting the faculty	1 2 3 4 5
45. Is slow to accept new ideas	1 2 3 4 5

—OVER—

46. Treats all faculty members as his/her equal	1	2	3	4	5
47. Is willing to make changes	1	2	3	4	5
48. Makes faculty members feel at ease when talking to them	1	2	3	4	5
49. Puts faculty suggestions into action	1	2	3	4	5
50. Gets faculty approval on important matters before going ahead	1	2	3	4	5
51. Postpones decisions unnecessarily	1	2	3	4	5
52. Is more a reactor than an initiator	1	2	3	4	5
53. Makes it clear that faculty suggestions for improving the department are welcome	1	2	3	4	5
54. Is responsive to one "clique" in the faculty but largely ignores those who are not members of the clique	1	2	3	4	5
55. In expectations of faculty members, makes allowance for their personal or situational problems	1	2	3	4	5
56. Lets faculty members know when they've done a good job	1	2	3	4	5
57. Explains the basis for his/her decisions	1	2	3	4	5
58. Gains input from faculty on important matters	1	2	3	4	5
59. Acts as though visible department accomplishments were vital to him/her	1	2	3	4	5
60. Acts as though high faculty morale was vital to him/her	1	2	3	4	5

• Questions 61-70 ask about yourself or the department in general. Use this answer code:

1 — Definitely False
2 — More False than True
3 — In Between
4 — More True than False
5 — Definitely True

61. I enjoy my work in this department	1	2	3	4	5
62. I have a positive relationship with the department chairperson	1	2	3	4	5
63. I agree with the priorities and emphases which have guided recent development in the department	1	2	3	4	5
64. The department has been getting stronger in recent years (use responses 1 or 2 if it has been getting weaker; use response 3 if there has been little change)	1	2	3	4	5

During the past 12 months, the department chairperson's/head's effectiveness has been seriously impaired by:

65. Enrollment/retrenchment problems in the department	1	2	3	4	5
66. Inadequate facilities for the department	1	2	3	4	5
67. Bureaucratic requirements and regulations	1	2	3	4	5
68. Inadequate financial resources to support departmental programs	1	2	3	4	5
69. A relatively low priority given to the department by the chairperson's /head's immediate superior	1	2	3	4	5
70. Obstructionism/negativism from one or more senior members of the faculty	1	2	3	4	5

• Your responses to the following questions will be returned to your chairperson/head. If you are concerned about anonymity, you may wish to type your responses or have them typed.

Which matters need priority attention in the department during the next year or two? ______________________

Identify any departmental policies or procedures which you feel need immediate improvement. ______________________

What is the most important observation you can make about the department chairperson's/head's:

a) administrative effectiveness? ______________________

b) administrative style? ______________________

Other comments: ______________________

Form 3

DECA REPORT

UNIVERSITY COLLEGE

J. J. DOE
DEPARTMENT OF ADVANCED STUDIES
SPRING 1976-77

NUMBER ASKED TO REACT: 10
NUMBER RESPONDING: 10
PERCENT RESPONDING: 100%

PART I. RESPONSIBILITIES

	IMPORTANCE			PERFORMANCE							
	HEAD	FACULTY		NUMBER RESPONDING							
		MEAN	S.D.	1	2	3	4	5	OMIT	MEAN	COMPARISON
A. PERSONNEL MANAGEMENT											
1. GUIDES FAC EVAL PROCEDURES	4	4.2	.7	0	0	3	5	2	0	3.9	HIGH AVG
2. REWARDS FAC APPROPRIATELY	4	4.5	.7	0	1	2	6	1	0	3.7	AVERAGE
4. ALLOCATES FACULTY RESPONSIBILITY	4	4.7	.5	0	0	1	4	5	0	4.4	HIGH AVG
9. MAINTAINS MORALE	4	4.4	.8	0	1	4	4	1	0	3.5	AVERAGE
10. FOSTERS FACULTY DEVELOPMENT	3	4.4	.8	0	0	3	6	1	0	3.8	AVERAGE
11. COMMUNICATES U. EXPECTATIONS	3	4.4	.8	0	0	1	6	3	0	4.2	AVERAGE
B. DEPT. PLANNING AND DEVELOPMENT											
3. GUIDES DEVELOPMENT OF PLANS	4	4.5	.7	0	0	2	6	2	0	4.0	HIGH AVG
5. FACULTY RECRUITMENT	2	3.6	.9	1	1	3	3	2	0	3.4	LOW AVG
6. FOSTERS GOOD TEACHING	4	4.4	.8	0	3	4	1	2	0	3.2	LOW AVG
8. GUIDES CURRICULUM DEVELOPMENT	4	3.9	.7	0	0	1	3	6	0	4.5	HIGH
15. ENCOURAGES BALANCED FACULTY	4	4.0	.6	0	0	2	3	4	1	4.2	HIGH AVG
C. BUILDING DEPARTMENT REPUTATION											
7. STIM RSCH/SCHOLARLY EFFORT	3	4.3	.8	0	2	1	2	5	0	4.0	HIGH AVG
12. COMMUNICATES DEPT'S NEEDS	3	4.8	.4	0	0	2	3	5	0	4.3	AVERAGE
13. FACILITATES OUTSIDE FUNDING	2	3.7	.8	1	1	3	2	2	1	3.3	AVERAGE
14. IMPROVES DEPT'S IMAGE	3	4.3	.8	0	0	2	3	5	0	4.3	HIGH AVG

PART II. EVALUATION SUMMARY	PERSONNEL MANAGEMENT	PLANNING & DEVELOPMENT	DEPARTMENT REPUTATION	TOTAL
A. PERFORMANCE WEIGHTED BY FACULTY IMP RATINGS	3.9 (HI AVG)	3.9 (AVG)	4.0 (HI AVG)	3.9 (AVG)
B. PERFORMANCE WEIGHTED BY HEAD'S IMP RATINGS	3.9 (HI AVG)	3.9 (AVG)	4.0 (HI AVG)	3.9 (AVG)
C. AGREEMENT AMONG FACULTY ON IMPORTANCE (INTRACLASS R)	---	---	---	.49 (AVG)
D. HEAD/FACULTY AGREEMENT ON IMPORTANCE (CORRELATION)	---	---	---	.47 (AVG)

J. J. DOE
DEPARTMENT OF ADVANCED STUDIES

UNIVERSITY COLLEGE
SPRING 1975-76

PART III. ADMINISTRATIVE METHODS

Item	Number Responding 1	2	3	4	5	OMIT	MEAN	DIFF FROM AVG	TRANSLATION
A. DEMOCRATIC PRACTICE — TOTAL SCORE = 3.9 (AVG)									
40. EASY TO UNDERSTAND	1	0	0	3	6	0	4.3	+0.4	FAV
(43.) REFUSES TO EXPLAIN ACTIONS	6	2	2	0	0	0	(1.6)	-0.1	-
(44.) ACTS WITHOUT CONSULTING FACULTY	4	4	2	0	0	0	(1.8)	-0.3	FAV
(45.) SLOW TO ACCEPT NEW IDEAS	9	0	0	1	0	0	(1.3)	-0.7	FAV
46. TREATS FACULTY AS EQUALS	4	1	0	2	3	0	2.9	-1.0	UNFAV
47. WILLING TO MAKE CHANGES	0	0	0	4	6	0	4.6	+0.6	FAV
49. PUTS FACULTY SUGGESTIONS INTO ACTION	0	1	5	1	3	0	3.6	0.0	-
50. GETS FACULTY APPROVAL BEFORE PROCEEDING	1	2	2	4	1	0	3.2	-0.8	UNFAV
53. WELCOMES FACULTY SUGGESTIONS	0	1	1	3	4	1	4.1	0.0	-
(54.) RESPONDS TO FACULTY CLIQUE	3	2	2	1	1	1	(2.4)	+0.4	UNFAV
57. EXPLAINS DECISIONS	1	0	2	3	4	0	3.9	0.0	-
58. GAINS FACULTY INPUT	1	1	1	4	3	0	3.7	-0.4	UNFAV
B. STRUCTURING — TOTAL SCORE = 4.2 (HIGH)									
31. MAKES ATTITUDES CLEAR	0	0	0	4	6	0	4.6	+0.6	FAV
(33.) WORKS W/O A PLAN	5	3	2	0	0	0	(1.7)	-0.2	-
34. MAINTAINS PERFORMANCE STANDARDS	1	1	0	5	3	0	3.8	+0.1	-
35. MAKES ROLE UNDERSTOOD	0	0	1	3	6	0	4.5	+0.8	FAV
36. LETS FACULTY KNOW EXPECTATIONS	0	0	2	3	5	0	4.3	+0.7	FAV
37. SEES THAT FACULTY WORK TO CAPACITY	0	0	2	5	3	0	4.1	+0.7	FAV
38. SEES THAT FACULTY WORK IS COORDINATED	0	2	3	3	2	0	3.5	+0.2	-
C. INTERPERSONAL SENSITIVITY — TOTAL SCORE = 3.3 (LO AVG)									
39. DOES LITTLE THINGS TO PLEASE	2	1	2	3	2	0	3.2	-0.3	UNFAV
(41.) KEEPS TO HIM/HERSELF	1	3	1	2	2	1	(3.1)	+0.8	UNFAV
42. LOOKS OUT FOR PERSONAL WELFARE OF FACULTY	3	1	0	3	3	0	3.2	-0.4	UNFAV
48. PUTS FACULTY AT EASE IN CONVERSATION	1	1	4	1	3	0	3.4	-0.7	UNFAV
55. MAKES ALLOWANCE FOR FACULTY PROBLEMS	2	0	0	3	3	2	3.6	-0.4	UNFAV
56. ACKNOWLEDGES GOOD WORK	2	1	2	2	3	0	3.3	-0.3	UNFAV
60. STRESSES FACULTY MORALE	2	0	2	3	3	0	3.5	-0.1	-
D. VIGOR — TOTAL SCORE = 4.7 (HIGH)									
32. TRIES NEW IDEAS WITH FACULTY	0	0	1	2	7	0	4.6	+1.0	FAV
(51.) POSTPONES DECISIONS UNNECESSARILY	9	1	0	0	0	0	(1.1)	-0.7	FAV
(52.) MORE A REACTOR THAN INITIATOR	8	2	0	0	0	0	(1.2)	-1.2	FAV
59. PLACES STRESS ON ACCOMPLISHMENT	0	0	1	3	6	0	4.5	+0.6	FAV

( ) INDICATES ITEMS WHERE LOW SCORES ARE DESIRABLE

J. J. DOE
DEPARTMENT OF ADVANCED STUDIES

UNIVERSITY COLLEGE
SPRING 1975-76

PART IV. CHARACTERIZATION OF DEPARTMENT

	NUMBER RESPONDING FALSE 1	2	? 3	4	TRUE 5	OMIT	MEAN
A. FACULTY							
61. ENJOY WORK	0	0	1	3	6	0	4.5
62. HAVE POSITIVE RELATIONSHIP WITH CHAIRPERSON/HEAD	1	0	4	4	1	0	3.4
63. AGREE WITH DEPARTMENT PRIORITIES	1	0	1	3	5	0	4.1
64. DEPARTMENT IS IMPROVING (3 = NO CHANGE)	0	0	3	6	1	0	3.8
B. CHAIRPERSON/HEAD PERFORMANCE ADVERSELY AFFECTED BY:							
65. ENROLL/RETRENCHMENT PROBLEMS	3	5	2	0	0	0	1.9
66. INADEQUATE FACILITIES	4	6	0	0	0	0	1.6
67. BUREAUCRATIC RED TAPE	0	1	4	3	2	0	3.6
68. INADEQUATE FINANCIAL RESOURCES	1	1	3	4	1	0	3.3
69. DEAN'S LOW PRIORITY FOR DEPARTMENT	0	0	1	3	6	0	4.5
70. NEGATIVISM FROM SENIOR FACULTY MEMBER(S)	4	4	0	1	1	0	2.1

PART V. DIAGNOSTIC SUMMARY

	PERF RATING	METHODS RELEVANT TO EACH RESPONSIBILITY[1]: WEAKNESSES	STRENGTHS
A. PERSONNEL MANAGEMENT			
*1. GUIDES FAC EVAL PROCEDURES	HI AVG	FAVORABLE RATINGS	35,36,51,40,44
*2. REWARDS FAC APPROPRIATELY	AVERAGE	46,42,39,56	35,36,47.40
*4. ALLOCATES FAC RESPONSIBILITIES	HI AVG	FAVORABLE RATINGS	35,36,51,40
*9. MAINTAINS MORALE	AVERAGE	46,41,50,48,42,58,55,39	32,35,45,47,40,44
10. FOSTERS FACULTY DEVELOPMENT	AVERAGE	46,42,58,55,39,56	35,36,37,40
11. COMMUNICATES U. EXPECTATIONS	AVERAGE		32,35,45,36,37,51,31,40
B. DEPARTMENT PLANNING AND DEVELOPMENT			
*3. GUIDES DEVELOPMENT OF PLANS	HI AVG	FAVORABLE RATINGS	52,32,35,45,36,37,51
5. FACULTY RECRUITMENT	LO AVG	46,58,55	52,32,59
*6. FOSTERS GOOD TEACHING	LO AVG	42,39	32,35,36,37,51,40
8. GUIDES CURRICULUM DEVELOPMENT	HIGH	FAVORABLE RATINGS	52,32,51,59,44
*15. ENCOURAGES BALANCED FACULTY	HI AVG	FAVORABLE RATINGS	35,45,36,37
C. BUILDING DEPARTMENT REPUTATION			
7. STIM RSCH/SCHOL EFFORT	HI AVG	FAVORABLE RATINGS	52,32,45,59,47,44
12. COMMUNICATES DEPTS NEED	AVERAGE		52,32,35,45,37,51,47,40
13. FACILITATES OUTSIDE FUNDING	AVERAGE	55,56	52,32,47
14. IMPROVES DEPARTMENT'S IMAGE	HI AVG	FAVORABLE RATINGS	52,32,35,45,51,47,40

*RATED AT LEAST "4" IN IMPORTANCE BY BOTH FACULTY AND CHAIRPERSON/HEAD
NOTE 1: SEE PAGE 2 TO IDENTIFY CONTENT OF THE ITEMS LISTED BY NUMBER

Form 4

(Please Do Not Sign Your Name)

Evaluation of the Academic Dean Rating Forms

The Academic Dean would appreciate your candid evaluation of his professional performance. Please elect a faculty member to pick up your completed questionnaires, collate them, and provide the Dean with the results. This will preserve anonymity.

There are no "correct" or "right" answers to any of these questions. Your opinion, along with the opinions of the rest of the faculty, will help the Dean recognize how well he is meeting your goals for him and his own professional goals.

Each item consists of four parts:

s. a statement concerning the Academic Dean's function
c. a continuum built on this statement
i. your estimate of where the "ideal" Dean in your college would be on this continuum
a. your estimate of the Dean's actual performance

Example:

s. Encouraging Faculty to Attend Professional Meetings
The Academic Dean is in a position to influence faculty to attend regional or national meetings dealing with their academic discipline.

	1	7
c.	The Dean actively discourages faculty attendance at professional meetings.	The Dean does everything he can to encourage faculty attendance at professional meetings.

i. Ideally, the Dean should be at point _____.
a. Actually, the Dean is at point _____.

Note:

Consider *c* above to be seven different points on a continuum. A rating of "4" would indicate complete neutrality or indifference on the Dean's part. A rating of "3" would indicate a slightly negative attitude, "5" a slightly positive attitude, "6" a very positive attitude, and "7" would indicate that the Dean goes so far as to keep a record of attendance at professional meetings and makes a point of putting pressure on individual faculty members to attend such meetings.

If you feel that *ideally* the Dean should encourage but not pressure faculty attendance at professional meetings, you would put down a "5" or a "6" for *i*.

If you feel that the Dean *actually* is ambivalent about faculty attendance at professional meetings, you would put down a "4" for *a*.

I. **Administrative Management**

s. The Academic Dean performs or supervises many administrative functions. This includes such things as class schedules, budgets, committee assignments, etc.

1	4	7
c. The Dean is efficient and effective in handling administrative functions.	The Dean handles some administrative functions well and some rather poorly.	The Dean is inefficient and ineffective in dealing with administrative functions.

i. Ideally, the Dean should be at point ____.
a. Actually, the Dean is at point ____.

II. **Executive Judgment**

s. As an administrator, the Academic Dean is called upon to make a number of significant decisions. Some must be made hastily and with little information. No one can be right all of the time. Here we are concerned with the ultimate wisdom of these executive actions or judgments.

1	4	7
c. When we look back at the Dean's judgments and the consequences of them, it appears that most of the time he has made a poor decision.	When we look back at the Dean's judgments and the consequences of them, it appears that one-half of the time his decisions have been good ones.	When we look back at the Dean's judgments and the consequences of them, it appears that nearly all of the time he has made a sound decision.

i. Ideally, the Dean would be at point ____.
a. Actually, the Dean is at point ____.

III. **Delegating Authority and Responsibility**

s. In carrying out the work of the college, the Academic Dean is in a position to delegate authority and the requisite responsibility to department chairmen, division chairmen, and administrators reporting to the Dean.

1	7
c. The Dean is not skillful in delegating authority and responsibility to appropriate persons.	The Dean is skillfull in delegating authority and responsibility to appropriate persons.

i. Ideally, the Dean would be at point ____.
a. Actually, the Dean is at point ____.

IV. **Providing Academic Leadership**

s. Some faculty groups need and want academic leadership. The Academic Dean is in a position where he can provide stimulating ideas to the faculty either through his own ingenuity or by using the ideas of others.

1	7
c. The Dean provides outstanding academic leadership. He brings many stimulating ideas to the attention of the faculty.	The Dean provides little or no academic leadership. He never brings stimulating ideas to the attention of the faculty.

i. Ideally, the Dean would be at point ____.
a. Actually, the Dean is at point ____.

V. **Acting Decisively**

s. The Academic Dean does not have complete freedom of movement in decision making. His authority is limited by faculty rights and procedures on one hand and the President and Board of Trustees on the other hand. In all situations, however, he does have some decision-making authority.

1	7
c. When most of the facts are available and a decision is needed, the Dean hesitates and is indecisive.	When most of the facts are available and a decision is needed, the Dean acts promptly and decisively.

i. Ideally, the Dean would be at point ____.
a. Actually, the Dean is at point ____.

Reminder:

Ratings of "1" and "7" are the extremes. Ratings of 2, 3, 4, 5, and 6 may be given.

VI. **Planning Ability**

s. The Academic Dean is often called upon to plan new programs, forecast future events, and prepare for them.

1	7
c. The Dean demonstrates little or no skill or foresight in college planning.	The Dean demonstrates great skill and foresight in college planning.

i. Ideally, the Dean would be at point ____.
a. Actually, the Dean is at point ____.

VII. **Encouragement of Faculty Research**

s. The Academic Dean is in a position to influence the research activities of faculty. Faculty research may be seen as more important in some institutions than it is in others.

1	7
c. The Dean does nothing to encourage faculty research.	The Dean does everything in his power to encourage faculty research.

i. Ideally, the Dean should be at point ____.
a. Actually, the Dean is at point ____.

VIII. **Improvement of Teaching**

s. The Academic Dean is in a key position regarding the quality of instruction. He may be able to influence teaching performance through the use of financial resources, consultants, etc.

1	7
c. The Dean does everything he can to help individuals and the faculty as a whole become better teachers.	The Dean does little or nothing to help individuals or the faculty as a whole become better teachers.

i. Ideally, the Dean should be at point ____.
a. Actually, the Dean is at point ____.

IX. **Dean's Role as Faculty Representative**

s. In most institutions the Academic Dean is responsible for representing the faculty to the President and the Board of Trustees.

1	7
c. The Dean can be counted upon to accurately and force-	The Dean does not represent faculty concerns to the Presi-

fully represent the concerns of the faculty to the President and the Board of Trustees.	dent and the Board of Trustees.

i. Ideally, the Dean would be at point _____.
a. Actually, the Dean is at point _____.

X. **Skill in Recruiting Faculty**

s. The Academic Dean is in a key position in the recruitment and selection of new faculty.

1	7
c. The Dean does a very poor job in the recruitment of new faculty.	The Dean does an outstanding job in the recruitment of new faculty.

i. Ideally, the Dean should be at point _____.
a. Actually, the Dean is at point _____.

XI. **Keeping Communication Lines Open**

s. The Academic Dean is in a position to keep college communication lines open. Occasionally he will have certain information that he should not divulge, but generally he can share, and encourage others to share, information about the college.

1	4	7
c. The Dean does everything he can to facilitate the flow of information to faculty and staff.	The Dean does little to facilitate or inhibit the flow of information to faculty and staff.	The Dean tries to keep information lines closed to faculty and staff.

i. Ideally, the Dean should be at point _____.
a. Actually, the Dean is at point _____.

XII. **Providing Academic Freedom**

s. The Academic Dean is in a key position in regard to academic freedom. He can act as a bulwark against attacks from both within and without the college.

1	7
c. The Dean does not provide or protect academic freedom.	The Dean can be relied upon to provide and protect academic freedom.

i. Ideally, the Dean should be at point _____.

a. Actually, the Dean is at point ____.

XIII. **Skill in Working with Groups**

s. The Academic Dean spends much of his time with committees and small groups. Most of those groups are engaged in defining and solving problems.

	1	7
c.	As a group member or leader, the Dean has little or no skill in helping the group define or solve its problems.	As a group member or leader, the Dean is very skillful in helping the group define and solve its problems.

i. Ideally, the Dean would be at point ____.
a. Actually, the Dean is at point ____.

XIV. **Communicating Ideas**

s. The Academic Dean is in a position to communicate ideas, solicit support for a program, explain curricular changes, or communicate other relatively abstract concepts to faculty and others.

	1	7
c.	The Dean communicates with clarity. After listening to him, you always feel you understand his meaning.	The Dean does not communicate with clarity. After listening to him, you are rarely sure of his meaning.

i. Ideally, the Dean would be at point ____.
a. Actually, the Dean is at point ____.

XV. **Sensitivity to Faculty Concerns**

s. The Academic Dean is in a position to be aware of matters that are of concern to academic divisions, departments, or individual faculty members.

	1	7
c.	The Dean is insensitive to faculty feelings and does not readily understand their relative level of concern about issues and problems.	The Dean is sensitive to faculty feelings and quick in discerning their relative level of concern about issues and problems.

i. Ideally, the Dean should be at point ____.
a. Actually, the Dean is at point ____.

XVI. **Handling Conflict**

s. The Academic Dean is in a position to be aware of any real or potential conflict between individuals or factions on the faculty or staff. It may not be wise to avoid conflict but his actions should help to reduce rather than increase disharmony.

	1	7
c.	The Dean does nothing to reduce intra-faculty conflict.	The Dean does everything possible to avoid or decrease unnecessary intra-faculty conflict.

i. Ideally, the Dean would be at point _____.
a. Actually, the Dean is at point _____.

XVII. **Acceptance of New Ideas**

s. In many institutions the Academic Dean is in a position where his attitude toward a new idea or academic program has a substantial influence upon institutional change.

	1	7
c.	The Dean is open to new ideas. He may not support every new proposal but his initial response is open and cordial.	The Dean is fearful of new ideas. His initial response to new proposals is negative.

i. Ideally, the Dean would be at point _____.
a. Actually, the Dean is at point _____.

XVIII. **Availability to Faculty**

s. The Academic Dean has a multitude of responsibilities. These responsibilities sometimes limit his time for personal consultation or discussion with individual faculty members.

	1	7
c.	The Dean usually avoids talking to faculty members. He prefers to be unavailable.	The Dean encourages faculty to talk to him whenever possible.

i. Ideally, the Dean would be at point _____.
a. Actually, the Dean is at point _____.

XIX. **Listening to Faculty**

s. The Academic Dean can learn little from faculty unless he "listens" to them. Listening to faculty does not necessarily mean agreeing with them. It does mean trying to understand their meaning.

1	7
c. The Dean seldom "listens." He is usually thinking of something else.	The Dean generally listens very carefully. He tries to understand the faculty member's meaning.

i. Ideally, the Dean would be at point ____.
a. Actually, the Dean is at point ____.

XX. **Honesty**

s. The Academic Dean deals with faculty on many important matters and over an extended time period. Faculty should not only have faith in the Dean's good intentions but confidence that his actions will not contradict his words.

1	7
c. The Dean is often dishonest or insincere. One cannot rely on his word.	The Dean is honest and sincere. One can always rely upon his word.

i. Ideally, the Dean should be at point ____.
a. Actually, the Dean is at point ____.

XXI. **Personal/Professional Stability**

s. As an administrator the Academic Dean should be reasonably resilient. When difficulties rise, his actions should be based upon logic and common sense rather than an emotional "set."

1	7
c. In response to difficult situations the Dean exhibits a high level of personal/professional stability.	In response to difficult situations, the Dean exhibits a low level of personal/professional stability.

i. Ideally, the Dean should be at point ____.
a. Actually, the Dean is at point ____.

XXII. **Fairness**

s. Like everyone else, the Academic Dean has social preferences. He should, however, separate his social and professional feelings so that his social preferences do not affect the instructional program.

1	7
c. Knowingly or not, the Dean "plays favorites."	The Dean never allows his social preferences to influence his professional responsibilities.

i. Ideally, the Dean would be at point ____.
a. Actually, the Dean is at point ____.

You have evaluated the Academic Dean on the following items:

____	I	Administrative Management
____	II	Executive Judgment
____	III	Delegating Authority & Responsibility
____	IV	Providing Academic Leadership
____	V	Acting Decisively
____	VI	Planning Ability
____	VII	Encouragement of Faculty Research
____	VIII	Improvement of Teaching
____	IX	Dean's Role as Faculty Representative
____	X	Skill in Recruiting Faculty
____	XI	Keeping Communication Lines Open
____	XII	Providing Academic Freedom
____	XIII	Skill in Working with Groups
____	XIV	Communicating Ideas
____	XV	Sensitivity to Faculty Concerns
____	XVI	Handling Conflict
____	XVII	Acceptance of New Ideas
____	XVIII	Availability to Faculty
____	XIX	Listening to Faculty
____	XX	Honesty
____	XXI	Personal/Professional Stability
____	XXII	Fairness

In the space provided please put a "+" mark in front of the seven items you regard as the most important.

Please put a " –" mark in front of the seven items you regard as least important.

XXIII. The best thing to be said for the Dean or his office is:

____

____

XXIV. The worst thing about the Dean or his office is:

____

____

Notes

[1]Sample DECA materials are available from William E. Cashen, Center for Faculty Evaluation and Development, 1627 Anderson Avenue, Box 3000, Kansas State University, Manhattan, Kansas 66502

[2]The material relating to Rasmussen's instrument comes in large part from his chapter, "Evaluating the Academic Dean" in Charles F. Fisher (Ed.), *Developing and Evaluating Administrative Leadership, New Directions for Higher Education 22,* San Francisco: Jossey-Bass, 1978 and is reprinted with permission.

[3]For sample materials and assistance in using this rating scale, contact President Glen Rasmussen, Findlay College, Findlay, Ohio 45840

Bibliography

Casteter, William B. and Heisler, Richard S. *Appraising and Improving the Performance of School Administrative Personnel.* Philadelphia: Philadelphia Graduate School of Education, Center for Field Studies, University of Pennsylvania, 1971.

Cowley, W. H. "Don of Higher Educationists: In Search of a Discipline." College and University Business (June 69): 61-64.

Fiedler, Fred E.; Chemers, Martin M.; and Mahar, Linda. *Improving Leadership Effectiveness: The Leader Match Concept.* New York: John Wiley & Sons, 1976.

Flanagon, John C. "Critical Requirements: A New Approach to Employee Evaluation." *Personnel* (1949): 419-425.

Lahti, Robert E. "Developing Leadership for the Management of Higher Education." *College and University Business* (May 1970): 61-64.

McClelland, Ben W. "Organizational Context for Administrator Evaluation." Paper prepared for the ACE Fellow Program in Academic Administration, Rhode Island College, 1977.

Pullias, Earl V. "Ten Principles of College Administration." *School and Society* (February 1972): 95-97.

———. "Ten More Principles." *Intellect* (April 1973): 428-431.

———. "Ten Additional Principles." *Intellect* (November 1973): 92-95.

Rasmussen, Glen R. "Evaluating the Academic Dean." In Charles F. Fisher (Ed.), *Developing and Evaluating Administrative Leadership, New Directions for Higher Education 22.* San Francisco: Jossey-Bass, 1978.

Charles H. Farmer is Director of Institutional Research, Executive Assistant to the Vice President for Academic Affairs, and Professor of Mathematics, University of Tulsa.

Chapter Five
Growth Contracting for Administrator Evaluation and Development

Neal R. Berte
Edward H. O'Neil

The formal process of performance evaluation in higher education has matured greatly during the past decade. In a number of areas it has become a priority concern as witnessed by the increasing number of performance evaluations of faculty, administrators, and even of boards of trustees. This development can be partially attributed to three reasons. The first reason is an increasing need for individual accountability in work performance as institutions of higher education have become more aware of the need to effectively manage limited staff and faculty resources. This is also related to the growing feeling that retirement should not be mandatory until age seventy, giving rise to the need for added opportunities to encourage growth and development in a tighter job market for higher education. The second reason corresponds to the first in that there is an ever-larger expectation that institutions must be responsive to the needs of their employees. In this context, it is important to be mindful that society's definition of what constitutes employee needs is not punitive but concerned with individual fulfillment. The third reason is that through the work of individuals such as Gail Sheehy (1976), Daniel J. Levinson (1978), and others there is a growing understanding of the stages of adult development. As this knowledge increases and becomes more widely available, there should be greater efforts to apply it to performance evaluations.

One technique of performance evaluation that is gaining acceptance within the higher education community is the use of growth contracts for faculty and administrator evaluation. Growth contracts in various forms have been initiated or experimented with in several institutions: New College at the University of Alabama, Tuscaloosa; College of the Mainland (Texas City, Texas); Wharton County Junior College (Wharton, Texas); Austin College (Sherman, Texas); College of Education, University of Massachusetts, Amherst; and Golden College (Wenham, Massachusetts) (Gross, 1977). By growth contracts we mean any one of the various evaluation plans that provide individuals the opportunity to deal consciously with, and to express in writing, their goals and objectives for personal growth and development over a designated period of time. Each individual would take time to develop personal goals, preferably over a one-year period. These goals might, and usually do, relate directly to job performance; however, many individuals establish goals and objectives which are in the broader context of the growth and development of a person and not just an administrative officer or faculty member of the college. Encouragement is also given to each administrative officer to use similar growth contracts in the evaluation process for all employees in their area.

Growth contracts are considered to be a viable way to demonstrate professional competence. This is one of the most suitable means of encouraging ongoing professional development and bringing a greater measure of integrity and fairness to the process of evaluating faculty and administrators (Gross, 1976).

We now understand more about the stages of adult development: The Trying Twenties, Traumatic Thirties, and mid-life crises of the Forties (Sheehy, 1976). This awareness makes us more sensitive to the needs for personal and professional development for men and women. Harold L. Hodgkinson (1974) believes that we should use the theories about adult development, "as a diagnostic tool—helping us to understand individuals in the formation and revision of their goals, helping to mediate their conflicts with institutions, other persons, and with themselves, and above all, helping them to realize that some crisis and reorientation are vital for continued personal growth; without it we continue to live last year over again."

Growth contracts can lead to improved individual satisfaction with professional and personal growth. It gives the individual something specific to strive for and a sense of accomplishment. This might tie into career counseling to help an employee determine where he or she wants to go in life. Accomplishment of these goals increases the effectiveness of the individual for the benefit of the individual and the institution.

Growth contracting plans generally include four elements: (1) Self-Evaluation, (2) Specified Areas of Improvement, (3) Plan for Improvement, and (4) Long-Range Goals. Form 1 in the Appendix presents growth contract procedures as used by the New College at the University of Alabama in 1974 and 1975.

Self-Evaluation. This is perhaps the most difficult skill to master for individuals using a growth contract for the first time. It is our nature to be reluctant to admit personal strengths and weaknesses, particularly when we are asked to convey these to a supervisor or peer. To overcome this reluctance, it is important to focus first on some area of improvement that is job related. This behavior may in time be related to some personal characteristic which needs attention. For example, it may be much more effective for an individual to acknowledge a communication problem in his or her working relationships with students than to identify an underlying problem causing the poor performance, such as insecurity. Self-evaluation is critical to the success of the growth contract. It may be wide-ranging over a number of characteristics or narrowly focused on a few criteria. Regardless, it is important that the individual gain an honest grasp of his or her own strengths and weaknesses. This self-assessment is the foundation upon which a good growth contract is built.

Areas of Improvement. This aspect of the growth contract focuses on those factors that have been identified through the self-evaluation which the contractor wishes to improve. These improvements or goal statements may be related to job performance, professional, physical, or personal development. Although the growth contract model addresses development in its broadest sense, it is important to focus on a realistic number of areas in a given time frame. Examples of areas of improvement would be: improving skills such as lecture style or group leadership; acquisition of a new hobby; giving attention to particular details of one's work (improving teaching skills or evaluation of student performance); participating in committee work or service activities associated with one's job; or building new professional competencies beyond one's discipline. In stating each goal area for improvement, it is important that the individual developing the contract avoid vagueness and generalities. A well-stated goal is specific enough to suggest means for accomplishment.

Plan for Improvement. Once an individual has identified certain areas for improvement, it is crucial that the contract contain a description of ways in which these areas are to be addressed. Developing a plan for improvement is just as critical as identifying those areas that need it. For many, it is the first time they have thought along these lines although they may have been teaching or administrating for years. A specific plan of action will allow the contractor to assess his or her progress toward achieving goals and objectives as well as providing a good basis for evaluating the success of the growth contracting experience. Individuals should describe the step or steps taken during the year to accomplish the stated goals. It is important to be as specific as possible. For each step, it is important to indicate the basis upon which the consultant evaluator will judge the extent to which the goal has been accomplished. The more specific the contractor can be, the more meaningful this process of assessment can be. Examples of such plans for improvement might be a detailed list of readings, plans to attend a professional meeting, identification of ways to acquire a new interest or hobby, exercise or diet plan related to physical development, plans to attend a "human potentials" workshop, participation in an "outward-bound seminar," or broadening one's readings in areas beyond formal training. Another example is the use of video tape equipment as a way for a faculty member to review his or her own lecture presentation or style of interaction with students. Administrators might select a similar technique to observe their own interpersonal skills.

Long-Range Goals. This last aspect of the growth contract is an essential point of reference. While the first three elements of the growth contract are focused on immediate self-evaluation and plans for improvement in the coming year, the long-range goal setting allows the individual to put the short-range goals within a larger context. This exercise in life-planning on a five- or ten-year basis is a way for an individual to establish priorities and to work actively toward achieving them. Bringing these aspirations to a conscious level and having the individual address them in a systematic fashion makes for a happier individual and for a more effective employee.

Long-range goals might include moving from administration to teaching or vice versa, moving from an academic institution into business, obtaining additional educational training, beginning a family, or running for political office. These long-range goals should be realistically addressed in the self-evaluation and in the immediate plans for the coming year.

Growth-Contract Procedure. While there are a number of ways of pursuing growth contracts, the following is offered as an example which some have followed successfully. Keep in mind that a growth contract is an effective tool only when the individual contractor recognizes it is important to his or her personal development. Otherwise, it will be of little benefit if it is a required exercise of personnel evaluation. The individualized growth contract designed by each person and the specific provisions which are self-imposed represent one of its principal strengths (Gross, 1976).

The first step is that the individual completing the growth contract should give careful consideration to the four elements discussed above. It may also be helpful at this point to discuss these ideas with a trusted colleague who can provide positive as well as negative feedback. These elements are designed to provoke thoughts and are by no means the only areas an individual may wish to include in his contract. However, all of these areas should be given some consideration in the growth contracting process.

Once adequate thought and discussion have taken place regarding the four elements, the person completing the growth contract should attempt to reduce these thoughts to several pages in a writing style with which he or she is comfortable. After a final draft of a growth contract is reached, the individual should make plans for discussing it with a person significant in his or her life.

This consultation may be with an immediate supervisor, peer, or someone else whom the contractor highly values. The consultant should be a person who is especially suited to assist the contractor in the design and implementation of the contract and in the evaluation of personal and/or professional growth. Potential consultants may include colleagues in the faculty or administration, students, alumni, or colleagues at other institutions. The consultation should consist of a fairly lengthy discussion of self-evaluation, goals for the coming year, and the plan for achieving these goals. The consultant should provide honest and candid input in each of these areas. Form 2 in the Appendix shows an example of a growth contract from the Dean of a College.

After this consultation, changes may be made in the contract and a final copy prepared and kept by both the contractor and the consultant. The process of developing a growth contract and negotiating it with a "significant other" person is far more important than the actual content of the contract. However, these matters should be kept in mind before finalizing the contract:

1) The contract should reflect an adequate first-year step toward the realization of the individual's long-range goals.
2) The plan for improvement should be specific enough to suggest means for accomplishment as well as means for assessing the extent and quality of accomplishment.

It is vital that the growth contract be reviewed by both the contractor and the consultant at a designated time. This time should be no longer than one year but may be, in many cases, much shorter. The contractor might also meet periodically with the consultant to discuss progress toward goals and seek additional assistance as problems arise while achieving them. At the close of the period of time, the contractor and the consultant should once again discuss the contractor's progress toward goal achievement. This might also be the opportunity to negotiate a new growth contract for the coming year.

A successful program of growth contracts could develop an increased sense of the faculty as a community of mutually respected teaching scholars. Faculty and administrator growth contracts are designed to individualize responsibilities in relation to each person's particular strengths, weaknesses, and interests; raise the performance level of individuals and the total personnel; and to provide a more precise and comprehensive basis for evaluation of faculty and staff to improve decisions relative to personnel matters. Recognition that each person brings particular strengths and weaknesses to the academic community should encourage the development of plans for comprehensive growth and improvement of the individual.

Self-renewal is one of the greatest challenges that anyone faces. Educators cannot afford to limit their concern for growth and development to their student constituency; to be a truly educational institution faculty and administrators must be concerned with the overall development of their colleagues as well as themselves.

APPENDIX

Form 1

GROWTH CONTRACT PROCEDURES

NEW COLLEGE, UNIVERSITY OF ALABAMA 1974-1975

Introduction: Many psychologists through studies of human growth and potential have found that there is in individual human beings a deeply felt urge to reach one's fullest potential development. A personal growth contract is a method for designing one's own program of development. Growth for each person will be unique. It may occur through job enrichment, through growth of a purely personal nature, or, more likely, through a combination of both. It has been shown that if one does a competent job of self-evaluation and follows through a consistent and conscientious program of self-development that one's job and personal life will have increased self-satisfaction. The following procedure may be followed in completing the personal growth contract:

1. The individual completing the contract should give careful thought to the areas covered in the growth contract. These are designed to provoke thought and are by no means the only areas for each individual to include in his or her contract.
2. The growth contract should be filled out in a consultation with someone whose opinion the person making the contract highly values. Often this is the immediate supervisor of the individual making the contract as he or she has had daily contact with the person and is usually qualified to give helpful advice. The consultation could, however, be with any colleague or peer whose opinion is valued by the maker of the growth contract.
3. Both the individual making the contract and the advisor should keep a copy of the contract so that it can be reviewed and updated periodically.
4. The growth contract should be reviewed by the person who made the contract and the advisor at least yearly and it should be updated more often if necessary.

Suggested Areas For Consideration

1. *Self-Evaluation:* Using available information, evaluate areas such as your job performance, which would include, budgeting, planning, leadership, follow-through on details, communications, evaluations, physical and personal areas of development, how you work with people, etc.
2. *Areas of Improvement:* In what areas do you need improvement

such as job performance, professional development, physical and personal areas of development, etc.

3. *Plans for Improvement:* How specifically do you plan to improve in needed areas and how can you be helped in these areas. Examples might be: professional readings, attending professional meetings, setting goals and attaining them, broadening your interests, exercise and diet as related to physical growth, and other matters related to personal growth.
4. *Long-Range Goals:* What would you like to be doing five to ten years from now?

Form 2

GROWTH CONTRACT

Dean of the College

I have attempted to itemize those areas that I think are most appropriate for self-analysis and hopefully growth in the course of the next semester. At the same time, I have attempted to suggest in each category fairly specific ways that this activity may be measurable within the limit of my ability to do so.

(1) *Goal:* Attempt to get more exposure to the teaching-learning process in the College.
Approach: Sit in on more interdisciplinary seminars.

(2) *Goal:* More contact with individual students and small groups of students.
Approach: Build on the number of interviews from this semester so that at the end of the spring semester I will have personally interviewed each student enrolled in the College. Also continuation of some involvement in Student Life Studies meetings.

(3) *Goal:* Attempt to get more closely allied to research activities in the College.
Approach: Personally review the faculty evaluation of student development forms and continue to review faculty evaluations by students as well as to administer the evaluation of the Dean again during the spring semester. On the latter, attempt to be conscious of the feedback and make appropriate plans for the future.

(4) *Goal:* Continue activities to develop contract and foundation support for the College.
Approach: Continue to assist with evaluation of faculty development proposals, respond to any inquiries on three recent private foundation proposals that have been submitted, and also to continue to be involved in general interpretation activities on

behalf of the University to the state at large and the College more specifically.

(5) *Goal:* Attempt more retreat-setting opportunities for the total staff and encourage faculty to participate in other development kinds of opportunities as well as to participate in these myself. *Approach:* Continue to speak and get involved in educational programs and institutional visits as appropriate. These may be measured at the end of this academic year as some indication of activity here.

(6) *Goal:* Attempt to continue operating on a personalized level as a way to contribute to the mission of the College as a place where humane education takes place.

(7) *Goal:* Attempt to remain open to new ideas with greater efforts at interpretation for students and staff regarding specifics such as the purpose of interdisciplinary seminars, concern for standards, evaluation activities, etc.

(8) *Goal:* On a more personal level, continue a program of physical exercise, involvement in the community through teaching Sunday school to 4th, 5th, and 6th graders, and spend more time with family.

Bibliography

Gross, Richard F. "Faculty Growth Contracts." *Educational Horizons* (Winter 1976-77): 76.

Gross, Richard F. "Facilitating Administrator Development through Growth Contracts." Council for the Advancement of Small Colleges/American Association for Higher Education's Conference on Evaluation and Development of Administrators, February 4, 1977, Airlie House, Virginia.

Hodgkinson, Harold L. "Adult Development: Implications for Faculty and Administrators." *Educational Record* (Fall 1974): 263-74.

Levinson, Daniel J. *The Seasons of a Man's Life.* New York: Knopf, 1972.

Sheehy, Gail. *Passages: Predictable Crises of Adult Life.* New York: Dutton, 1976.

Neal R. Berte is President, Birmingham-Southern College.

Edward H. O'Neil is in Cultural Foundations of Education and American Studies, Syracuse University.

Chapter Six
The Ad Hoc Committee Model for Administrator Evaluation

G. Lester Anderson

This chapter sets forth a paradigm for the evaluation of academic administrators which we shall call the ad hoc evaluation committee model.[1] This model is analogous to the ad hoc search committee model used by colleges and universities to select faculty and administrators. The model has the following characteristics:

- Each evaluation is made by an ad hoc committee appointed for the purpose of making a specific evaluation.
- The committee is made up of members chosen from the constituent bodies of the college or university served by the administrator being evaluated and deemed significant enough to have a participant member on the committee.
- The committee is, in relative terms, small—perhaps as few as four and seldom as many as ten.
- The method of selection of committee members, their authority, mode of operation, and a statement as to their accountability should be codified and recorded in the college's or university's articles of governance.
- The authority of the governing board of the college or university (or like body) to make the determinative evaluation of the chief academic officer is complete. The ad hoc committee's evaluation of a president is thus subject to board review and possible rejection.
- The authority of the board of trustees to continue in office or to remove from office an academic administrator on the recommendation of the president is also complete. The ad hoc evaluation of administrators other than the president is subject to presidential review, and its evaluation with the president's view is subject to definitive action by the institution's governing board.

Sections of this chapter will set forth in greater detail the 1) criteria against which evaluation judgments are made, 2) composition of an ad hoc evaluation committee, 3) methods of selection, 4) principles basic to the use of an ad hoc evaluation committee, 5) nature of the evaluation process, 6) nature of the evaluation report, and 7) the principles, assumptions, and caveats relevant to the work of an evaluation committee.

The logic for evaluation of academic administrators is set forth in Section I of this volume. Alternatives to the ad hoc committee model are also presented in other chapters. In the larger frame of reference that supports the case for formal administrator evaluation, there are, however, aspects that particularly support the ad hoc committee model as an alternative to others in colleges and universities. These aspects, in association with a definition of academic administration and of evaluation, will be noted at this time.

While logic for the evaluation of administrators in large complex organizations (businesses or industries) also supports the evaluation of academic administrators, it does not necessarily or unequivocally support the view that the processes in colleges or universities should be modeled on the processes of business. Institutions of higher education do not conform to the norms of organizations in business, industry, or government. This deviance has to do with constituencies and the decision-making process in colleges and universities (Mortimer and McConnell, 1978).

It is to accommodate the peculiar nature of the college and university—the various roles that administrators carry; the nature of authority shared by trustees, administrators, and faculty in the decision-making process; and the special role of students that binds them into the institution in a way distinct from that of a consumer—that directs us to present our ad hoc evaluation committee model as an alternative to more conventional models.[2]

But, first, two definitions:

Academic administration is leadership and managerial activity associated with teaching, research, educational services (such as counseling or placement), and extension activities including continuing education.

Evaluation is a process to review and assess the performance of academic administrators and to make a value judgment concerning this performance.

Criteria and Conditions

There are numerous criteria that evaluators should or can be aware of; criteria that illuminate an area of administrative responsibility, provide indicators of performance, and help to define, describe, or measure performance. Criteria signifying failure or success in administration are imperfectly expressed. They are not amenable to universal agreement as to their utility. In addition, they often do not lend themselves to measurement and quantification in ways that will win acceptance or please students of measurement and quantification of human characteristics or behavior.

On the other hand, those who work in or study the academic world (faculty and others) do have considerable experience as to what the successful administrator should do and what he or she should be. These persons have set forth many elements relevant to judgments of success or failure in administrative roles, and these elements have an empirical wisdom. It is in this sense of pragmatic considerations, of the insights that win the approval of those who are experienced and who have an intuitive sense of the rightness or wrongness of administrative acts, that we move now to the discussion of criteria from which judgments can be made.

The competencies that an administrator must demonstrate over time are multi-faceted, overlapping, and often contradictory. To say that a president or dean must on occasion be bold is a valid statement. To say that a president or dean must on occasion be cautious is also valid. The consequence is that there is no way to identify a few qualities, characteristics, habit patterns, competencies, or performances that will permit a valid evaluation of academic administrators on all occasions. It is reasonable to suggest that all require a complex of attributes. Likewise, the situation in which administrators operate is, in almost all instances, an environment of complexity rather than simplicity, of ambiguity rather than clarity.

Finally and as noted earlier, the college or university is an organization that, if not unique, is representative of a very small class that is not to be perceived, or judged, or managed by conditions operating in the worlds of business and industry. We will make no further attempt here to be definitive about colleges and universities as organizations, but we will be suggestive and thus hope to indicate the variety of talent academic administrators need.

First, faculties of the nation's colleges and universities enjoy freedoms known to few others in our society, *i.e.* they are autonomous professionals. They claim and receive a considerable participation in the governance (management) of colleges and universities. Few other organizations have such a complex management system where the workers have such a high degree of self-governance and policy control and are permitted to assume that administrators are in many respects responsible to the members of the organization.

Second, colleges and universities operate in the public interest in a very special way. They provide the nation's workers whom we call professionals, they are the chief knowledge producers, and they are one of but a few institutions that serve as the nation's conscience and the nation's critic. In these terms, they are accountable and their administrators are accountable in ways that are faced by few other institutions. This statement should establish the uniqueness of the college or university administrative task.

Let us now record a list of criteria that may be valid for ad hoc evaluation committees to use in judging academic administrators and are relatively complete. The classes of criteria are as follows:

1. Criteria related to education and training
2. Criteria related to experience
3. Criteria related to organizational production
4. Criteria related to organizational efficiency
5. Criteria related to performance as an academic leader
6. Criteria related to performance as an academic manager
7. Criteria related to personality, health, energy, personal values, and administrative style
8. Criteria of educational statesmanship
9. Criteria related to astuteness and sophistication in such affairs as are political, economic, social, and involving interactions with persons on and off campus
10. Criteria that would seem to be related to institutional uniqueness or special institutional attributes
11. Criteria, if satisfied, that counterbalance weaknesses elsewhere
12. Criteria that, if not satisfied, guarantee failure

Education and Experience. Criteria related to education or training and experience would seem more valid to a search process than to performance or current status as an administrator. After a person holds an academic administrative position, evaluators will give more attention to "on-the-job" displays of performance, character, and so on. Hence, these criteria will not have a significant place in the list of criteria against which academic administrative performance is judged.

Productivity and Efficiency. Criteria of productivity and efficiency seem, on first consideration, to be extremely important. Evaluation of administrators in the business and industrial world, in the management of athletic teams, and in some other occupational groups give great weight to productivity and efficiency criteria. However, their use in judging academic administrators has grave limitations.

Colleges and universities and their academic administration can be evaluated best in elementary terms of productivity and efficiency only. Other criteria frequently take precedence—morale, spirit, creativity, loyalty, spectacular success in a single sphere of effort, deferred satisfactions not measured in terms of months or a few years, and so on.

Productivity in colleges and universities often can only be crudely quantified and quality is often not ascertainable except over extended periods of time, often as long as even fifty years or more. If one counts number of degrees, student credit hours generated, number of dropouts, journal articles or books published, or costs per student, much additional information is required before one knows whether or not the "countings" have any validity; in some respects, the validity may be nonexistent or highly ambiguous.

Likewise, evaluations of presumed efficiency standards are treacherous to interpret, even by the wisest of informed persons. Is a system with high admissions standards and low dropout rates presumed to be better in terms of efficiency standards than one with open admissions and higher dropout rates? One does not dare to say "Yes" except as much, much more information is available, and then not always with certainty. Much more, of course, can be said as an interpretation of this idea.

Finally, it is hazardous, at best, to relate such measures of productivity and efficiency of colleges and universities as organizations as may be valid to the *performance of academic administrators of a given time.* The quality of a faculty recruited by a dean may not be clearly evident until some years after the initial acts. This is particularly true if the dean has been a bold, courageous, and risk-taking recruiter rather than a recruiter of a "safe" staff. Practices presumably developed and made operational in terms of efficiency may, over time, be discovered to be actually counterproductive. For example, it has been said that the "search committee" idea for recruitment of faculty and administrators assured uniformly *good* appointments but seldom brilliant ones. Time alone will reveal an aberration.

The consequences of the above statements, if they have validity, lead to the conclusion that evaluation of academic administrators must be designed in other terms than their presumed productivity or efficiency. That is, there are few criteria available in colleges and universities comparable to those in the business and industrial world, *e.g.* sales made in units of time, items of a given quality processed in a given time, reduction in process time (efficiency) resulting from modernization, and so on.

Performance Criteria—Leadership, Management, Personal Performance. Performance criteria are at the heart of academic administrator evaluation. Obviously, productivity and efficiency are important indicators of performance. But we have just said that these indicators are not particularly useful in academic evaluations. We must treat performance criteria in some other way. It is recommended that performance criteria be satisfied by evaluation under three categories: (1) performance that demonstrates or is otherwise indicative of leadership; (2) performance indicative of managerial skills; and (3) performance specifically related to work habits, interactions with others, and patterns of response in a variety of situations related to administrative demands.

Criteria related to leadership produce a complex of interactions and activities. Leadership per se is activity of a particular kind and has as its essence preserving, maintaining, interpreting, and enhancing the worth of the college or university as an institution—that is, an organization infused with value.[3] An academic leader must interact with a broad spectrum of persons who have an "interest in" a specific college or university. They include faculties, other administrators, trustees, students and alumni, and persons in the community, the state, and the nation. Much of a president's time is devoted to activities that either directly or indirectly seek to enhance the image or prestige of the college or university or to establish an environment in which the college or university can thrive. The same can be said for a comparable use of time by an academic dean. The evaluation process should bring forth the dimensions of the administrator's activity related to his or her leadership role and also attach value judgments to this activity.

Criteria related to an administrator's managerial role relate to his or her skill in such areas as budget preparation and control; personnel management, involving such aspects as recruitment skill, judging the performance of others, negotiating faculty union contracts, being sensitive to organization forms and their consequences and reorganizing as it seems indicated; and sensitivity to the operations and use of resources by support systems, the library or building maintenance. The role of administrators, presidents, deans, or others, as "managers" of students in all their interactions can be of utmost importance in judging the success or lack of success of administrators (Selznick, 1957).

A third dimension of performance relates to such matters as the following: How well does the administrator use his or her time? Is the administrator competent in communication activities? Can he or she manage conflict? Does the administrator comprehend the breadth of activities he or she is engaged in and the judgments that are being made about performances in relation to a broad spectrum of constituencies?

Personal Qualities. Criteria of personality, personal values, presence, health, and energy are often critical in evaluations. The significance of these criteria is almost a given in evaluation; in fact, they often receive the bulk of attention of evaluations particularly at the executive level in business and industry as well as in education. In somewhat technical or conceptual terms, we are involved in evaluating the effects of the "socialization" that an academic administrator has received. In fact, we say about the administrator: "Does he or she look like an administrator? Does he or she talk like one? What are his or her values? What does he or she stand for? Is his or her health good? Will he or she support academic freedom? Will this administrator respect faculty values? Does he or she have a high energy quotient and health that is not handicapping?"

Subsystems of criteria in this realm could also include the following: (1) integrity; (2) good will; (3) health and energy; (4) sympathy for and understanding of people—with their troubles, sorrows, flaws, and joys; (5) openness and candor; and (6) intelligence. Many additional dimensions or facets can be identified.

Administrative Style. Most students of administration recognize the concept of administrative style. What is implied is that operations of a given administrator take on a characteristic of wholeness that can be characterized by just a few words, *e.g.* authoritarian and demanding, low-keyed and permissive, aggressive and dominating. In and of itself, style may have little significance. On the other hand, a given style may be essential in a given institution, *e.g.* Reed College seems unable to tolerate an administrator who is in the least authoritarian.

Cohen and March (1974) discuss performance of presidents associated with certain metaphors. Criteria of style can be developed that deal with such characteristics as authoritarian, democratic, judicial, conciliating, and so on. The point is that style may be an important element of success or failure as a college is unionized, as the adversities of inflation and unemployment bear heavily on an institution, or as emotions rise when minority groups become aggressive or politicians infringe on institutional autonomy and academic freedom.

Educational Statesmanship. The statesmanship criterion may be subsumed under other criteria just described, particularly personal values and presence. Statesmanship also relates to other criteria to come, *e.g.* political astuteness and economic and fiscal sophistication. Some might say that educational statesmanship represents the "highest value" in appraising a college president. It can also be important in the evaluation of vice-presidents or deans. But we list here certain items that could elicit judgments in an evaluation that seem relevant to statesmanship.

1. Is the academic administrator *committed* to the values of the life of the mind, the value of the examined life, the essentiality of academic freedom, the recognition of the need for autonomy for the scholar-researcher, respect for higher education as valuable in and of itself, and to the fundamental character of higher education as an institution that is a preserver and critic of western culture?
2. Does the academic administrator have personal courage in the face of adversity, conflict, or unpleasantness?
3. Is the academic administrator temperate in nature, not overly given to fault-finding, open in interactions with associates at all levels, considered to be fair and evenhanded in dealing with people?
4. Does the academic administrator keep abreast of problems, obligations, and issues, including national issues? Does he or she face up to problems and issues when they arise? Does the administrator deal constructively with crises, seek consultation, and accept advice?
5. Is the academic administrator known as a person of complete integrity?

Political and Fiscal Astuteness. Some persons have said that all educational decisions are, in the end, political decisions. Academic administrators have to be alert to the political effects of institutional decisions, both *internal* and *external.* Examples that test political astuteness are of this order: methods of handling student aggression, consequences of a deficit, interpretation of athletic policy, support given an academic senate or a faculty council, rules concerning alcohol on the campus. The interests of the variety of constituencies of a college or university are not homogeneous; in fact, they are often in conflict. In the current milieu, decisions of an economic or fiscal character constantly are being made not only by presidents but also by vice-presidents, deans, and directors. Projections or alternative decisions can be critical to institutional well-being. Decisions in this area are often of concern to many. Examples are of the following type: Shall a deficit be budgeted? How are merit increases to be handled? How should surplus funds in auxiliary enterprise accounts be invested, if at all? How can "soft money" be handled with minimum hazards to institutional stability? Should the institution grant honorary degrees?

The academic administrator will understand these types of situations and be aware that decisions that please one constituency may offend others. The academic administrator is constantly tested and evaluated by those within the institution and by those without to determine how he or she handles conflicting demands.

Unique Criteria. It has been noted by Burton R. Clark (1970) that on occasion a president will have a special quality and a special vision that force circumstances to conform to his or her will and thus dominates an institution. Such a person, as president, may be assessed in the terms we have just outlined, but such an evaluation is, in a sense, irrelevant because of the overriding power of a president to make the institution seem his or her own. The same may be said for a college dean. The words "charisma" or "charismatic" are often used to describe or define such persons. Charisma denotes and connotes powers beyond the norms, powers that define the evaluation without reference to norms.

It also must be recognized that certain characteristics of an administrator may be fatal to success and require an unfavorable final evaluation despite other qualities highly esteemed. Such characteristics, if successfully concealed, may not be influential but, if known, make tenure hazardous or impossible. They are normally flaws of character—moral lapses or failure in financial integrity—but they may also be perceived as complete ineptness in, for example, a managerial role, misplaced trust in others, or an incapacity to delegate to others until a situation assumes pathological characteristics. An evaluation committee should be sensitive to the occasions when the administrator possesses a "fatal flaw."

The Criteria Situation–A Summing Up. We have frequently inferred that each evaluation is a unique event. It is thus to be acknowledged that each assessment should be based on criteria relative to it. It should be noted constantly that evaluations almost always involve qualitative judgments. Involved committees should not be fearful of making or recording such judgments. When considering the varieties of criteria, one should recognize that performance criteria carry a special power. Other criteria should not be downgraded; yet the old saying, "Judge me by what I do, not what

I say," has to be respected.

The application of the criteria to a given situation requires sophistication. Such sophistication involves a general understanding of colleges and universities, of the diversity of administrative roles, of the subtleties involved in superior versus modest performances, and in the nature of special cases. The sophisticated evaluator has a sense of a given institution's history, its traditions, even its mythologies. He or she knows that strength can be weakness and vice versa, that expenditure of great energy or long working hours may represent weakness rather than strength, and finally, that *all human beings are flawed* and should be understood and judged as such.

Evaluation of administrators requires the application of multifaceted criteria, the willingness to make value judgments, and the courage to put institutional values on a level with personal commitments.

The Ad Hoc Evaluation Committee

Earlier, it was suggested that the search committee model be used in the evaluation process and that the evaluation model be designated as an *ad hoc evaluation committee*. This committee can take several forms. While an evaluation committee and a search committee have somewhat different tasks, in both instances there is an "evaluation" of a "person" in relationship to a specific "task." A *search committee* evaluates in order to predict to what degree the evaluated person will in *future time* perform a set of tasks in a satisfactory manner. An *evaluation committee* assesses the performance by an administrator of a given set of tasks and makes a value judgment about how well the person performed in *time past*. Where colleges and universities have standardized the composition and procedures of search committees, they may become the model for evaluation committees, with any modifications that seem desirable. The following system is offered as one workable for evaluating presidents, and is then used as a base for generalizing the model for all academic administrative groups, *e.g.* vice presidents, deans, directors, and so on.

Composition of the Ad Hoc Evaluation Committee. The ad hoc committee for the evaluation of presidents[4] should have a membership of no less than eight,[5] consisting of the following:

1. Two members of the board of trustees to be selected by the board
2. Two members of the senior administrative staff (deans, provosts, or vice presidents) selected by the board of trustees from a list of four provided by the president. The members shall be considered peer members[6]
3. Two persons selected from the tenured faculty by the generally recognized faculty organization and by methods of the organization's own choosing. If the college or university has an academic senate, this body may be designated. If there is no senate but there is a faculty union organization, this body may make the

selection

4. There shall be one student selected by the recognized student governance association by methods of its own choosing
5. There shall be one alumnus or alumna selected by the alumni association by methods of its own choosing if such an association exists. If such an association does not exist, the board of trustees shall make the selection

The board of trustees should, on its own authority and in terms of the ad hoc nature of the committee, modify the above composition by adding members to achieve ethnic, racial, or sexual balance not otherwise achieved or to provide for other constituencies that the board believes should be represented. The chairperson of the ad hoc committee may be a trustee named by the board, or the board may ask the committee to select its own chairperson.

It is suggested that the committee membership be modified for all evaluation of academic administrators other than the president as follows:

The board of trustees will not be represented on these committees. The faculty should be asked to name three persons to the committee and the president should appoint three persons from the administrator peer group. He may name one of his appointees as chairperson; or, he may ask the committee to name its own chairperson. One student and one alumnus or alumna should be named as stated above. For academic administrators of a constituency that does not encompass the whole institution, *e.g.* dean of a college, the faculty and student members should be selected by that administrator's constituency.

Though the board of trustees will not be represented on the ad hoc committee, the board will receive the committee's evaluation reports through the president. The president will make his own evaluation of the administrator under review and make a recommendation to the Board as to the administrator's continued status.

Again, the governing board or president may desire to modify the committee's composition regarding the review for any particular administrator and should do so to achieve a balance or to otherwise secure a committee that would be appropriate for a given evaluation. This modification may include naming one or more trustees to the committee.

The nature of the ad hoc evaluation committee model precludes an expertness in evaluation that would characterize evaluators in such organizations as business, industry, or government bureaus. Evaluations are made a part of the managerial role of persons responsible for the work of subordinates. Business, industry, and government create within their structures a "personnel bureau" that gives general supervision to all evaluations in a formalized process. A part of the training of managers is working in cooperation with a personnel department to make evaluations as professionals. As noted—the ad hoc committee model precludes such professionalism. The members of an ad hoc committee do not have a hierarchical relationship to the evaluated administrators, nor are they trained in evaluation techniques. For this reason, the variety of aspects of an ad hoc committee functioning are set forth.

Responsibilities of the Ad Hoc Evaluation Committee. Now let us turn to the task of the committee which is to prepare an *assessment portfolio* for the administrator under review. The portfolio is a document that includes a self-assessment and the committee's full appraisal. The nature of the portfolio is discussed in more detail later in this chapter.

The following procedure is recommended:

1. For all evaluations except his or her own, the "assessment portfolio" will be delivered to the president. The president's portfolio will go to the board. It is assumed that each administrator under review is directly responsible to the president, *e.g.* vice presidents, deans, directors. The cases of administrators not reporting to the president will be handled as exceptions, as the president determines.
2. The president will review each portfolio other than his or her own and prepare an assessment. In some circumstances the president may delegate this task but not the final responsibility. He or she will discuss the evaluation with the administrator under review, transmit to the board of trustees the appraisal, and retain the resulting portfolio in the personal file.
3. The board of trustees will review the president's portfolio, make an evaluation, and discuss it with the president.
4. If the college or university is part of a state system for higher education, then after the board of trustees' review with the president, the portfolio with its evaluation should be forwarded to the appropriate authorities.

Role of Ad Hoc Committee Members. Each of the members of the ad hoc committee, as noted, will be representative of a constituency or other legitimate interests. It must be recognized that each member is able to speak from a limited perspective only and then in representative terms, *i.e.* students can hardly speak as representatives of the faculty or the faculty as representatives of the administrative hierarchy. *However,* each of the ad hoc committee must assume personal responsibility for statements he or she makes. Each must know that he or she can in no way express the variety of judgments that members of a given constituency will always hold. To maintain a responsible role, in what at best can be perceived as a paradoxical situation, requires wisdom, courage, and tact from each person on the committee. Each group of two or three represented on the ad hoc committee will prepare its own statement. Each will attempt to convey the consensus or the variety of points of view of its constituency, *but* it will be discreet in seeking this consensus of these points of view. It will not poll or survey its membership or seek interviews with a random sample. Finally, each group will make a statement believed to be a fair representation and will include its own point of view.

Roles of Each Constituent Group. We will now attempt to clarify in a preliminary way the perspectives the representative groups bring to the evaluation and indicate what each might contribute to the assessment portfolio.

The trustees have a special responsibility in the evaluation of the presidents. As members of the ad hoc committee, they will bring understandings between the president and the board at the time of and subsequent to the initial appointment. For example, the board may have stated to the president that external relations (with the community, with alumni/alumnae, and with governmental bodies) should have high priority in his performance in a variety of roles. This perspective may be unknown to other constituencies. Other situations that the board has agreed to or considered with the president should be known. The board members should make their evaluations in terms of board interests, perspectives, and concerns.

The peer members of an ad hoc committee bring different perspectives. They see their fellow administrators in action more frequently than any other group and know the freedom and constraints imposed by the board, the environment, and significant others. They can see more of the "warts" but can also have greater empathy. They may well be comrades, displaying a fellowship of peers. As they make their evaluations, they should not attempt to escape from these interactions, but should consider them opportunities to "know better than others" what a given academic administrator is doing and how well or ill he or she is doing it.

The faculty members carry the value system of the college or university; *i.e. they are the institution* in terms of performance, values, interactions, meaning, significance, and, in the end, they satisfy that crass word, productivity. While faculty can on occasion be insensitive, even cruel, they must tell it as they perceive it regarding academic administrators. If an administration or administrator is brilliant, let the faculty say so; if shabby, let them report it in the same fashion. They should be guided by their professionalism and by their professional or disciplinary perspectives and commitments. They should be forthright, open, and, if necessary, courageous in making their evaluations.

The students are unique among the groups represented for they are here today and gone tomorrow. They have little sense of institutional history and are often indifferent to institutional tasks other than that of the faculty serving the students as instructors. Yet students are everywhere about the institution; they expect it to command and deserve their loyalties now and after graduation. The college or university will be alma mater to them. While their evaluations inevitably will be restricted by their own limitations, the perspectives they will bring to the assessment portfolio will be significant and useful.

The alumni, as former students, may have a greater sensitivity to human fallibility than current students. Their judgments will probably be more tempered by the passage of time and the perspectives brought on by added experience, maturing, and aging. Their contribution to the evaluation will be complementary to that of students and useful in what will normally be its tempering effects.

Committee Processes. The task of the ad hoc committee has been defined, *i.e.* to prepare an assessment portfolio. The role of the representatives of each of the constituencies has also been described, *i.e.* each constituency prepares its statement in terms of its particular role; it does not presume to speak for the committee as a whole. The committee as a whole normally prepares a condensed statement that represents the views of the entire committee; however, minority or dissenting statements may be included. The statement defining roles suggests that each of the constituency members should strive to interpret the view of the total constituency, but the committee should not determine such views by public hearings, survey instruments, or such.

The committee will first meet on call of its chairperson who will have been named by the trustees or president or otherwise selected. This first meeting will be organizational. The chairperson will review the nature of the committee's task and the role of each of the members. This may be done by reviewing the substance of this chapter. Understandings will have to be developed by mutual exchange. These will include such items as role expectation, the substance of each member's report, the nature of the criteria for evaluation, and expectations of confidentiality, candor, accuracy, committee accountability, and fairness. The committee will normally agree that whatever occurs in committee discussions is assumed to be privileged information. The administrator's self-evaluation should be made available to the members at this time.

The second meeting should be the occasion for a review of the administrator's self-evaluation. This will also be an opportunity to discuss further and answer questions about issues and processes reviewed at the committee's first meeting. It should be agreed that each constituency group or member will prepare a first draft of its evaluation to be sent to the other members before and for discussion at the third meeting.

The third meeting should provide an opportunity to review first draft evaluations and look forward to securing a final draft from each group for the fourth meeting. At the fourth meeting final drafts should be reviewed and a plan developed for preparation of the total committee statement.

A fifth meeting may be used to review the summary draft, suggest revisions, and present an opportunity for dissenting opinions. A sufficient consensus may be achieved at this meeting to permit the group to ask the chairperson or another member of the committee to prepare the final and complete evaluation portfolio to be distributed to members for approval before its submission to the president or board of trustees.

Limited experience of the member institutions of the State University of New York indicates that as few as four meetings of a committee can suffice, that six or seven should be a maximum, and the process can normally be completed in a period of four to six weeks. The experience of these institutional committees is that the task is not onerous for any one person nor is it disruptive of the institution's normal functioning.

The Assessment Portfolio. The assessment portfolio begins with the administrator's self-evaluation, which may be accompanied by a statement concerning the development and current status of the institution or appropriate subunit. The portfolio then incorporates statements of the groups represented on the ad hoc committee. Finally, it should contain a statement that sums up and represents the committee's judgment concerning the evaluee. Statements by a dissenter or minority should be included if so requested. The assessment is descriptive, analytical and evaluative, or judgmental. However, it does not represent a final or definitive evaluation. As noted earlier, this definitive evaluation is to be made by the board for presidential evaluations and by the president for all others.

The assessment portfolio need not have a standard format. Criteria to assist evaluators in making their statements have been presented earlier. Some evaluators will prefer to use checklists and similar forms to seek objectivity. Others may write extended analytical essays and not fear to be personal, qualitative, or even sentimental. All evaluators should remember that their observations will be part of a whole and will be tempered, strengthened, or even negated by others' evaluations. Truth and reality are multidimensional, and the evaluation should be that as well as value-oriented and judgmental. The total evaluation should also be descriptive and have face validity, *i.e.* it should state what is generally known but not always articulated. It should reflect an attitude of fairness, responsibility, and concern. It should neither be prepared in haste, nor of personal rancor, nor out of the narrow issues or problems of the day. It should be worthy of the individual being judged and of the bodies making the judgments.

Responsibilities of the Board of Trustees and President

As indicated above, the board of trustees will receive the portfolio and the evaluation report of the president. The president will receive the evaluation and portfolio of other academic administrators. Each should acknowledge receipt of the evaluation and then thank and dismiss the committee whose work is over. There is one exception: after studying the evaluation, the board or president may wish to meet with the committee for clarification or a more analytical discussion of the assessment portfolio and the summary evaluation. This meeting should not be deemed irregular.

After receiving the evaluations and entering into a discussion or clarification with the committee, as is deemed desirable, the trustees or the president should prepare a *final* and *definitive* evaluation. It should be short, but reveal strengths and limitations, make an overall estimate of administrative performance, and, if suitable, make suggestions such as a shift in style, better utilization of time, or greater sensitivity in relations with others.

The trustees should review with the president the substance of the assessment portfolio, the committee's evaluation, and the board's definitive evaluation. In some instances, this discussion will be pro forma—even congratulatory. In others, it can be prolonged, in depth, even severe and traumatic. The governing principles should be respect for human dignity and the welfare of the institution.

The president should conduct a similar review with each of the evaluated academic administrators. It should represent the processes and concerns just discussed.

Due Process in Administrative Evaluation. The evaluation of administrators is an act of accountability in harmony with current trends. Due process is a complementary act of accountability. As a board of trustees and a president commit themselves to evaluation, it is essential that those who will be affected know the process. If a board or president uses the model provided in this chapter as it is, all should know and understand the process. As the process is modified by a board or president, the nature of the modifications should be made known.

However, an integral part of the process, the right of review or the use of an appeals procedure, has not yet been discussed. It has been assumed and stated that with presidential review there will be an interaction between the president and the board at which the character and finding of the review will be discussed. This discussion itself can be used as a review mechanism if the president asks for it and the board agrees. Should there be no meeting of the minds by the president and board, the decision of the board is determinative.

Other academic administrators should have the right to ask for a review or to file an appeal regarding an evaluation. Again it is assumed that in each instance of evaluation there will have been interaction between the evaluee and the president when the process and findings of the evaluation were discussed. Should the discussion or findings prove unsatisfactory to the evaluee, he or she should have the opportunity to ask for a further review or to file an appeal. It is suggested that the president and the board have a formal process for conducting a review or hearing an appeal and rendering a decision. If the institution does not have a process, the following is suggested as a model. The board shall name two of its members, and the president shall name a peer administrator who shall constitute a *review and appeals board or committee* for academic administrators (other than the president) who have undergone evaluation. This review-appeals board may hold such hearings or arrange interviews with such persons as it desires. It shall hear the person aggrieved who may offer materials in writing and bring to the interview his or her personal counsel. The review board shall prepare a written finding and make copies available to the person aggrieved, the president, and the board of trustees. The president and the governing board will make a final disposition based on recommendations of a review-appeals board committee and on legal constraints.

Uses of the Evaluation

The final and definitive use to which an official evaluation report points is continuance in office, removal from office, or advice and counsel concerning future services and tenure. But it is to be assumed that normal, systematic evaluations at regularly specified times will not be harshly concerned with a decision to remove from office. Indeed, it seems that the removal of a president is characteristically related to an idiosyncratic situation such as unanticipated and climatic "occurrences" often following a breach of trust, a serious legal offense, insubordination, or a blatant failure of integrity.

It is assumed, then, that a formal evaluation made periodically will fall into place as part of the continuing activity to improve institutional processes and decision-making. The evaluation should be expected to serve both the evaluee and the college or university without threatening either.

The evaluation should be of use to governing boards and in some respects to the institutional constituencies. The board of trustees will better understand the president, other administrators, and also the situations (with their demands and constraints) in which administrators work. Finally, as institutional constituencies understand that administrators are being evaluated, all should have increased confidence in the well-being of the college or university—the trustees and president will be perceived as truly tending the store.

In the end, and as noted earlier, an evaluation is an accountability document and should be so viewed. It should be looked upon as part of the system by which an institution maintains itself. The ad hoc evaluation committee model should reinforce the concepts. of an accountability document.

It should be clear that the ad hoc evaluation committee system presents issues, problems, opportunities, and consequences that are not normally associated with conventional administrative personnel evaluation. These unique issues stem from the committee's openness, its formalization of an informal process wherein the variety of constituencies are involved in making judgments, and its vulnerability to "mistakes of the amateur evaluator." There is also the easy loss of confidentiality when committees are at work. For these reasons, a rationale is presented for the "formal system" along with certain caveats.

Need for a Formal Evaluation System

It should be noted again that every institution will contain an informal evaluation system at work. Presidents, vice-presidents, deans, and others will be continuously subject to conversations by their peers, the faculty, and the students. Such activity is the sign of an open institution and is normal organizational behavior, in no way pathological. Astute administrators will know how to handle—*i.e.* evaluate—and use the messages they are receiving through the informal system. There is much to be said that is favorable about an informal system.

But it also has its limitations. As colleges and universities become more complex the informal system often proves insufficient. It is now apparent as a general consensus that an institution will increasingly be required to be formally responsive in assessments of its operations. Fiscal operations are routinely assessed by auditors, some institutionally selected and others representing state and federal governments. The federal government and other official bodies now routinely review employment practices of colleges and universities, particularly in relation to employment and salaries of women and minority groups. Such reviews more and more often will include formal assessments of administrative personnel.

Caveats Regarding the Formal System. It is appropriate, then, to review briefly some expectations and some caveats regarding a formal system of administrator evaluation particularly as it involves an ad hoc committee. These include the following:

1. The formal system will complement an informal evaluation system. It will not—it cannot—replace the normal day-to-day judgments, praise, scoldings, and questioning that administrators experience, but it should add to it, stabilize the total process, and as is sometimes necessary, bring about judgments that require official notice and action.
2. While the strengths of a formal system can be noted, the limitations should also be recognized. Even in the name of accountability or of democratic governance, institutions cannot keep responding to whims of the disgruntled; the vagaries of shifting styles and values; or the variety of claims and counter claims made by religious, civic, social, or patriotic groups that require administrative attention. Colleges and universities have great inherent stability. Evaluation should be a stabilizing process, not a disrupting one.
3. All constituencies, particularly the faculty, trustees, alumni, and supporting agencies of government, need to have a clear understanding of the process and potential of administrator evaluation. Without such understanding, unattainable expectations

will often be expressed or the process may be deemed a boondoggle, a whitewash, a "con- or snow-job."

4. All who participate in any evaluation need to have an enlightened sense of responsibility; they should be persons of wisdom and judgment, sensitive to human feelings and conscience.
5. While it will be known that administrator evaluation processes exist and their natures should be understood, confidentiality dare not be abridged. Authority must be delegated and accepted with full faith and trust if administrator evaluation is to succeed. General findings will be known, but intimacies should not be fully shared.

Some Dicta and Final Caveats

Certain assumptions or presuppositions seem to be called for and accepted as given as we strive for an effective evaluation system based on ad hoc committee activity. These items seem to be relevant:

1. An appraisal system must never fail of dignity and confidentiality.
2. The nature of the human condition—that all of us are flawed—should be understood by all. Perfection as an ideal may be entertained, but it is desirable for those who evaluate the evaluation and deal directly with the evaluated administrator to understand human limitation—that all of us err, that understanding of potential human response is essential, and that all evaluation inherently involves criticism.
3. An evaluee has a "right to know" how he or she was evaluated, the criteria involved, and how he or she rated.
4. So many variables are involved that are qualitative, subtle, and complex that an evaluation does not produce a simple document; or a checklist of modest length; or a score, ratio, quotient, or other quantified, simplistic measure.

While the statements about to be made may seem to be truisms, they are often overlooked in evaluating evaluations. Evaluations or assessments are multifaceted. In some areas, the securing of relevant data is not difficult; in other areas it is almost impossible. Production criteria are almost impossible to evaluate in the academic world on a short-run schedule. The proper weightings are difficult to give. On occasion, "one flaw" may outweigh a preponderance of favorable evaluations. On other occasions, one great strength may more than compensate for an unfavorable assessment elsewhere.

Recognition of a second condition is also fundamental. The same qualities may be nearly ideal in one time or place and quite inappropriate in another. Valid evaluations can only be such as they are related to specific tasks in a specific place at a specific time—when they have an accurate frame of reference.

Specific in Time and Place. Again, because the ad hoc evaluation committee system of evaluation gives power and authority to amateurs in the field, we will now express certain realities concerning the process that may not be self-evident. Evaluation must be conducted within a frame of reference. It should be specific in time and place as well as in the role of the one evaluated.

The constraints of time and place must be considered with care because the situation of an institution may at one time be so critical as to almost foreclose a favorable review while at another time an administrator may create a situation that will assure his or her success. In any event, when making a judgment concerning an administrator, the freedom and the constraints the situation presents must be at least implicitly reviewed.

Expectations of the Administrator and Institution at Time of Appointment. During the evaluation process, the evaluators must learn what the trustees and the president deemed the institutional mission to be at the time of appointment. It should be determined if mission and role were mutually understood or were ambiguous. The situation for other academic administrators can also be analogous, *i.e.* presidents and deans may or may not understand the expectations that were held by each at the time of a dean's appointment. Unfortunately, the situation is too often ambiguous or one party or the other has misunderstood. This type of situation has to be handled in the evaluation. It is a necessary condition in evaluating to understand the degree of responsibility that a given administrator possesses.

Specific Issues at Time Administrator was Hired. A statement of mission and role requirements may be complemented by a statement of specific issues or situations that existed as an administrator "came on board" and to which he or she was charged to give explicit attention.

Finally, as a preview to evaluation, it should become apparent to the evaluators who the primary and secondary constituencies are that administrators need to relate to. These constituencies help define the freedoms and constraints under which administrators operate.

A Summary Statement

This chapter has presented an ad hoc evaluation committee model as a basis for the evaluation of academic administrators. The system is rationalized in terms of the peculiar nature of colleges and universities in that typical line/staff relations do not operate in these institutions. Rather there are a variety of constituencies that require accountability of the academic administrator—governing boards, faculty, students, alumni, and administrative peers. These constituencies choose members of an ad hoc committee that will carry out a specific evaluation of an individual administrator.

Because members of the committee are not professional evaluators, the chapter spells out the roles of the various members of an ad hoc committee, sets forth a process for evaluation and review, including criteria, and describes the assessment portfolio which is the primary evaluation product. The chapter also emphasizes the subjective nature of administrator evaluation, cautioning committees as to the ambiguity, complexity, and confusion that is inherent. It calls for prudence and points out the need to observe due process and the right of those evaluated to ask for review.

Notes

1. This paper is largely drawn from the experience the author had in preparing a monograph-manual for the Council of Presidents of the Pennsylvania State Colleges and University and the President and Provost of the Pennsylvania State University in 1975. G. Lester Anderson, *The Evaluation of Academic Administrators; Principles, Processes, and Outcomes.* Center for the Study of Higher Education, the Pennsylvania State University, University Park, Pa., 1975 (72 pp.). Materials from the monograph are used with permission.

2. The distinction of students as contrasted with clients and consumers is symbolized in the phrase *alma mater.* A college, once chosen, *demands* certain behaviors from the students who enroll, and the college assumes obligations for the student that are rooted in tradition and culture.

3. It requires considerable training to evaluate the tasks a professional performs. The members of an ad hoc committee cannot be expected to secure training comparable to that of a professional in order to serve on an evaluation committee. Nor does amateur status mean incompetence. But a committee member may wish to review certain materials in addition to that included in this chapter that would acquaint him or her with the task. The bibliography furnishes such a list of materials.

4. The office and person of the president is deliberately used as a base to describe the composition of the ad hoc committee and how it operates. Modifications of the committee and process will be presented in terms of evaluations of academic administrators other than the president. To use the "presidential review" as a model has certain advantages. First, it seems that the president is currently more subject to review than other administrative officers. The reasons are two-fold: (1) boards of trustees are at the forefront in asking for review, and it is the president they want reviewed; (2) other administrators are more amenable to subjecting themselves to review if the president has had to consent to review. Second, the process of review of a president is seemingly more complicated, the committee more complex. In modifying a review process it is seemingly easier to simplify the structure of the committee and its processes as one moves to a discussion of the review of vice presidents or deans, than the reverse.

Above we have noted that presidents have seemed to be more subject to review in terms we are describing than other administrative officers. (See Chapter Ten.) It might be claimed that such is true only of state-wide systems with more than one campus responsible to a single board. However, approximately 40 percent of all students are enrolled in such multi-campus institutions. States with multi-campus systems in whole or in part include California, New York, Texas and Pennsylvania, the four most populous states, but also Massachusetts, New Jersey, North Carolina, Ohio, Illinois, Florida, Oregon, Arizona, New Mexico, Colorado, Minnesota, and Wisconsin among others. It also seems that the pressures for academic review are more intense in the public than in the private sector.

5. The case study of this model used by the State University of New York presented in Chapter Ten has a committee of four plus a convenor. The model presented here was proposed by the author in the monograph cited earlier.

6. Some presidents may protest that other senior administrators are not their peers. It is

the author's position that the perceptions of presidential role, performance, and constraints held by vice presidents and deans are often as valid as the president's and who may thus be considered the president's peers.

Bibliography

Anderson, G. Lester. *The Evaluation of Academic Administrators: Principles, Processes, and Outcomes.* Center for the Study of Higher Education, the Pennsylvania State University, University Park, 1975, 72pp.

Baldridge, J. Victor. *Academic Governance.* Berkeley, California: McCutchan, 1971.

———. *Power and Conflict in the University.* New York: John Wiley & Sons, 1971.

Bolman, Frederick deW. *How College Presidents Are Chosen.* Washington, D.C.: American Council on Education, 1965.

Clark, Burton R. *The Distinctive College: Antioch, Reed, and Swarthmore.* Chicago: Aldine, 1970.

Cohen, Michael D., and March, James G. *Leadership and Ambiguity: The American College President.* New York: McGraw-Hill, 1974.

Corson, J.J. *Governance of Colleges and Universities.* New York: McGraw-Hill, 1975.

Drucker, Peter F. *The Effective Executive.* New York: Harper & Row, 1967.

Ferrari, Michael R. *Profiles of American College Presidents.* East Lansing: Michigan State University Press, 1970.

Gould, John Wesley. *The Academic Deanship.* New York: Teachers College Press, 1967.

Kaplowitz, Richard A. *Selecting Academic Administrators: The Search Committee.* Washington, D.C.: American Council on Education, 1973.

Kauffman, Joseph F. *The Selection of College and University Presidents.* Washington, D.C.: Association of American Colleges, 1974.

Mortimer, Kenneth P. and McConnell, T.R. *Sharing Authority Effectively.* San Francisco: Jossey-Bass, 1978.

Remmers, H.H., and Hobson, R.L. *The Purdue Rating Scale for Administrators and Executives.* West Lafayette, Indiana: Purdue University Book Store, 1951.

Selznick, Philip. *Leadership in Administration.* Evanston, Illinois: Row, Peterson, 1957.

Stoke, Harold W. *The American College President.* New York: Harper & Row, 1959.

Wiggin, Gladys A. "Selecting and Appraising Personnel." In Harold Benjamin (Ed.) *Democracy in the Administration of Higher Education.* New York: Harper & Brothers, 1950.

G. Lester Anderson is Professor Emeritus of Higher Education, State University of New York, Buffalo and Pennsylvania State University.

Chapter Seven
MBO and Administrator Evaluation

Philip C. Winstead

Among the most serious tasks facing administrators in higher education are solving the problems of evaluating the performance of individual staff members and evaluating the performance of the institution as a whole. Management processes need to be developed which will allow these institutions to achieve optimum results while maintaining their capacity to change, to be relevant, to be meaningful, and, most important of all, to be accountable.

Accountability is a "catch-phrase" that has been used in educational circles for a number of years, but which still has tremendous implications for administrators. It means, in effect, that these schools and those who are responsible for their operations will be judged by results and not by promises. Accountability refers to the process of expecting each person within the institution to be responsible for accomplishing outcomes. These outcomes are based upon specified goals and objectives and are measured against stated criteria. We must answer not only the key question of what has been done, but also how much it has cost, and, ultimately, whether it was worth the price. The assumption of accountability is that all resources within the institution must be committed to achieve basic purposes. Management by objectives (MBO) is a results-oriented concept that stresses both effectiveness and efficiency.

MBO is based on the premise that no individual can direct all the activities of a complex organization. Complex institutions must be managed by outcomes. MBO is a technique whereby the goals of the institution are clearly stated and measurable objectives for each organizational unit are derived from these goals. Each person periodically agrees to major responsibilities in terms of the objectives and the results expected in light of the resources available. During the designated time period, the individual is given wide latitude in choosing a method of achieving the objectives. At the end of the period the actual results are jointly reviewed against the agreed upon goals and objectives. The strength of the MBO process lies in its focus on results, its provisions for evaluative feedback on performance, and the commitment of participants involved in the process.

Readers wishing to proceed directly to a discussion of administrator evaluation within MBO may be somewhat frustrated in the following pages which discuss MBO at large. MBO is a systematic planning and management process where evaluation is only a by-product. Figure 1 depicts a simplified view of the MBO process and the critical factors which form its foundation. The point here is that performance review only becomes a relevant matter after its context has been established through goal clarification, measurable objectives, unit and individual self-analysis, action planning, and implementation.

Not only is it illogical to hastily focus on evaluation without giving due consideration to MBO's preceeding elements, it is also self-defeating. L. James Harvey (1976) has warned about ways to destroy MBO in higher education: one good way is "focusing on MBO primarily as an evaluation system." Administrators who believe their president is using MBO to pin down their performance rather than for institutional development will play games to begin with and soon assume the role of saboteurs.

Historical Perspective

Management by objectives is not a new concept; in fact, managers, including college administrators, have always managed by objectives. When a college administrator got a task, he or she decided what needed to be done, undertook activities to accomplish the task, and then took a look at whether or not the job was done successfully. Although these activities may have been identified by various terms such as planning, organizing, budgeting, or controlling, this was management by objectives. What is new in this system for higher education is the increased emphasis on results, better team work, improved motivation, increased participation, stronger commitment, and more objective performance appraisal.

Peter F. Drucker (1954) was probably the first person to specifically label the concept "management by objectives." Eleven years later George S. Odiorne (1965) published *Management by Objectives: A System of Managerial Leadership,* and this treatment firmly entrenched the term in the literature as he tied the MBO concept to the systems approach by describing how MBO works in the organization. Many other books and articles on the subject have followed, either under the term management by objectives or related terms such as management by results, management by participation, or administration by objectives, etc. Among recent writers, Dale D. McConkey (1974) has made significant contributions, especially in the area of relating MBO to the budgeting process.

During the 1950s and early 1960s, the thrust of MBO was in the area of performance appraisal. The intent was to move away from how a person

Figure 1
MBO Process and Foundation

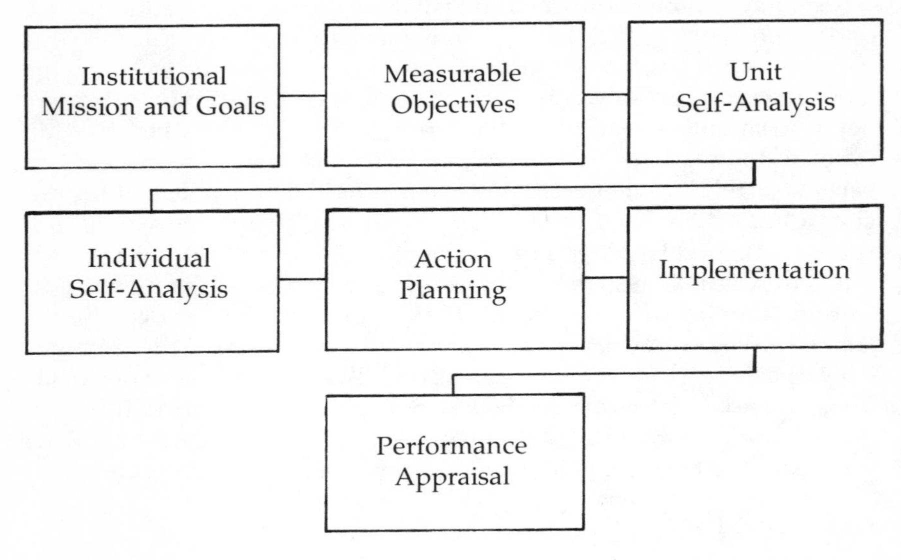

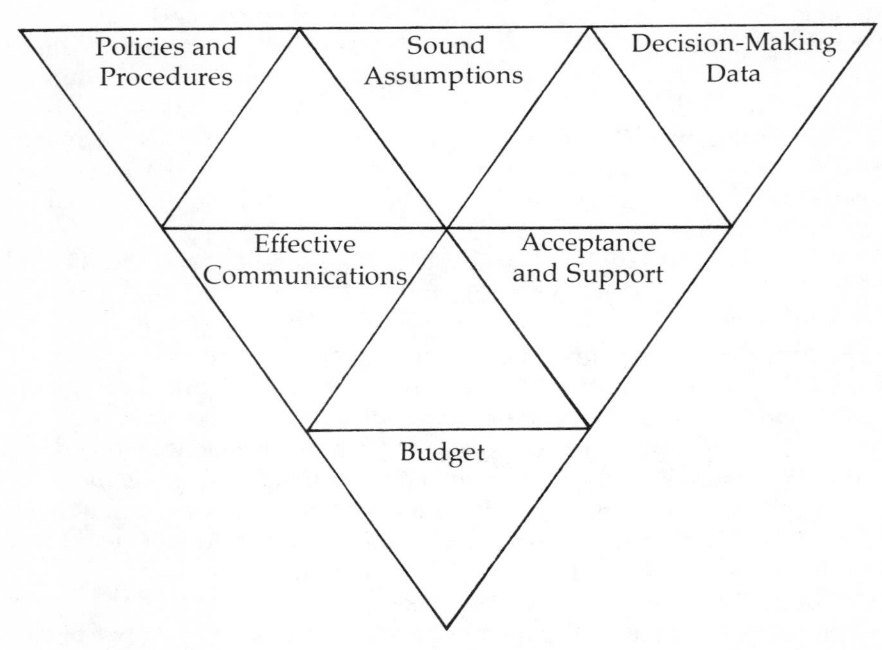

approached his or her job (for example, with enthusiasm) toward the results he or she achieved. In the mid-sixties, the emphasis moved toward making MBO an integral part of comprehensive planning related to the overall decision-making process.

MBO in Colleges and Universities.

In the early 1970s a number of colleges and universities began developing formal MBO programs. Moreover, some schools utilized systematic planning programs undergirded by MBO (Winstead, 1975). Such processes can take many forms but generally include the follow ing distinct steps or activities.

1. Identification and evaluation of problems and opportunities
2. Clarification and evaluation of mission, goals, and objectives
3. Determination of priorities
4. Analysis and evaluation of capabilities
5. Development and execution of programs of action
6. Identification and monitoring of future developments that will have a major impact on performance or results
7. Allocation of essential resources
8. Acceptance and support of key people who are involved or affected

It is steps two, five, and seven which comprise the MBO thrust of a systematic institutional planning program. These three steps illustrate that there must be a program of action developed to support valid objectives. Essential resources must be allocated to support the program of action. These requirements are crucial in reducing the quantity of possible worthwhile objectives to those which can have a meaningful effect on the administration of the college. The coupling of objectives to programs and consequently to the budget forces MBO to be an integral part of management planning. Experience has shown that the selection of objectives is very important to the success of MBO. If this aspect is handled improperly, the result is an over-emphasis on activities rather than on key result areas. This over-emphasis can result in a system too encumbered with paperwork for effective utilization. The key is to include in the MBO system only those objectives which can have a major impact on the performances of individuals and of the institution.

Pros and Cons. Before making MBO sound like the answer to all of the planning and management problems of a college or university, including administrator evaluation, it must be pointed out that management by objectives has as many potential disadvantages as advantages. Failures in effective use of the MBO process are just as numerous as successes. As with most organizational processes, the critical elements are the personnel involved and the commitment to giving the system a fair chance to succeed. If implemented and conducted with care and concern, the potential for success is great, and the results of a successful MBO program are well worth the risks involved. But the risks are present. A poorly implemented and conducted MBO program will most likely lead to failure, and the resulting failure is likely to cause very serious harm to the organizational and administrative life of the institution. Table 1 compares the possible advantages and disadvantages of a management by objectives program.

Table 1

Comparison of Possible Advantages and Disadvantages of a Management by Objectives Program

Advantages	Disadvantages
1. Improves communications, especially with feedback provisions	1. Threatens some individuals
2. Clarifies responsibility	2. Can have the appearance of simplicity
3. Fosters accountability	3. Terminology is alien to some
4. Emphasizes results rather than activities	4. Creates measurement problems
5. Enhances continuity	5. Tends toward too much paperwork
6. Assists in goal clarification	6. Requires additional time in some cases
7. Aids evaluation process	7. Can result in overcontrol
8. Improves budgeting procedures and resource allocations	8. Identified with industry and government rather than education
9. Increases internal consistency of administrative practices	9. Some aspects, like profit motive, are not applicable in higher education
10. Applicable at all levels of the organization	10. Often viewed as a panacea
11. Fosters collegiality	11. Cited by some as non-humanistic
12. Based on tested management principles	12. Works better in some areas of a college or university than others
13. Helps in team-building and leadership development	13. Can stifle creativity
14. Lessens dependence on individual personalities	14. Can become too authoritarian
15. Can overcome fragmentation	15. Can confuse efficiency with effectiveness

MBO Process Components

Goal Clarification. At the present time few activities of college administrators are more important than clarifying the purpose and directions of the institution. Yet many administrators are so fully occupied with day-to-day pressures and unique responsibilities that they lose sight of the institution's goals. The result is often a lack of congruence between the actions of individual administrators and the goals of their schools. If this congruence were confined to isolated instances, there would be no problem, but in the larger perspective it can be harmful.

Colleges and universities, therefore, need explicit goal statements to provide necessary focus and direction to their institutional planning. Only after an institution decides what it should do, wants to do, can do, and how to go about it will it be able to maintain its autonomy and integrity and accomplish its chosen mission. Also, to remain viable in a climate of change, schools must continually work toward achieving relevant priorities. To be achieved, these goals must be clearly articulated to receive the necessary support from the institutions' constituencies.

Clarifying goals and receiving the necessary support from the institution's constituencies can be time-consuming tasks, but no planning or management by objectives system can operate effectively without cornerstones on which to test its programs and activities and without the understanding and support of those who are important to the institution. Another very important reason for goal clarification is the fact that most colleges and universities can no longer be all things to all people. In a climate of scarce resources, goals are necessary to distinguish between many worthwhile aims the institution could pursue and those it should pursue.

Goals, because they only provide focus and direction, are open-ended and not necessarily measurable. They should be consistent with the purpose (reason for being) of the institution and inclusive enough to cover the legitimate objectives of the college or university. For example, for a traditional liberal arts college, the purpose of the institution may include, ". . . a community of scholars which introduces students to the methods and concepts of liberal learning and prepares them for the lifelong process of becoming educated." A goal for the institution may be: "To educate qualified students in the liberal arts tradition and to guide them in the quest for intellectual, spiritual, physical, and social and cultural wholeness; to help them achieve appropriate learning objectives; to satisfy their personal growth needs; and to help them become socially responsible individuals." For the academic affairs area of the college or university, a goal may be, "To encourage students to become acquainted with and develop an appreciation of the concepts, techniques, and values of the humanities, fine arts, natural sciences, and social sciences."

Goals, however, because they are broad and general, can take on different meanings for different constituencies within the institution. Depending on a person's background and interests he or she may attach different meaning to and place a different value on a possible institutional goal. Understanding and agreement among constituent groups is essential if goals are to serve as useful bellwethers within the planning and management structure of the institution.

One procedure for articulating institutional goals is the Delphi method used to obtain goal agreement among constituent groups. Although it was developed mainly as a forecasting technique, first used about twenty-five years ago by senior scientists at the Rand Corporation (Dalkey and Helmer, 1962), the Delphi method has been used as a device to encourage consensus or convergence of opinions. The purpose of the procedure is to elicit agreements from different persons without face-to-face confrontation. The Delphi technique, applied to goal clarification, involves having each participant make anonymous ratings concerning a series of possible goal statements. Each participant then gets composite feedback of the way others responded to the goals and is then asked to respond again to the same statements as they view this summary information. The purpose of additional iterations is to discover the intensity of agreement or disagreement with each of the possible goals. The process may be repeated as often as desired. The result is to determine the consensus arrived at by repeated questioning with feedback.

One advantage of the Delphi technique is that it avoids the dominance in decision-making of persons with strong personalities who tend to exercise weight in a general meeting beyond the logic of their argument. Does a faculty member's judgment receive the same consideration in an open forum as the president of the institution? Is a newcomer to the organization listened to as closely as a distinguished member of the community? The intent of the Delphi method is to increase the chance for a decision to be made on the basis of informed opinion rather than "who says what." Through this process the belief is that agreement can be reached on the proper goals of the institution and thereby increases the usefulness and degree of support for the institutional goals.

Measurable Objectives. Achieving reasonable agreement on goals, however, is only the first step. And if succeeding steps are not taken, there is a high probability that the resulting "mission" statements will be no more meaningful than many such statements now found in college catalogs. By translating goals into measurable objectives the incremental progress can be measured. More importantly, activities may be directed toward the achievement of specified outcomes in light of those objectives.

Although a goal provides focus and direction, it is not necessarily measurable. An objective should be measurable. Objectives may be revised as the situation demands. No objective should be set without the ability to allocate and acquire the necessary resources. One does not have an objective, in the MBO sense, unless a program of action has been developed and resources are allocated. Although some practitioners in the field define these terms in the opposite way and some use the terms interchangeably, it is necessary in an effective MBO program to distinguish the broad and general goal from the narrow and specific objective. In MBO, measurement is necessary for control purposes. Since there are some legitimate "results" areas where focus and direction are needed but quantification is difficult, the distinction becomes important because there are times when only general guidance is needed but not necessarily firm measures. Also, in a system such as the one being described, management is not by goals; rather, management is by objectives.

For an objective to be measurable and thereby suitable for the process of MBO, it should contain the following six elements: time, outcome, performer, action, accomplishment level, and method of measurement. The time is the completion date. The outcome is the expected accomplishment. The performer is the one responsible for the action. The action is what is to be done. The accomplishment level is the acceptable level of proficiency. The measurement technique consists of how the extent of accomplishment is to be determined. For example, the following is an illustration of a measurable objective in college or university fund raising which identifies the six elements:

By *June 1979,* the *Development Office will solicit by mail* all alumni
time performer action

and parents for *financial support* and obtain *positive responses* from
outcome measurement

15 percent to produce an income of $125,000.
accomplishment level

An objective is generally one of three types: (1) routine—those of a repetitive nature; (2) problem-solving—those responding to a particular need or dysfunction in the system; or (3) innovative—those which attempt something which has not been done before (Deegan and Fritz, 1975). It should be stressed to administrators that most (60-70 percent) of what they do is routine and ongoing. It is in the budget this year, it was in the budget last year, and it will be next year. The administrator should specify objectives in the routine area only if one or more of these three things is true: (1) it is a result that the supervisor wants to monitor; (2) it is a result that the administrator wants the supervisor to monitor; or (3) the objective directly affects someone else's planning.

One must be careful not to oversimplify the process of MBO. A simplistic approach does not deal adequately with the problem of limited resources present in most educational institutions. A viable school never has enough resources to do everything that its leaders justifiably want to do. Therefore, to be practical, MBO must be related to the setting of institutional priorities. In order to help discriminate among the many desirable objectives which are proposed, each should be weighed against the following criteria before it is authorized.

1. Is the objective suitable; does it relate to a stated goal?
2. Is the objective feasible; can it be done?
3. Is the objective acceptable; is the institution willing and able to pay the cost?

4. Is the objective valuable; is it worth the cost?
5. Is the objective achievable by the institution?
6. Is the objective measurable; does it contain the six elements required of an objective?
7. Is the objective flexible; can it be changed if necessary?
8. Is there firm determination to succeed by those responsible?

Self-Analysis and Action Planning—Unit and Individual. Just as clarifying goals and deriving measurable objectives from goals are critical to an effective MBO program, so is the element of self-analysis. All too often objectives become delusions because of a lack of basic understanding about institutional and individual capabilities. Much energy and resources are wasted because objectives are pursued which have little chance of being accomplished, because necessary skills and resources are unavailable, or because of circumstances within the environment.

One technique for conducting an appropriate self-analysis is to do a SWOTs analysis. SWOTs is an acronym for a self-appraisal in which an organizational unit or an individual can look inwardly at *s*trengths, *w*eaknesses, *o*pportunities, and *t*hreats. Figure 2 shows a SWOTS format.

Figure 2
SWOTs Analysis

Strengths	Weaknesses	Opportunities	Threats
Area:			
Area:			

The SWOTs analysis can provide a framework for assessing needs and environmental conditions which can influence the MBO process. As a result, objectives can be authorized which maximize strengths, minimize weaknesses, capitalize on opportunities, and eliminate or minimize threats.

For example, a SWOTs analysis developed for the academic area of a college or university may include among its strengths the following:

1. The overall quality of the faculty with some departments outstanding

2. A library which is attractive and generally well-kept, conveniently located at the center of the campus, and with ample space for growth
3. Gift support for the university among alumni and friends of the institution

Among the weaknesses stated may be:

1. Declining aptitude test scores of entering freshmen
2. Failure of book budget to keep pace with increase in cost of library materials
3. Salaries and fringe benefits for faculty and staff have not kept pace with rate of inflation

Among the opportunities for the institution may be:

1. Strengthen the agreement among faculty and administration of the university with respect to current academic goals and priorities
2. Rearrange library floor plan in order to increase reading and study areas
3. Develop a stronger continuing education program in order to better serve the needs of the community

Among the threats stated may be:

1. Inadequate security for non-tenured faculty
2. Inadequate student center and campus-wide lack of meeting rooms
3. Shifts in academic interest of students

Likewise, a SWOTs analysis for an individual administrator may include among the strengths the following:

1. Proven organizational and administrative ability
2. Willingness to experiment with new ideas and innovative administrative practices
3. Responsiveness to administrative expectations (meeting deadlines, serving on committees, etc.)

Among the weaknesses stated may be:

1. Difficulty in keeping abreast of major developments nationally in administrative field
2. Insufficient expertise in the use of the computer and other technological advances in educational administration
3. Interpersonal relations, especially communication skills

Among the opportunities may be:

1. Increase personal interaction with other administrators at same managerial level
2. Engage in special programs (workshops, seminars, etc.) to improve communication skills
3. Increase visibility among colleagues at other institutions via publications and presentations at professional meetings

Among the threats stated may be:

1. Becoming obsolete in needed areas of expertise
2. Uncertainty of the university's commitment to needed level of professional growth and development
3. Lack of precise long-range career goals

Therefore, using the SWOTs analysis technique to provide a framework, objectives developed for the institution may include:

1. For Fiscal 1978-79, see that the budget includes increased funds for the purchase of library materials in a sufficient amount to maintain the present acquisition rate and offset rising prices
2. For Fiscal 1978-79, see that faculty compensation increases by a minimum of 8 percent for all full-time teaching personnel
3. See that the average aptitude test scores for freshmen entering the university in the fall of 1978 do not decline from the scores of freshmen entering the previous year
4. By January 1, 1979, complete plans and secure construction funds for expansion of university student center

Also, objectives developed for an individual may include:

1. By January 20, 1979, complete reading program designed to upgrade knowledge of administrative uses of the computer
2. During March 1979, successfully complete announced professional association workshop (one week) on "Communications Skills and the Manager"
3. By May 1, 1979, complete and have accepted for publication by refereed journal manuscript on "Staff Development at a Small College"
4. During 1978-79, develop and begin implementation of personal five-year professional growth plan

Measurement Problems. Another aspect that is critical for an effective MBO program is that of appropriate measurement. Many MBO programs have failed because of a misunderstanding over what constituted acceptable measurement. One hears the comment, "You can measure other areas of the college, but you can't measure mine." "My work involves too much creativity or critical thinking." Acceptable measurement which is simply agreement between the persons involved can be at one of three levels. First is the generally recognized level of quantifiable data, at times difficult or even impossible to find or develop. Therefore, a second level is that of performance indicators. These are evidences that by recording certain actions or results one may conclude that the objective has or has not been accomplished. For example, a person's improved voting record might be a performance indicator for improved citizenship. But at times even performance indicators are difficult or impossible to find. The third level is simple "effort toward." "I don't know what happened as a result, but I conducted certain activities which were designed to accomplish certain objectives," *e.g.* "I held a class or conducted a meeting." In an MBO process, agreement can usually be reached on at least one of these three levels of measurement. The key is agreement between the administrator and his staff as to exactly which measurements are acceptable in assessing performance.

Performance Reviews. An inherent part of a viable MBO system is performance review. Although the person responsible for accomplishing an objective is given flexibility as to choice of methods, review sessions are needed to monitor progress, to take corrective action or revise objectives when necessary, and to encourage optimum results. There is no magic frequency concerning the timing of review sessions. Once a year is not enough because this prevents mid-year corrections. One a week or once a month is probably too often because the time involved could be disruptive rather than constructive. Each administrator, therefore, should develop with his or her staff a workable schedule for review.

The manner in which the review sessions are conducted is essential to the success of an effective MBO program. During the session discussion should focus on the present and the future: how well tasks are being accomplished and how the individual hopes to expand his or her competence. It is an opportunity for checking results against plans and re-allocating resources if necessary as well as recognizing a person's professional aspirations and seeking ways to achieve them.

The reviews should be seen as help sessions rather than as punitive. The focus should remain on achieving optimum results rather than on seeing to what limits of productivity one can force those in the system (maximum results). Working at an over-extended pace can cause greater adverse consequences than the possible short term gains. Non-recognition of this factor is why so many MBO programs have started with initial success and then deteriorated into subsequent failure. Therefore, it is suggested that the review sessions be organized around the following five questions:

1. What progress is being made toward the accomplishment of objectives?
2. What can be done to help?
3. Are there additional policies needed to accomplish objectives?
4. Are their policies in existence that hinder accomplishing objectives?
5. Do objectives need to be changed?

A maxim to remember is that for optimum results, any time the environment fluctuates it is necessary to make changes in the resource allocation, the program of action, and the objectives.

Conducting a performance review is seldom an easy task, especially in academic settings where a premium is placed on maintaining collegial relationships. A number of good reasons have been noted as to why college and university supervisors are sometimes less than candid during a performance review (Deegan and Fritz, 1975):

- If performance has been excellent, high praise may well lead to a request for a salary increase or promotion which is nearly impossible during a period of across the board budget cuts.

- If performance has been marginal, it is difficult to substantiate shortcomings in the professional arena, and in all likelihood the result will be bad feelings rather than improved performance.
- If performance is clearly substandard, the individual may be so well-protected by tenure or personnel policies, that little real pressure can be applied.

Although conducting a performance review is inherently difficult, previously agreed upon goals and objectives with corresponding criteria and performance standards makes a tough task easier by raising the discussion above emotion and opinion to a rational level.

MBO Foundation Components

A successful MBO process rests on a firm foundation of policies and procedures, assumptions, decision-making data, effective communications, acceptance and support, and budget process.

Policies and Procedures Appropriate policies and procedures must be in existence and clearly in focus for effective MBO. MBO is a move toward decentralized, participative planning and management. With MBO involving more people throughout the organizational structure, it is necessary to have understood what a staff member is expected to do. Policies furnish the framework for plans, decisions, and objectives and are broad statements of general intent that tell what is permitted or expected. A procedure is specific instruction that tells how to do something that is permitted or expected. For an effective MBO program, two basic types of policies and procedures should be implemented: (1) in areas where policy/procedure guidance is needed to perform more effectively, and (2) in areas where existing policies/procedures prevent optimum performance. An example of how one might obtain a firm grasp of which policies are needed and which policies may need revising is to conduct a brief survey annually asking faculty and administrators to respond to their needs and constraints in the area of policies and procedures.

Assumptions. In a viable MBO program, reaching agreement on desirable objectives cannot be done if isolated from other key factors in the environment. Therefore, the development of pertinent, reliable assumptions is important in planning where MBO is taking place. An assumption is a careful estimate regarding a very important probable development over which administrators have no significant control but which will have a major impact on activities or results. For example, for the university business office the future national rate of inflation is an assumption. The future room and board charges for the university are not. These latter prices can be controlled. In general, assumptions are divided into two categories—those about the world in which the institution exists and those specifically applicable to the institution or its functioning. The first category might include economic, business, socio-political, and educational assumptions. Assumptions applying directly to the institution might include the school's environment and its future capabilities. Also, assumptions should be dynamically quantified if possible (*i.e.* expressed in a chart or graph, over periods of time, with historical data, current status, and future projections). Examples of assumptions pertinent to higher educational institutions are: (1) the complexity of the social and physical environment will place increasing demands on a highly literate, well-informed citizenry (Social/Political); (2) salary levels nationwide for college and university faculty will increase at approximately the same rate as the consumer price index (Business/Economic); and (3) students will have increased interest in academic majors more directly related to career preparation (Educational).

Decision-Making Data. Just as policies and procedures are essential in a decentralized, participative management style, good decision-making data is indispensable. A frequent weakness in MBO programs is the failure to recognize that if more people in the lower echelons are to be directly involved, (*e.g.* developing plans and objectives and participating in a MBO style of administration), then the people down the line must have the same information as those in top positions. There is a cliche in the planning field that the quality of plans and decisions cannot consistently rise above the quality of the information on which they are based. If an effective MBO program is installed, the availability of information thoughout the organization is crucial; moreover, data generated should be action-oriented and designed to provide basic information and alternatives for planning and decision-making. Appropriate data categories are purpose and scope, environment and competition, capabilities and opportunities, assumptions, goals and objectives, policies and procedures, strategies and programs, priorities and schedules, organization and delegation, budgets and resources, and evaluation.

The distinction between action-oriented data and non-action-oriented data is in the intended use. Some information is interesting to have and nice to know but does not influence administrative plans and decisions. Action-oriented data are designed to contribute toward some pending decision or issue under discussion. For example, studies such as "An Analysis of Academic Prediction as it Relates to the Admissions Process and Academic Sources," and "Academic Performance and Attrition Rates for Freshman Students in Triple Rooms" produce information which is useful for administrators as they wrestle with the problem of ways to improve the chances for academic success of entering students.

Effective Communications. Data gathering is, of course, just the first step to ensuring that all those who need pertinent information have it. The data must be available when and where needed and in a usable form. Some people will require an entire computer printout, while others will need only a one-page summary.

Regular lines of communication and authority should be maintained with an emphasis on the "need-to-know" concept. Reports, meetings, and other types of formal and informal communications devices should be utilized when appropriate. One possible aid to effective communications is the use of a "planning book" or "fact book" which contains pertinent institutional information. This is a way in which MBO and other elements of systematic planning can be integrated into the ongoing administrative structure. The book can be looseleaf (so each page can be updated individually), color-coded with pages keyed for distribution on a need-to-know basis, and organized around *specific* data categories *previously mentioned.*

All institutional information cannot be in one planning book. If it were, the book would be unmanageable and would defeat the very purpose of the system. Also, if information is distributed on a need-to-know basis, the contents will differ for each book holder depending on his area of responsibility; the material applicable university-wide will be found in all planning books.

Acceptance and Support. Systematic planning undergirded by MBO can lead to the achievement of optimum results in colleges and universities. However, a move toward decentralized, participative planning and management can present some difficulties. In spite of the difficulties, the participative style of planning and management holds tremendous promise because most institutional problems are people problems. People today want greater fulfillment of psychological needs—acceptance, recognition, participation, involvement, self-realization. When people are reasonably well-compensated and have some feeling of job security, one of the strongest motivating factors is an opportunity to plan for one's own future activities in the institution. MBO with its personal interaction can contribute to this desire.

It is imperative that one does not take for granted the support of those people involved in the MBO program. People who do not fully understand MBO may feel threatened. They may view it as a punitive system or as a way to increase efficiency rather than to increase effectiveness. Efficiency may only be "spinning the wheel faster." Effectiveness means making sure "the wheel is carrying the load in the right direction." The same type of distinction is made between "maximum results" and "optimum results." Maximum is a quantitative term implying the most. Optimum is a qualitative term implying the best, *i.e.* the best possible results with due regard for the prevailing circumstances.

The key is to take each step seriously and deliberately and to stress the morale and team-building factors as well as the results-oriented emphasis. By all means, however, one should be aware that any management style will not produce the optimum results unless the process has the acceptance and support of the people involved.

Budget Process. MBO becomes a trap and delusion unless adequate resources are provided to accomplish the agreed-upon objectives. A realistic budget must include the price tag on programs of action. If a budget is not an integral part of the management planning process, MBO will not survive as a part of the system. It is like an orchestra playing a musical composition. The music is nothing more than symbols on paper until the orchestra performs. The orchestra, of course, cannot perform without the proper equipment and other resources. Thus, objectives are meaningless until programs of action have been devised with resources allocated. Therefore, an organization's budgeting process must be made compatible with the MBO program. The emphasis must be changed from viewing budgets as an estimate of future income and expenses to emphasis on allocation of anticipated resources to programs with the aim of optimizing results.

Conclusion

As a process, management by objectives requires that objectives for a given organizational unit be derived by members of that unit and reviewed by appropriate higher echelons of the organization. At this point, before they are authorized, the objectives are checked for consistency with those of the institution. Responsibility for each is then assigned to the appropriate person and he or she is notified of available resources. During the designated period, the person is given the choice of methods and provides periodic updates using milestone reporting techniques. Regular review sessions, designed to monitor progress and encourage optimum results, are held for the purpose of involving each person with his or her supervisor. At the end of the period, unit results and individual performance are jointly reviewed against the agreed-upon goals and objectives. The strength of the process is in the focus on results, the provisions for feedback, and the commitment arising from participant involvement in the process.

Finally, MBO is certainly not a panacea for deep-rooted management ills. It is an approach to management which is conceptually sound and compatible with our collegial norms and values. Although there are other viable alternatives to MBO, it is a process which should be given serious consideration when one is considering effective management and sound administrator evaluation.

Bibliography

Dalkey, Norman and Helmer, Olaf. "An Experimental Application of the Delphi Method to the Use of Experts." Memorandum R-M-727-PR, Rand Corporation, July 1962.

Deegan, Arthur X. and Fritz, Roger J. *MBO Goes to College.* Boulder, Colorado: University of Colorado, 1975.

Drucker, Peter F. *The Practice of Management.* New York: Harper & Row, 1954.

Harvey, L. James. *Managing Colleges and Universities by Objectives.* Wheaton, Illinois: Ireland Educational Corporation, 1976.

McConkey, Dale D. "The Position and Function of Budgets in an MBO System." *Business Quarterly* (Spring 1974): 44-50.

Odiorne, George S. *Management by Objectives: A System of Managerial Leadership.* New York: Pitman, 1965.

Winstead, Philip C. "Furman University's Management Planning Model for Liberal Arts Colleges." Final Report to the Ford Foundation and Exxon Foundation, Furman University, Greenville, South Carolina, November 1965.

Philip C. Winstead is Coordinator of Institutional Planning and Associate Professor of Education, Furman University.

Section III
Practices of Administrator Evaluation

The four approaches presented in the previous section have been tried at several colleges and universities and subsequently refined. In reviewing their experiences the authors of this section provide insights and recommendations which can guide new administrator evaluation programs around barriers and to goals.

Charles H. Farmer's work at the University of Tulsa is presented in Chapter Eight. A rating scale was developed and implemented to evaluate the president, vice president, and deans. Although much care and attention was given to instrument design and construction, it did not achieve its stated purpose of improving administrative performance. In retrospect fundamental issues were glossed over and no provisions were made for using the data collected. It was naive to assume information alone would be sufficient for improvement.

In Chapter Nine Dan T. Bedsole describes Austin College's use of the type of growth contracts Berte and O'Neil introduced in Chapter Five. The Career Development Program applies to administrators as well as faculty and non-managerial staff. Individuals write development plans with long-range and short-range goals, including specific projects for attaining these goals. The plan is reviewed at least once a year.

Chapter Ten contains reactions from presidents and evaluators to the ad hoc committee model proposed by Anderson in Chapter Six. Murray H. Block chronicles the development of SUNY's presidential evaluation program. Twenty presidents have been evaluated by the process.

Philip C. Winstead returns in Chapter Eleven to report how Furman University uses performance appraisal in the context of institutional planning/MBO which he described in Chapter Seven. In the early 1970s Furman began a comprehensive effort to revitalize its management, planning, and evaluation processes. Achieving agreed upon objectives influences salary and promotion decisions, but other leadership aspects, such as communication skills and initiative, are also taken into account.

Chapter Eight
University of Tulsa: Overrated Rating Scales

Charles H. Farmer

In recent years, colleges and universities have given serious thought and have taken action to find ways to make their administrators more responsive to the needs and interests of their diverse constituencies. In particular, ways have been sought to promote broader and more democratic faculty participation in decision-making areas which traditionally were reserved for the administration.

The idea of involving faculty in the decision-making process was at the core of the University of Tulsa's effort to design and implement an administrator evaluation system. Ostensibly, faculty evaluation of administrators was to improve the performance of Tulsa's top leaders, but unfortunately the system did little more than provide a formal vehicle for faculty to express their opinions about how well the president and deans did their jobs. Rating scales were carefully constructed, approval was gained through proper governance systems, data was collected and given to both administrators and faculty, and nothing as far as anyone could see resulted from the exercise.

It is hoped that an account of Tulsa's attempt to "power-share" through administrator evaluation will help other campuses repeat what was done right, avoid what should have been done differently, and build an evaluation system that has a more constructive impact on its leaders.

Source of Demand for Administrator Evaluation

Demands for administrator evaluation typically originate from one of three sources: (1) faculty interest—often motivated by faculty evaluation by students; (2) administrator interest—motivated by institutional self-study or the need for individual self-improvement; or (3) state-level interest such as coordinating boards and trustees—motivated by the need for public accountability. Very often it comes from the first source—a by-product of the continuing press for more meaningful faculty accountability. As the limits of academic freedom and responsibility are debated and faculty realize student evaluation of teaching is here to stay, a notion of "do unto them as is done to us" emerges. The notion of formally evaluating administrators may be the result of spite more than thoughtful consideration.

The source of demand for administrator evaluation by faculty at Tulsa can be traced back to the faculty's attitude toward the formalized program for student evaluation of instruction. In the early 1970s faculty were required to use the Student Instructional Report, a rating scale produced by the Educational Testing Service. They did not particularly like it but accepted it as an inevitable fact of academic life.

With the acceptance of student evaluation of instruction came a desire to put the administration in a similar position as reported in the 1972 *Report of the Committee on Faculty Responsibility* prepared by the Tulsa chapter of the American Association of University Professors. Originally the report was undertaken to deal with the need for establishing more precise criteria to be used in tenure and promotion decisions and better communication to individual faculty members. It also stated:

> What may be called downward evaluation is standard and orthodox practice. The Board of Trustees evaluates administration, the administration evaluates the faculty, faculty evaluates students.
>
> The *Statement on Student Rights, Freedoms, and Responsibilities,* released October 11, 1972, states (Section I,F.): . . . the students should have the opportunity to evaluate the faculty. We have accepted the first stage of what may be called upward evaluation. Having accepted this step, the committee (Committee on Faculty Responsibility) recommends that upward evaluation be carried one step further with an acceptance of the proposition that the faculty should have the opportunity to evaluate the administration.

Getting Started

Without support from either the governing board or the president of an institution, administrator evaluation will not be formalized. At Tulsa, the support came from the President who took the position that if faculty wanted to rate the administration, then they should be permitted to do so. He instructed the Office of Institutional Research (OIR) to investigate the evaluation of administrators and offer a proposal for proceeding onward to the faculty. However, as is the case in most academic institutions, the committee system moves at less than lightning speed. A short chronicle of events occurring over the next three years demonstrates the point.

The *Report of the Committee on Faculty Responsibility* was presented to the University Senate on November 16, 1972. It was five months before the portion of the report involving administrator evaluation was considered. The next event in the chronology occurred in a meeting of the University Senate two years and five months later on September 25, 1975, where it was announced that the Academic Affairs Council had endorsed and approved the OIR proposal for faculty evaluation of administration which would later be presented to the Senate for approval.

There was another delay at the next meeting of the Senate where the main topic of discussion was whether or not the proposal should be presented to the entire Senate for approval. The Chairperson of the Academic Affairs Council expressed the opinion that the OIR proposal was for information purposes only and not for approval. The Executive Council felt that since a standing committee of the Senate had endorsed the proposal, the proposal should be submitted to the Senate for action. The Vice President for Academic Affairs stated his feeling that the implementation should be a concern only for the administration, but if the Senate wanted this responsibility, he had no objection. At the President's suggestion, it was decided that the proposal would be placed on the agenda for Senate approval.

Three years from the origin of the request, on November 10, 1975, in a memo to all of the faculty from the Secretary of the University Senate, there was a proposed resolution under new business that stated, "Be it resolved that the University Senate supports the proposal for the faculty evaluation of the positions of president, vice president for academic affairs, collegiate deans, and graduate dean."

After a lengthy discussion of the proposed resolution at the November 20, 1975 meeting of the University Senate, the resolution was voted on and approved with a roll call vote of 27 yes votes, 4 abstentions, and 4 no votes. The President turned the details of designing an evaluation for academic administrators over to the Vice President for Academic Affairs. Since the Director of Institutional Research serves in a staff function to the Vice President's office, OIR was asked to develop a workable system—immediately.

Designing the System

One of the great comic scenes in literature, the birth of Laurence Sterne's Tristram Shandy, depicts the rage and frustration of a male midwife as he attempts to untie the knots of his instrument bag while Tristram, upstairs, threatens to be born without him. Readers will recall, however, that complications occur and the frantic midwife finally severs the knot with a knife, cuts his thumb, and, in pain and haste, misapplies the forceps, drawing poor Tristram into the world with a smashed nose.

There are a number of warnings in Tristram's birthing for educators designing any evaluation system. There is the possibility, of course, that campuses may engage in such painstaking deliberations that their program finally bursts into the world without any professional assistance. It is more likely, however, that this complex issue will not receive the extensive attention it requires due to an imposed time deadline.

In Fall 1975, Tulsa's administration did not want to further delay the design process and therefore set a Spring 1976 target date for the first round of administrator evaluation. The fear that delay would lead to terminal inaction may have been well-founded, but in retrospect resulted in hastily conceived instruments and procedures that could have damaged both the administrators under review and the institution.

If administrator evaluation programs are to be successful, they require the close involvement of both administrators and faculty throughout planning, implementation, and monitoring phases. This was not the case at Tulsa. OIR was told to develop a questionnaire and an implementation process to evaluate the president, vice president, and deans, and to do so in a few months time. Originally it was thought that OIR would be a valuable "buffer" between the administration and faculty and help preserve anonymity. As it turned out, OIR functioned more as "insulation" than as "buffer" between the administration and faculty.

During the design process, there was no collaboration and little liaison between OIR and the faculty and administration. Besides the fact that the implementation date was fast approaching, the faculty seemed more interested in implementing some kind of a formal system to evaluate administrators than in agreeing in advance on what purposes it should serve or how it should be done.

A review of the literature in 1975 revealed that little had been written about administrator evaluation other than at the chairperson level. Telephone calls to NEXUS at the American Association for Higher Education and to the Educational Testing Service were equally unproductive in providing guidance. There was no choice but to develop our own approach, but at least we did not feel we were re-inventing the wheel.

The central administration decided that a single set of criteria and questions should be incorporated into one evaluation instrument for all administrators to be reviewed. Since every faculty member must have the opportunity to participate, to present his or her view of the truth, a rating scale approach seemed to be the only viable option. The instrument should meet at least four requirements: (1) allow for diverse administrative styles, (2) avoid assumptions concerning the "ingredients" of administrative excellence, (3) encompass total administrative performance, and (4) concentrate on specific characteristics which are likely to affect performance in diverse administrative tasks.

With the requirements in mind, OIR sifted management appraisal literature from business and industry as well as systems for evaluating high school principals, and developed a form which provided scaled performance ratings for forty specific items categorized in four areas: (1) Leadership, (2) Relationships with Faculty, (3) Supervision and Evaluation of Personnel, and (4) Personal Qualities. Form 1 was used for administrators other than the President. Form 2 includes, in addition to the performance areas above, items unique to the president's position such as resource development and effective representation of the university to external agencies. (See Appendix)

Implementing the System

The raters for each administrative position were designated by the University Senate as follows:

- The President—evaluated by all teaching faculty, collegiate deans, and members of the administrative staff
- The Vice President for Academic Affairs—evaluated by all teaching faculty, collegiate deans, and members of the administrative staff
- Each collegiate dean—evaluated by all faculty members affiliated with the respective dean's college and teaching during the semester of the evaluation
- The Graduate Dean—assessed by those designated as graduate faculty and teaching during the semester of the evaluation

The rating scales were distributed by campus mail. Upon completion, the forms were returned to OIR. In addition to specific response items, each instrument included a comment section designed to be anonymous. During the computer processing, individual comments were transcribed by an outside firm onto a single typed sheet and returned to the administrator. When the evaluation was completed, all forms were destroyed.

Completed instruments were processed by Tulsa's computer facilities to provide arithmetic means for each specific item. These statistics were originally to be reported according to respondent classification including academic college, rank, tenure status, and age group. In order to preserve anonymity, however, only results by college were used and no distinctions were made between faculty and administrative staff raters.

The Quality of the Instrument

Throughout the process of developing and using the instrument, there were concerns for its validity and reliability. Is it valid—does it measure what it is supposed to measure? If it is valid, can it be relied on—how accurately does it measure critical aspects of administrative performance? Within the constraints imposed by the lack of research defining administrator effectiveness in higher education and by limited time for implementation, both issues were addressed.

The issue of validity must proceed from a good answer to the question, *What is administrator effectiveness?* In developing the four criterion areas and corresponding sub-items, an assumption was made about the relationship between successful leaders in business, industry, and secondary education and those in colleges and universities. Although the organizations perform different functions, the human side of each enterprise has more similarities than differences. Therefore, criteria ranging from leadership to personal qualities are critical to all successful administrators.

As the sub-items were developed in each of the four criterion areas, further, albeit less than rigorous, attention was given to validity. First, the

President and Vice President of Academic Affairs were asked to "jury" the instrument's content. They felt that from their point of view the items covered most of the behaviors critical to their performance and that of the deans. (Later, when they saw the data, they said the deans' scores contained "no surprises.") Second, five faculty from each college were asked before the instrument was distributed to give an overall rating of each administrator under review. Subsequently, these ratings were used as "anchor points" to compare data collected by the instrument. The early ratings turned out to be very similar to the instrument's area scores for each administrator tabulated by averaging the ten items in the four areas. The close similarity added a measure of confidence that the instrument addressed the same traits and processes that faculty thought were important.

Equivalent terms for reliability ("rely-ability") are dependability, consistency, and stability. Reliability coefficients provide estimates of the consistency or precision of measurements. Assessment instruments cannot be classified as "reliable" or "not reliable" since the concept is one of the "degree of reliability" which depends upon the size of the coefficient. Reliability coefficients can vary through a range from zero (no reliability) to 1.00 (perfect reliability). The classic question which must be answered to evaluators is this: "In view of the importance of the judgments I shall make, is the reliability coefficient large enough to warrant my use of the assessment results?" As an arbitrary guideline, reliabilities of .8 or larger are considered adequate for most types of instrumentation. As shown in Table I, the instruments' reliability coefficients, determined by the Kuder-Richardson Formula 20 measure of internal consistency, all surpass the .8 level of adequacy.

Data Feedback and Initial Reaction

The evaluation results were reported to individual administrators in two ways—mean scores and comments. Also, average scores in each evaluation category for each administrator were released in bar graph form and were available through deans' offices or the library to everyone in the academic community. As shown in Table 2 and Table 3, the bar graph format facilitated comparisons between all administrators. Since individual scores were also released, the faculty did in fact know which dean was which in Table 3.

The initial reaction from administrators to their data was a combination of perplexity and self-satisfaction. First of all, the aggregate scores for each of the four areas were difficult to decipher, let alone use for improvement plans. There were often wide ranges of scores on items within an area such as Relationship with Faculty so that the overall mean score did not prompt any action. Furthermore, administrators did not take into account that the faculty were very generous raters. Similar to student ratings of faculty, the "average" evaluee received a rating of 5.5

Table 1

Reliability of Questionnaires

Reliability Coefficients	Evaluating Group	N	Return Rate
	Reliability of President's Questionnaire		
0.98	All Participating Groups	127	45%
0.98	Arts and Sciences	55	52%
0.99	Business Administration	8	28%
0.98	Education	14	40%
0.97	Engineering and Physical Sciences	24	48%
0.98	Law	7	41%
0.99	Nursing	6	46%
0.94	Administrative Staff	12	34%
	Reliability of Vice President's Questionnaire		
0.98	All Participating Groups	116	41%
0.98	Arts and Sciences	51	49%
0.99	Business Administration	8	28%
0.98	Education	12	34%
0.98	Engineering and Physical Sciences	20	40%
0.99	Law	7	41%
0.99	Nursing	6	46%
0.97	Administrative Staff	11	35%
	Reliability of Graduate Dean's Questionnaire		
0.97	All Participating Groups	71	48%
0.98	Arts and Sciences	34	52%
0.96	Business Administration	6	35%
0.88	Education	12	44%
0.97	Engineering and Physical Sciences	17	44%
	Reliabilities of Deans' Questionnaire		
0.97	Arts and Sciences	51	49%
0.97	Business Administration	9	31%
0.95	Education	16	46%
0.94	Engineering and Physical Sciences	24	47%
0.99	Law	7	41%

Table 2

Faculty Evaluation of the Vice President for Academic Affairs

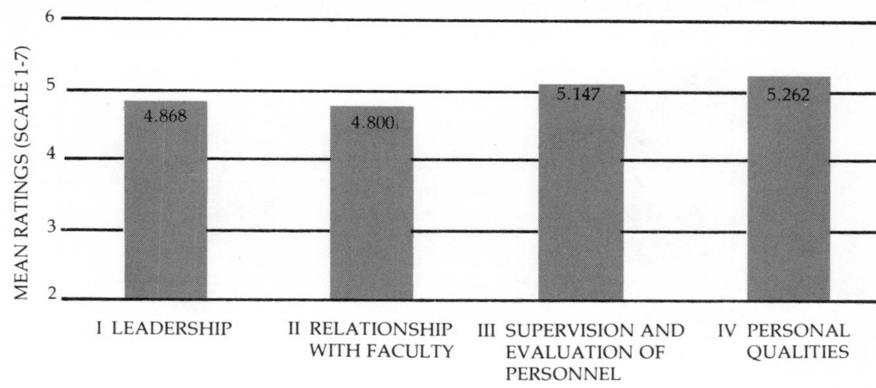

Faculty Evaluation of the Dean of the Graduate College

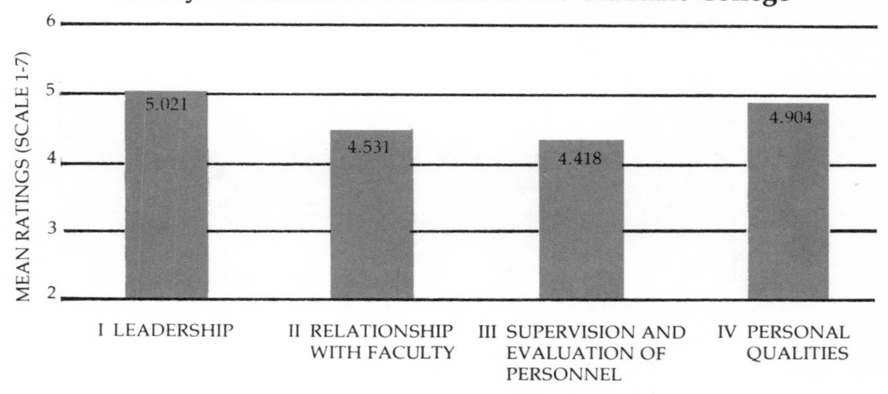

Faculty Evaluation of the President

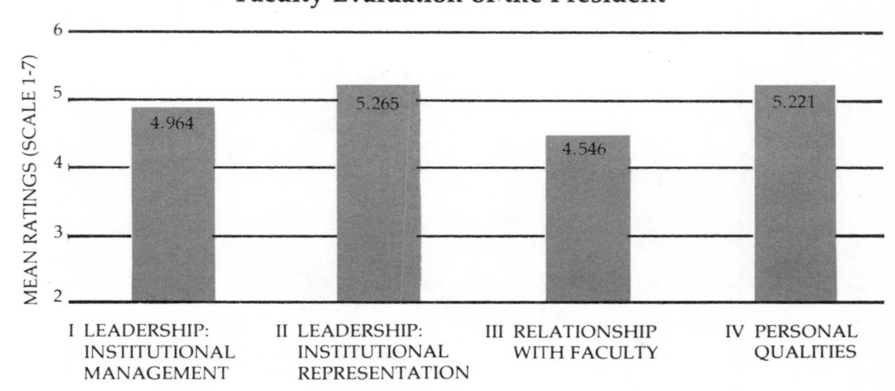

Table 3
Comparative Faculty Ratings of College Deans

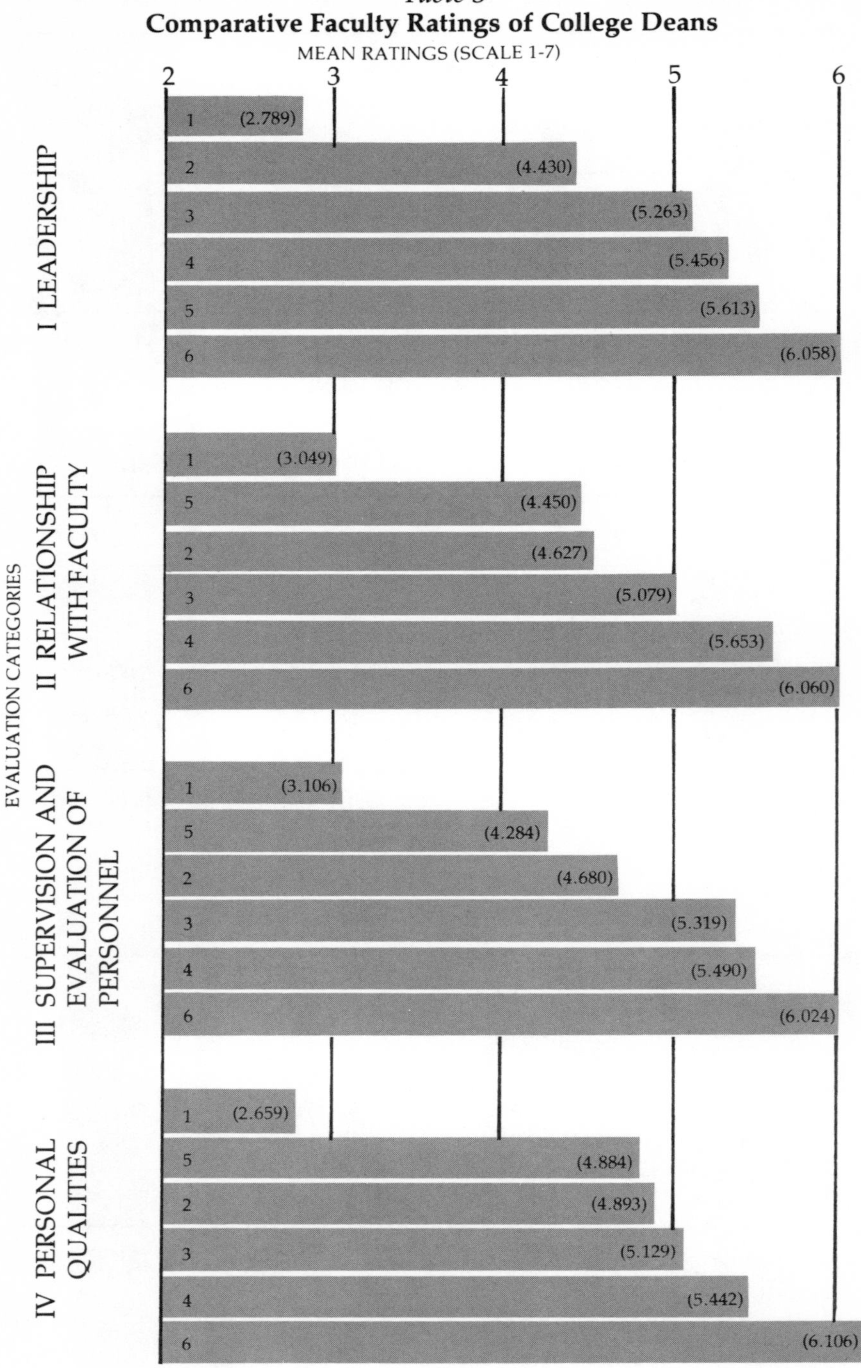

on a 7-point scale. Apparently many administrators thought that the faculty graded them on a bell-shaped curve, saw their marks as high, and therefore were quite smug about the grades they received on their symbolic report card.

Impact on Administrative Performance

In a study of the development of an administrator evaluation process, a section about impact on administrative performance would ideally be one of the longest. The section would detail how the data helped administrators identify and maintain their individual strengths and map strategies for improving on their shortcomings. This section, however, will be short. As far as anyone can see, the evaluation results brought about no change in administrative performance, constructive or otherwise.

What went on behind closed doors between dean and vice president, vice president and president is impossible to say. From the outside, from the faculty rater perspective, business continued as usual. A certain amount of speculation went on when administrators stepped up to new positions or stepped back to the faculty, but it was also noted that administrative personnel shifts occurred as frequently before the evaluation. For the most part, the evaluation process appeared to be similar to the interminable scorekeeping required by the university, state, and federal bureaucracies where data is gathered and forgotten.

Although a case could be made for peripheral benefits from Tulsa's administrator evaluation process, the benefits seem slim compared to what might have been. Communications were improved between faculty and administrators as a formal channel was established, and perhaps a precedent was set for involving faculty in other areas of decision-making, but to focus on such spin-off benefits obscures the fact that they did not spin off of the achievement of the core function of the evaluation process—to improve performance. In the next section, a rearward look at the Tulsa experience will give guidance to other institutions in achieving a better cost-benefit ratio for implementing administrator evaluation.

Reflection and Recommendations

Despite the considerable length of time it took for Tulsa to adopt and implement administrator evaluation, the system was narrowly conceived and narrowly executed. That is not to criticize Tulsa's administration, staff, or faculty. The limitations reflect an all too typical set of assumptions and perspectives. First of all, it was assumed that valid information gathered by accurate means from the faculty would be sufficient for improving administrative performance. Second, there was a prevalent belief that rating scales were not just the best way but the only way to carry out the process.

Looking back over the three years it took to complete the administrator evaluation cycle, there are a number of critical points where "what was done" now seems very different from "what should be." Tulsa's effort would have been more rewarding if more attention had been given to program ownership, purpose and process, data feedback, and follow-through support.

Program Ownership—What Was Done. No one really "owned" the administrator evaluation program in a way that leads to a commitment for effectiveness. The administration saw it originate from the faculty and considered it something *they* wanted to do. On the other hand, the faculty viewed it as an administration controlled effort since OIR was the builder. OIR, in an effort to stay neutral, acted independently. The result was that most of the administrators viewed their evaluation by faculty as faculty viewed their evaluation by students—as a fact of life that must be endured but not embraced.

What Should Be. For evaluation to be growthful, it must be something that is done with you not to you. Rather than having the issue be passed from one segment of the university to the other, a task force of administrators and faculty is needed to move the process from start to finish. A unit similar to OIR can be a useful technical resource to react to questions and pursue ideas, but should not be placed in a position where it was seen as the primary proponent.

Purpose and Process—What Was Done. The purpose for administrator evaluation was never clearly articulated. On one hand it was assumed that opinions from below, like the student evaluation of faculty, would be growthful. On the other hand there was a covert political reason also linked to the student evaluation of faculty. Upward evaluation in the classroom would be more tolerable if a "what is good for the goose is good for the gander" notion was accepted in other quarters of the university. Faculty objections to student ratings would be deflated if administrators could show they were under the same gun. Thus, the purpose for administrator evaluation focused from the beginning on the activity not the results. The driving force was to be able to say, "We are doing administrator evaluation at Tulsa." There was less concern for the question, "What is administrator evaluation doing for Tulsa?"

Given the political reasons underlying the initiation of administrator evaluation, it is little wonder that the process turned out to be strikingly similar to the student evaluation of faculty. Both rely on rating scales with opportunities for written comments. Not only could administrators say to the faculty that they faced the same gun—it was the same caliber.

What Should Be. Administrators and faculty need to push hard from the beginning at "Why undertake administrator evaluation?" Performance improvement and legitimate political purpose can be accommodated. However, the perspective should change from focusing on common administrative characteristics rated by faculty on a single form to identifying unique aspects of individual administrators documented by the most appropriate means from the most valid sources. Administrators should be active in determining the criteria relevant to their role at that time. The administrator's own view of his or her performance in these situationally specific areas needs to be mixed with the views of everyone in a position to make a value judgment—faculty, peer administrators, superiors, and even students and secretaries.

Rating scales provide a convenient and politically sound means for collecting the views of a large number of individuals. However, anyone who has pondered his own data from rating scales soon realizes that numbers do not speak clearly and comments are difficult to interpret. Data from interviews, structured narrations, and documents related to achievements set in the context of the institution's and the administrator's goals paint a more vivid picture of what is done right and what needs to be changed.

Data Feedback—What Was Done. The honest intention of the data feedback process was to be reasonably open about the evaluation while maintaining a reasonable degree of confidentiality. Therefore, numbers from the rating scales were made public but written comments remained the private matter of each administrator. It is important to note a contradiction in the general purpose of administrator evaluation and the way the data was publicly displayed. The intended purpose was formative—to improve individual performance—but the thrust was clearly summative. By presenting the data for chief officers and college deans in a rank order fashion, the tendency was to see it as proof of who is doing their job and who is not. Evaluation was cast in the light of trial and punishment rather than growth and development.

What Should Be. Comparisons between administrators should be avoided while meeting the legitimate need for feedback to faculty raters. Some form of summary is obligatory, but it is easy to see how an administrator who appears in "last place" would be crippled and almost impossible to retain even with hard data to support his or her talents and achievements. The most positive way to get back in touch with raters is to look to the future not the past. Rather than dwell on the actual ratings, the administrator should outline his or her development plan and may even ask the faculty and others to help determine the best measures of future success. "Here is what I intend to do" and "How will we know?" is a far more positive stance than defensiveness and recriminations.

Follow-Through Support—What Was Done. Since growth and development was not the driving force for administrator evaluation at Tulsa, little attention was given to subsequent steps in the change process. At best, there was a naive assumption that information alone would be sufficient for improvement. Embedded in that primary assumption was the belief that individual administrators could, without assistance, interpret data, analyze performance, set priorities, map strategies, secure resources, monitor progress, and that his or her improvement efforts would be supported and rewarded by the institution. Without all of these abilities and conditions, constructive change is less than likely.

What Should Be. Strategies for administrative development need to be planned concurrently with those for evaluation. Collegial support is one of the most critical factors. A number of options are available to administrators, but the choice is up to the individual about how he or she would prefer to carry on the planned change process. Administrators may wish to work with immediate superiors, a small group of peer administrators, or a support group of trusted colleagues. An administrator may be able to find all the help needed in the collective wisdom of colleagues, but more formal resources such as readings, on-campus workshops, and off-campus consultants should also be available. Finally, the institution must decide and make known what will happen to administrators who demonstrate improved performance. Professional improvement is assumed to be in large part internally motivated, but few administrators would say that recognition, salary, and promotion are irrelevant.

Conclusion

Since 1976 there has been a moratorium on administrator evaluation at Tulsa. Besides the unimpressive results of the first evaluation cycle, an unusually high turnover at the vice president and dean's level has created a situation where many administrators simply have not been on the job long enough for an assessment to be worthwhile. During this period, an administrator/faculty task force has been at work on administrator evaluation and is due to report the results of its deliberations in early 1979. They returned to the very beginning to take up the hard design questions such as *Why?*, *How?*, and *Who?*, and moreover, the *Then What?* question which will link administrator evaluation to administrator development.

Over six years have passed since the idea of administrator evaluation was accepted in principle at Tulsa. It has been a slow and at times disappointing process, but there is a strong note of optimism. The first evaluation cycle was a learning experience which, if properly utilized, will help close the gap between what was and what should be. Tulsa is in a perhaps enviable position to quite literally follow the kind of advice given by Robert Nossen (1976):

> **Never start your first program for administrator evaluation. You do not know enough about it. Start with your second.**

APPENDIX

Form 1

Administrator Evaluation Rating Scale

For rating Vice Presidents, Deans, Department Heads: For Vice President to rate Deans and for Deans to rate Vice President; For Deans to rate Department Heads and for Department Heads to rate Deans; For the President to rate the Vice President

Administrator under Review: ______________________________

Instructions

1. Please complete the attached rating form as outlined in the instructions below.
2. Please do not identify yourself or your department in any manner.
3. Return your completed form to ______________________________

This rating form is designed to give you an opportunity to express the extent of your satisfaction or dissatisfaction with the capability and effectiveness of those administrators who directly affect the academic environment in which you work.

If you do not feel that you have sufficient information to evaluate the individual administrator, please leave the question or form blank.

Write the number in the blank space that describes your judgment of that factor. Rate the administrator on each item that is appropriate, giving the highest scores for unusually effective performances. The end of the survey allows for a narrative description.

Highest	*Average*	*Lowest*	*Don't Know*	*Not Appropriate*
7 6	5 4	3 2 1	0	

I. Leadership

_______ 1. Makes timely *and* effective decisions
_______ 2. Plans imaginatively for the future
_______ 3. Works for creative consensus
_______ 4. Maintains efficiency through delegation of responsibility *and* commensurate authority
_______ 5. Works effectively in the community for the support of the university
_______ 6. Displays concern for basic issues rather than trivia.
_______ 7. Inspires enthusiasm for university goals

_______ 8. Maintains clearly-defined standards of performance
_______ 9. Evokes a receptive attitude toward evaluation
_______ 10. Creates an atmosphere of integrity

II. Relationship with Faculty and Other Administrators

_______ 1. Encourages a high level of academic performance
_______ 2. Encourages individual professional growth
_______ 3. Promotes a high standard of faculty conduct and citizenship
_______ 4. Evidences a recognition of the faculty role in academic governance as established by the university
_______ 5. Evidences a recognition of the role of other administrators in academic governance as established by the university
_______ 6. Promotes a good relationship between faculty and higher authority
_______ 7. Promotes a good relationship between other administrators and higher authority
_______ 8. Gives recognition to faculty proficiencies and accomplishments
_______ 9. Gives recognition to the proficiencies and accomplishments of other administrators
_______ 10. Evidences trust in the faculty to exercise good judgment
_______ 11. Evidences trust in other administrators to exercise good judgment

II. Relationship with Faculty and Other Administrators Continued

_______ 12. Displays flexibility and patience toward delays
_______ 13. Displays ability to mediate and resolve human conflicts
_______ 14. Regularly maintains effective lines of communication
_______ (a) Supports two-way communication with faculty
_______ (b) Supports two-way communication with other administrators
_______ (c) Displays willingness to explain his/her actions
_______ (d) Provides advance notice of changes
_______ (e) Defines explicitly what is expected of faculty
_______ (f) Defines explicitly what is expected of other administrators
_______ (g) Communicates a counter position effectively
_______ (h) Provides feedback upon the completion of assigned tasks

III. Supervision and Evaluation of Personnel; Management Procedures

_______ 1. Evaluates personnel with fairness *and* objectivity
_______ 2. Practices effective management procedures
_______ 3. Displays ability to give constructive criticism in a positive manner

_______ 4. Recognizes the merits of differing methods and techniques
_______ 5. Cooperates in effecting solutions to identified problems
_______ 6. Maintains an "open door" policy
_______ 7. Accepts suggestions on professional matters
_______ 8. Processes detailed *and* routine tasks efficiently
_______ 9. Turns in reports on time
_______ 10. Establishes uniform procedures
_______ 11. Issues suggestions instead of directives where appropriate
_______ 12. Expresses appreciation for a job well-done

IV. Personal Qualities

_______ 1. Displays an active interest in major issues and innovations in post-secondary education
_______ 2. Possesses broad intellectual and cultural interests
_______ 3. Displays physical and mental vigor necessary for the position
_______ 4. Relates effectively with faculty
_______ 5. Relates effectively with other administrators
_______ 6. Evidences impartiality in assessing problems, people, and issues
_______ 7. Displays a sensitivity to the feelings of associates
_______ 8. Relates effectively with different types of people
_______ 9. Possesses a personality to which associates can easily adjust
_______ 10. Is aware of the impact of his/her day-to-day operation on the various publics served

V. Additional Comments

1. What general suggestions do you have which might assist this administrator in improving his/her performance?

   a. What specific activities does this administrator engage in that help you to be more effective?

   b. What specific activities would you like to see this administrator either improve or initiate that would allow you to be more effective?

2. Compared to other academic administrators with whom you have worked, how would you rate this administrator overall? (Check one.)

   Outstanding_______ Satisfactory_______ Unsatisfactory_______

Form 2

The University of Tulsa

Faculty Evaluation of President

Respondent Characteristics: (In order for your evaluation of the President to be scored, please check the item in each category which best describes your position).

1. Primary University Affiliation

   (a)__Arts and Sciences
   (b)__Business Administration
   (c)__Education
   (d)__Engineering & Physical Science
   (e)__Law
   (f)__Nursing
   (g)__Administrative Staff

2. Academic Rank

   (a)__Professor
   (b)__Associate Professor
   (c)__Assistant Professor
   (d)__Instructor
   (e)__Teaching Assistant
   (f)__Visiting Faculty
   (g)__Other
   (h)__No Academic Rank

2. Tenure: Yes__ No__

4. Age: (20-35)__
   (36-50)__
   (over 50)__

Instructions

1. Please complete the attached rating form as outlined in the instructions below.
2. Please do not identify yourself or your department in any manner.
3. Return your completed form to the Office of Institutional Research.

This rating form is designed to give you an opportunity to express the extent of your satisfaction or dissatisfaction with the capability and effectiveness of the President.

If you do not feel that you have sufficient information to evaluate the President, please leave the question or form blank.

Write the number in the blank space that describes your judgment of that factor. Rate the President on each item that is appropriate, giving the highest scores for unusually effective performances. The end of the survey allows for a narrative description.

Highest	*Average*	*Lowest*	*Don't know*
7 6	5 4	3 2 1	0

I. Leadership—Institutional Management

_______ 1. Evidences awareness of his multiple roles and responsibilities toward faculty, students, governing board, and community

_______ 2. Directs an administrative organization and management structure which is effective in carrying out policy decisions

_______ 3. Evidences ability to work effectively within the formal governance structure of the university

_______ 4. Supervises the efficient and equitable allocation of institutional resources

_______ 5. Always displays leadership in directing the current and long-range planning of the institution

_______ 6. Maintains an appropriate balance of support for the academic research and social service functions of the university

_______ 7. Maintains appropriate responsiveness to suggestions and ideas of others

_______ 8. Inspires enthusiasm for university goals

_______ 9. Processes detailed and routine tasks efficiently

_______ 10. Establishes uniform procedures

II. Leadership—Institutional Representation

_______ 1. Works effectively for development of facilities, equipment, and funding necessary to support functions of the university

_______ 2. Represents the university effectively in its relationship with the governing board

_______ 3. Projects an effective national image of the mission and role of the university

_______ 4. Encourages faculty and staff members to promote university interests through professional memberships, community services, and other individual activities

_______ 5. Supports disciplines in individual projects for student recruitment

_______ 6. Maintains appropriate commitment to the social service role of the university

_______ 7. Works effectively in the local community for the support of the university

_______ 8. Evidences capacity to maintain institutional integrity against any outside pressure groups

_______ 9. Works effectively to obtain research and program funding for university projects

_______ 10. Maintains appropriate interest and involvement in outside agencies for the support of private higher education

III. Relationship with Faculty

_______ 1. Encourages a high level of academic teaching performance
_______ 2. Encourages individual professional development
_______ 3. Promotes a high standard of faculty conduct and citizenship
_______ 4. Evidences commitment to the full exercise of academic freedom
_______ 5. Involves individuals responsible for implementing programs in preliminary planning and decision-making
_______ 6. Maintains an appropriate interest and involvement in college and departmental activities
_______ 7. Supports an effective structure for the recruitment of faculty members
_______ 8. Supports an effective structure for the reward of faculty members
_______ 9. Displays ability to mediate and resolve human conflicts
_______ 10. Regularly maintains effective lines of communication
_______ (a) Supports two-way communication with faculty
_______ (b) Displays willingness to explain his actions
_______ (c) Provides advance notice of changes
_______ (d) Defines clearly what is expected of faculty

IV. Personal Qualities

_______ 1. Displays an active interest in major issues and innovations in post-secondary education
_______ 2. Possesses broad intellectual and cultural interests
_______ 3. Displays physical and mental vigor necessary for the position
_______ 4. Works effectively with faculty members
_______ 5. Works effectively with other administrators
_______ 6. Evidences impartiality in assessing problems, people, and issues
_______ 7. Displays a sensitivity to the feelings of associates
_______ 8. Works effectively with different types of people
_______ 9. Possesses a personality to which associates can adjust easily
_______ 10. Is keenly aware of the impact of his day-to-day operation on the various publics served

V. Additional Comments

1. What suggestions do you have which might assist the President in improving his performance? (Your written comments will be transcribed to a typed comment sheet and forwarded to the President.)

2. To assist in planning future administrative evaluation please indicate your response to this evaluation:

	Yes	No	
(a)	_____	_____	I favor mandatory review of specific administrators.
(b)	_____	_____	I believe such evaluation is an effective means for improving administrative performance.

Bibliography

Nossen, Robert. "Peril and Pitfalls: Limitations of Evaluation Systems." Paper presented at the American Association of University Administrator's Conference on Administrator Evaluation, November 19, 1976, Pittsburg, Pennsylvania.

Charles H. Farmer is Director of Institutional Research, Executive Assistant to the Vice President for Academic Affairs, and Professor of Mathematics, University of Tulsa.

Chapter Nine
Austin College: Institution-Wide Career Development

Dan T. Bedsole

In view of prevailing norms and common practices relative to administrative appointments, evaluation, and management development, it may appear presumptuous to propose an *institutional* program of career development for administrators. But the experience at Austin College has demonstrated that such a program can be viable and have positive benefits for individuals and for the college as well. We believe this approach could be adopted beneficially by many other colleges and universities wishing to encourage creative, informed leadership.

Before describing the experience with this approach at Austin College, it is appropriate to indicate several assumptions on which our program is based. These assumptions give perspective in building a case for the need for an institutional program of career development for administrators.

One assumption is that the faculty members and administrators at Austin College and at most colleges, we would suppose, are quite willing to work hard to become more proficient at their duties. While some may be more talented than others, all want to make a strong contribution, continue to grow personally and professionally, and be well respected by others. It is a responsibility of the College to provide an environment and support structure which will encourage each teacher and administrator to perform up to capability and continue to grow, stay current in his or her fields, and improve skills. Recognition and reward are important aspects of a broad support structure designed to help each individual teacher and administrator achieve and maintain his or her full potential.

While it is essential that highly qualified people be appointed to the various positions, simply securing able, well-motivated individuals whose goals are in harmony with those of the college is not enough. The environment or organizational climate in which a person works can challenge and support the individual so that he or she develops even beyond expectations, or it can have a neutral or even negative impact on the individual's growth.

When you analyze it, in spite of how carefully each search committee has done its job, every person appointed to an administrative position at any level brings a mixture of strengths and weaknesses, abilities and shortcomings, with both insights and blind spots as well as some unknown or untested qualities. If one wants to look at labels, to some degree as individuals we may be at the same time dynamic and trustworthy, aggressive and sensitive, committed and adaptable, hardworking and devoted to family and community, knowledgeable and forward-looking, and perceptive and flexible. At least this would be a fairly common self-characterization. But does it really say that much about administrative *effectiveness* this year or ten years from now? Probably not.

We assume that the goal of any administrative evaluation and development program is to improve administrative *effectiveness* for the particular institution. Administrative effectiveness, like managerial effectiveness, however, appears to be highly particularized for the individual college or university. A successful academic vice-president in a certain liberal arts college might not be so successful in a different liberal arts college, and even less likely so in a junior college or in a university setting, where his or her strengths may be somewhat out of place. A dean in a faculty-dominated college may not function so well in a college which has a tradition of strong administrative leadership. Even the same college may need different types of administrators at various times in its life. A relatively comfortable college which suddenly faces financial crises may need a new style of administrative leadership. Sometimes in such a situation the administrators can change their styles and preoccupations to meet the new needs, but this is not always the case.

This leads to another assumption which is sometimes overlooked. For any administrative position there is not a single style which is necessarily preferable or more successful. Even for the role of president widely different styles seem to work equally well at similar colleges. One president may not be good at speechmaking but still be quite successful overall. In many institutions, particularly small colleges, it is the administrative *team* or group of administrators working together which should be the focus of concern. A college needs a group of administrators who are able to work well together to meet the administrative and relational needs of the institution. Not all administrators have to be strong at public relations or development work but several should be; not all need to be analytical problem-solvers but some should be; and not all need to be good at designing systems. A strong case can be made that administrative evaluation and development programs as well as selection and appointment processes need to give as much attention to the functioning of the administrative team and the immediate and future needs of the institution for leadership as to the functioning of individual administrators.

With these assumptions in mind let us examine the institutional program of career development used for administrators at Austin College, a residential liberal arts college related to the Presbyterian Church which has 1,100 full-time students and a faculty of eighty full-time teachers.

Career Planning for Administrators

Since 1972 Austin College has had a Career Development Program involving all of its faculty and administrators. The major emphasis and raison d'etre for the program at the beginning was career planning and development for individual *faculty* as described in detail in a recent article (Bedsole and Reddick, 1978). But from the very beginning the career development concept was applied to administrators of the College as well. By now all of the College's administrators have been actively participating in the Career Development Program. The designations "administrator" and "manager" can be used either broadly or narrowly. At Austin College there are presently some twenty-three individuals who devote over half of their time to administrative or managerial functions, but about half of them also hold faculty rank and teach regularly or occasionally as part of their duties. In the College's Program Management System there are eight divisions which include some sixty programs, each of which has a program director. Examples of programs are English, Chemistry, Heritage of Western Culture, Computer Services, Religion, Purchasing, Constituency Relations, etc. Over half of the forty-five program directors who direct one or more programs are full-time faculty who may or may not have some release time because of this responsibility. Thus, a large number of faculty have important administrative duties and major roles in managing the College. Obviously, the distinction between the categories "administrator" and "faculty member" becomes somewhat fuzzy at times.

Having a Career Development Program which involves faculty, administrators, and staff makes for continuity and consistency. A faculty member who progressively becomes more heavily involved in program management and other academic leadership roles may wish to explore the possibility of moving into academic administration on a half-time or full-time basis at some point.

The Career Development Program furnishes the ideal structure through which the person with administrative ambitions can be counseled, coached, and trained for managerial and leadership roles. There can be a sharing of information about various positions, what these require, and possibilities for the future. Career paths may vary greatly. This can be a time of experimentation, testing, and communication which will benefit both the individual and the institution. It can also be an appropriate time to assess the realism of personal ambitions.

Career Development Program Elements

The process of the Career Development Program at Austin College applies in a similar fashion to both faculty and administrators, but the descriptions below and the examples used have been chosen in relation to administrators rather than faculty or staff. Additional details on the process are available in the article cited previously (Bedsole and Reddick, 1978).

Advisors and Consultants. Each individual has a "Career Development Advisor," typically the person's immediate supervisor; *e.g.* the President serves as Career Development Advisor for those administrators who report directly to him. The individual's Career Development Advisor serves as "coach" for the process and representative of the College relative to the individual's career planning process. A special additional resource is the Career Development Consultant, an emeritus professor of education and psychology who serves on a part-time basis as a career counselor for faculty members and administrators. Other administrators and faculty may also assist the individual in career planning, evaluation, and implementation efforts.

Development Plans. Periodically, usually at least every five years, each individual prepares a long-range plan for personal and professional growth, typically a five-year projection. This written statement outlines the individual's background, present roles, desires for exploration, aspirations, concerns, and plans for development during the five-year period ahead. Even concerns about interpersonal relationships, work loads, and assignments are appropriate for inclusion. Both long-range and short-range goals are described and specific projects for attaining these goals outlined.

Such Career Development Plans are similar to growth contracts described in Chapter Five by Berte and O'Neil, but the term Career Development Plan is more appropriate for the process at Austin College for several reasons. As indicated above, the plan deals with long-range and short-range goals, plans for growth and renewal, immediate concerns, and long-range ambitions. The review and discussion of life planning and career stages, values, and aspirations are encouraged. The mid-life crisis phenomenon, career progression concerns, and phasing into retirement are suitable topics for discussion along with a realistic assessment of the College's needs and capabilities for support for the individual. A written plan is developed and submitted but in no sense is it to be considered a contract which would be binding on one or both parties. Rather it is considered to be a definite statement of intentions and a valuable communications device for describing the individual's situation, goals, and probable plans.

Annual Review. At least once a year, usually in May or June, the administrator meets with his or her Career Development Advisor to review the goals previously set for that year and to assess whether these have been attained. At that time the plan may be updated and revised to reflect changes, new conditions, and additional possibilities. If the administrator has been unable to fulfill projected goals this is acknowledged and the individual's situation is reviewed. Mutually acceptable new goals are then set. As with faculty, conscientious participation in the Career Development Program is part of the individual administrator's professional responsibilities.

Evaluation is an integral aspect of the annual review, first in relation to the individual's degree of success in meeting the goals and fulfilling the plans described in the Career Development Plan, and secondly, in relation to evaluation of courses taught, evaluation by peers and subordinates, etc. Both positive and negative feedback can be given as appropriate in a very direct, open way. If an individual has what appear to be exaggerated perceptions of his or her capacity or potential, ways to test the latter may need to be developed. In any event honest feedback in a climate of trust is encouraged, since this will be of much more benefit to the individual than overly generous or nonspecific feedback or "pablum."

Last year a series of personal interviews involving some sixty administrators and faculty members were conducted by the Career Development Consultant for the purpose of obtaining evaluations of key administrators by those working most closely with and for them. The results of this series of confidential interviews were summarized for review by each administrator being evaluated and by the President and Executive Vice President.

The administrative team and the President in particular are evaluated at least once each four years by the Board of Trustees. This fits into the plan the Board of Trustees utilizes for reviewing all college operations periodically. Each summer the Board participates in an intensive two-day workshop on campus reviewing one of the four major operational areas of the College: (1) educational programs (2) business affairs (3) college relations and development, and (4) long-range planning and administration/governance. By focusing on one of these areas in turn each summer, over any four-year period, all aspects of college operations are carefully reviewed by the trustees who thus become rather well informed about all areas of college operations and policies.

During the year in which long-range planning and administration/governance are reviewed, there is a major evaluation of the President and his administrative team, with the evaluation procedures being approved in advance by the Board. Naturally, the primary focus is on the evaluation of the President and his overall effectiveness. Two years ago, when the last such evaluation was conducted, the Career Development Consultant held a number of interviews to obtain confidential evaluations. An outside consultant was also utilized in an independent evaluation effort. This whole process appeared to be well organized with suitable direction and participation by the Board of Trustees. A special committee of the Board discussed the findings with the President who in turn reviewed these with his administrative team. The process was a positive one for the

President and other administrators, and the importance of evaluation at all levels was reinforced for members of the college community.

At Austin College periodic evaluation is viewed as a stimulus for change and growth as well as a basis for providing recognition and rewards. To be valid it must be direct and candid and also be related sensitively to the reward structure. From our experience we believe the Career Development Program provides a suitable vehicle for accomplishing this.

Statements of Individual Goals

Most administrators are rather closely tied to their institution and their future relates rather directly to the success of the institution. Many started out as full-time faculty at the College and moved into full-time administration after years of successful teaching. Their ambitions typically assume that they will remain at this college. Even so, the Career Development Program really focuses on the total *career* of the individual, indeed lifetime planning. In some instances this involves planning for possible advancement to a suitable position at another college, either in the near future or several years hence.

A few excerpts from four particular Career Development Plans will be given below to illustrate some of the types of goal-setting and career planning issues which may be involved in this process. Since most Career Development Plans are twenty to thirty typewritten pages in length, only a few of the aspects of any one plan are included here.

One of the younger administrators described the sequence of his participation in the Career Development Program as follows, illustrating how a person's ambitions can be spelled out and taken into account:

> I would like to take this opportunity to use my Career Development Plan to portray how the process can actually stimulate a person into thinking and achieving goals in a much more rapid fashion than one might ordinarily expect. In order to do this, I am referring you to a list of some 10 goals which were designed by me in April 1973. After you have read through these 10 goals, I would like to reflect on where I stand at this point with reference to these 10. Then I will project the directions that I have been encouraged to go based on the success of my 1973 set of goals . . .
>
> I have found the administrative side of my experiences at Austin College gratifying, and the ones I continue to pursue and enjoy with great vigor and excitement. Out of my two and one-half years of experience with the Educational Advising Office, my administrative experience in being [a program director] and having had what I consider a unique opportunity at this institution to preview a large portion of its operation; *I now commit myself to the long-range goal of looking toward a time*

when, with additional administrative opportunities at this institution, I will be ready to assume a role of Presidency of some institution similar to Austin College.

In order to keep abreast of college administration and particularly to understand the more complex personnel issues of college administration, it is apparent that some form of training, either within our institution or outside of it, is necessary. One possible avenue for that type of training would come in the form of participation in the Institute for Educational Management held at Harvard University each summer. I am not aware of other types of opportunities that would be more germane to my interests, but I assume that my executives could tell me of such. I am interested in the content of the Institute for Educational Management and would like to have this opportunity for additional training. I will leave the question of the specific summer for participation to my executives . . .

In summary, my commitment continues to be concomitant with Austin College and the liberal arts tradition. Again my aspirations and goals tend to be administrative as compared to discipline-oriented. I am by nature an energetic and goal-oriented type person; therefore, I will always seek to rise to higher levels of the organization by the very nature of my own drives. I contend that my skills in interpersonal relations with the constituency of the College will serve me well in this capacity . . .

Career Development at Austin College has proven very successful for me personally. It has provided me with the opportunity of stating my goals and having reaction from my executives in whether or not those goals were, in their opinion, realistic. It has also been very meaningful for me to see that many of my original goals and objectives have been considered and indeed acknowledged in terms of reality. Likewise, the discussions which I have had recently with the administration tend to encourage me further in terms of the role and scope of the Career Development system in an institution like Austin College. My personal commitment remains as high as ever to the institution, and I assume the institution will acknowledge back to me in a realistic and open manner its evaluation of my goals and objectives.

In contrast to this are the comments of another administrator in his Career Development Plan:

In the course of nearly three years, while I have moved from my early to middle fifties and thus lost professional mobility, I have reevaluated my status and perspectives relative to ad-

> ministrative assignments. At first reluctantly and afterward with somewhat better grace, I have concluded that advancement in academic administration is probably not a reasonable prospect and that the kinds of partially administrative posts that might become available to me are not likely to be very different from the ones I presently hold . . . I must conclude that I should project a low-profile position within Austin College . . .
>
> Consistent with such a projection is my intermediate goal of developing further competence in my [teaching specialty], with its short-range relationship to the project described more fully below . . . But in longer range, seven to ten years or so, I need also to explore possibilities for non-teaching employment beyond retirement. When the time comes for me to leave teaching—whenever that might be—I want to have some reasonable options. I think that [my present age] is an appropriate time to start preparing for that circumstance because I expect more of my preparation may have to be managed piecemeal over weekends and holidays through several years. Some of my informal contacts within the College may be especially helpful to me in directing my study and getting it underway.

Another administrator at the College speaks quite personally:

> During [this year] I have spent time, energy, and money in attempts to formulate long-range plans. Although I do not yet see all the answers, I think that these expenditures have been worthwhile in indicating a direction in which I should go. The work with a career consulting firm included some psychological analysis and some advice on techniques to be used when and if I decide to seek other employment. I have no regrets about having spent my money for this purpose. I think I got some helpful insights about myself and about how to compete in the job market. Suggestions by the consultants have started me on some readings in psychology and about the executive life.
>
> I believe that my best contribution can be made by moving away from teaching into administration. I have tried very hard to avoid neglecting my teaching in favor of administrative tasks, but I am not satisfied with either kind of effort. I need to do a better job of interacting with area faculty regarding their career development plans and evaluation of their work. I need to be more familiar with what goes on in the area. Too much of what I do is reaction to a deadline or crisis. I need to initiate as well as react.

There is evidence to support the view that the higher the level of the executive the less control the individual has over his or her time. It may seem a contradiction, therefore, to move further into administration when one is seeking more time to do things right. My justification is that the greatest frustration of all is to feel unprepared to give the student what the student needs, and that the other problems are to be preferred over this one. I have long envied those people who can function well with only four or five hours of sleep out of a 24 hour day. I am convinced that I am not so constituted and that I cannot accomplish much more than I now do by spending much more time at it. Indeed, I might accomplish more by spending less time trying and more time guaranteeing some minimum amount of rest and/or relaxation each day.

I see the installation of program management and career development for faculty as offering quite a challenge for the next couple of years. Beyond the installation phase there will remain room for improvement in utilization of individual talents and interests. I do not yet know how to achieve a better match between individuals and jobs needing doing, but I feel that serious attempts need to be made, and I would like to help make them during some part of the next five years.

To function well as an executive I need to change certain habits. For example, I need to make some decisions more quickly. Some improvement can be realized by deliberate and constant effort, but formal training might be helpful. I would like to investigate some of the training opportunities available for college administrators.

Another administrator had this to say:

In the area of personal development, I believe that I can identify a number of characteristics which add significantly to my performance. These include a sense of commitment, some analytical ability, some quantitative ability, a degree of objectivity, and even a tendency to work toward perfection when it is kept under control. I believe that I can also identify two characteristics which have significantly limited the benefits of these strengths, and I wish to make a special effort to improve in these areas during the coming months. The first limitation is attempting to do everything myself. I have at times told myself that I had to do something either because there appeared to be no one else immediately available with the set of skills required or because everyone else was already too busy. In fact, even if there is no one immediately available with the *set* of skills required, almost every task can be broken down into elements that others can do—often better than I can myself. Further, if I made better use of the skills and help of others, I might find that I had more help available when I need it. Therefore one of my resolutions for [the year ahead] is to move as rapidly as possible to develop for as many of my responsibilities as possible a set of standard operating procedures that will permit me to draw upon the abilities and commitments of others. I feel very strongly that the normal, routine operation of an office should be so established that it will function quite satisfactorily whether I am present or not. This approach will lead to the development of others, and it will free me to deal with the non-routine and to focus on planning to avoid crises rather than continually being in the middle of one. (I might note that I have intellectually held this position for some time, but certain recent experiences with a computer have encouraged me to take positive steps to translate my belief into action.)

The second limitation I plan to give special attention to has to do with the scheduling of work and the accepting of assignments. I find that I have a tendency when responding to new opportunities and assignments to evaluate my ability to get them done on the basis of whether or not I personally had the technical skills required. I plan to be much, much more careful in maintaining an appropriate balance among the *total* resources available to me, the *total* responsibilities I hold, and the appropriate level of perfection to aim for on each task.

In both of these limitations I may well 'overcorrect' before I find and learn to work at the appropriate balance point. I ask your help and indulgence should this happen.

Even the President of the College is involved in the process of Career Development Planning. Two years ago, the President developed his own Career Development Plan and discussed it with the Chairman of the Board of Trustees, who served as the President's Career Development Advisor. In so doing, the President began, for the first time, to face up realistically to the prospect of some approach to phasing into retirement over a five to ten year period with the appointment of a new president. This resulted in the adoption of a leadership transition plan whereby the President was appointed Chancellor and the search for a new president was initiated and successfully completed.

Like most other colleges, Austin College does not grant tenure for administrative positions, although some administrators hold tenure appointments earned when they were full-time faculty. The same rules concerning notice of termination apply to administrators as for non-tenured faculty. This means that any administrator with over four years of full-time service at the College must be given at least a year's notice of nonrenewal of contract. With the flexibility of the Career Development Program in recent years, no administrator at the College has been terminated but several have modified their career directions.

Administrators as well as faculty are eligible for regular sabbaticals and study leaves. The College provides the time off without loss of salary and in addition assists with related expenses such as travel, housing, tuition, etc. An example of such a leave for an administrator is given below:

> I would like to apply for a sabbatical for the spring semester of [next year] to be spent studying at Stanford and the University of California at Berkeley. In the 18 years I have been at Austin College, I have had little time to spend on preparation for my courses due to heavy involvements in teaching, administration, and area or college-wide involvements. I need an extended period of time for study to improve my competence and bring myself up to date in my major fields of interest. Consequently, I want to study at least one semester at one of the best graduate schools and one that has an outstanding law school. If possible, I would prefer to take my sabbatical at two such institutions rather than one because I intend to attend classes in several fields of [my discipline] and this would enhance the opportunity to do so.
>
> In addition, I hope to do some research on higher education administration, issues, and directions. And, finally, I want to visit a select member of graduate and law schools in California to develop contacts and to learn more about their programs in order to better advise and to increase opportunities for our students who want to enter graduate or professional schools.

If it is more practical for the administrator to take a mini-sabbatical for the summer, for the January term, or for part of the fall term or spring term, then such an option can be utilized. An example of such a mini-sabbatical is the one taken last year by the College Librarian for an eight week period:

> Because of the potential value to our faculty and our students of online searching of a variety of data bases, I would like to undertake a few weeks' training in the art of "searching" at the Lockheed Research Laboratory, Palo Alto, California. Attached is a letter from one of their representatives, and a brief outline of the proposed internship. It is quite likely, through our membership in the AMIGOS Bibliographic Council, that we will have access to these data bases in fiscal 1977-78. The library will be responsible for acting as interpreter between user and system; therefore, the better trained we are, the better service to our users. In addition, if time allows, I should like to visit a few of the college libraries in northern California to compare our OCLC system of cataloging with that of BALLOTS at Stanford.

Funding

Financial assistance in the form of Career Development Implementation Grants to cover expenses is available to administrators as well as to faculty for sabbaticals and study leaves, attendance at special conferences, workshops, seminars, etc. Such grants cover extra expenses incurred by the individual but are not used for salary payments or for release time, which are covered as needed in other ways.

Several years ago, the College concluded that an expenditure of at least one percent of its Educational and General Funds each year would be justified for supporting career development activities and related expenses. Setting this as one of its highest priorities, the College sought and obtained a grant of $50,000 per year for three years to provide such funding. After demonstrating the benefits and importance of such funding, the College was then able to obtain a commitment from a foundation to establish a one million dollar endowment which will provide about $50,000 a year for such Career Development Implementation grants to faculty members, administrators, and staff.

A few examples of such grants given to administrators for career development activities and related expenses during recent years are given below:

- Graduate work which culminated in the Doctor of Public Administration Degree from Nova University (Assistant President)
- Full-time study at Texas A & M University leading to completion of the Master of Agriculture degree in Floriculture (Grounds Supervisor)
- The six-week Institute for Educational Management, Harvard University (Dean of Humanities)
- A one-week Summer Institute on College Admissions, Harvard University (Director of Admissions)
- A Lifework Planning Workshop; visit to another college (Director of Career Planning and Placement)
- A one-week Institute for Chief Student Personnel Administrators (Dean of Educational Administration)
- A three-day Seminar on Time Management at the SMU School of Business Administration (Registrar)

To qualify for funding, such endeavors must be shown to have a logical tie-in to the individual's Career Development Plan. There are specific guidelines as to the types of expenses which may be reimbursed and certain limits are specified. Such support is in addition to periodic attendance at professional meetings which is generally covered out of regular travel budgets.

Such support helps make it possible for academic administrators to keep up with their teaching fields of specialization, with the art of teaching, and with administrative skills and new developments in higher education. To stay at the forefront of such a wide range of topics taxes the individual's time and energy and finances as well, so the College's support is essential if its administrators are to be encouraged to be active at the task of staying current and continuing to grow personally and professionally.

Not all of the activities have to be pursued on an individual basis. Austin College, like many other colleges, has begun to offer management training workshops periodically for a group of its administrators or for a mixed group of faculty and administrators. Much of this type of activity was carried out within the framework of the College's four-year long Total Institutional Project during the years 1971-75 with financial support from The National Endowment for the Humanities and the National Science Foundation (Austin College, 1976).

Teaching improvement centers and management development programs have become common for many institutions. A difference here is that the Austin College program involves *all* faculty and administrators as well as selected staff. We are convinced that institution-wide participation with strong, tangible institutional support will be of more benefit to individuals and to the college than self-improvement efforts which are strictly voluntary. The latter can easily become somewhat isolated from the main thrust of the institution. They often are viewed as personal "bootstrap" efforts which have little lasting impact.

The support of all career development activities at Austin College becomes much more meaningful for the individual in our Career Development Program because of the direct relation these have with the individual's career development plan. The President, Executive Vice President, the person's Career Development Advisor, and others can be supportive and reinforcing of the goals and endeavors of an individual's activities which are planned, particularly as they become fully aware of goals, concerns, needs, and aspirations of the individual. Assignments can then be arranged so as to maximize the attainment of individual and institutional goals.

The approach is highly personal and individualized. Some faculty may move into full-time administrative work at the College for a few years then return to full-time teaching. Others may be shifted to different responsibilities which may be at a higher level, or at the same or lower level. Still others may move on to new positions at other institutions. While it continues to be somewhat difficult for the administrator to make definite long-range plans because of the many contingencies, the Career Development Program with its extensive communication process facilitates such planning and provides a fairer, more open approach. Both the individual and the institution have much to gain from this active planning and free flow of information.

Participation by Staff Employees (Non-Managerial)

Staff employees may also participate in the Career Development Program upon nomination by the employee's divisional executive. Such nominations are made when it appears a Career Development Plan will be mutually advantageous to the College and to the individual.

In relation to improving job skills, the staff employee may receive permission to take time off from work to attend Austin College classes at a rate of ten percent of tuition cost, attending special institutes, etc. Tuition costs for courses at other colleges and universities may be reimbursed if such courses relate directly to enhancement of job skills or possible career advancement at Austin College. In such cases or similar ones, the employee can apply for funds, with each case being reviewed and decided individually.

Success of the Career Development Program

After six years of experience with the program, the College has learned much about its operation. It is evident that the program has been very well received by the College's faculty, administration, and staff. It is viewed as a positive means of support for individual self-renewal and growth efforts and a valid approach for matching the personal goals of the individual with the institution's goals, priorities, and educational needs. It enhances open, direct, and frequent communication so that individuals are much less likely to be taken for granted. It provides an incentive for administrators to be active in carrying out creative projects and varied participation in management development activities. Rewards and recognition come not only through promotion and merit salary increases, but also through financial support provided by the institution or sabbaticals, leaves, and other career development activities of the individual.

This is not to imply that this program will be a panacea for any institution. To have a viable, productive career development program requires a college to be fully committed in theory and practice to providing strong leadership. There must also be a climate where administrators are challenged to provide effective leadership and are provided support so that risk-taking is encouraged. Unless there is funding for career development activities, the program could be shallow and lacking in enthusiastic participation.

Some problems have arisen. For busy administrators it is hard to find enough time to prepare one's own Career Development Plan and to respond to the plans and needs of others. It is not that the program is so time consuming, it is just that this type of activity does not have the immediate, pressing urgency of the many day-to-day demands, crises, appointments, meetings, etc. As with long-range planning efforts generally, that which can be deferred without immediate negative impact will often be delayed. To counteract this tendency probably requires either a firm schedule or continual pushing from a conscientious coordinator or top administrator.

Some administrators as well as some faculty initially may not be very specific or candid in their career development writeups. Generally, however, given encouragement, they will freely expand on their comments and make stronger commitments, and be more candid in sessions with the Career Development Consultant and with their Career Development Advisors. The fact that Career Development Plans are shared with only a few administrators except at the request of the individual (and otherwise are treated confidentially) apparently has a positive impact on the degree of honesty and candor displayed in these writeups.

It is all too easy for anyone, particularly an administrator, to be responsive and reactive but not creative and aggressive. Strong leadership takes a great deal of determination and a tough hide. An administrator may just drift along from year to year without a major stock-taking or re-charting of career direction. Properly carried out the Career Development Program can be a positive intervening force. While all aspects of the career development process may not be completed by an individual each year, the approach does much to assure that periodically there will be a facing up to the imperatives of the future. Overall, the Career Development Program appears to have worked very well at Austin College.

Guidelines for Establishing a Career Development Program

Based on the experience at Austin College several suggestions may be given to other institutions wishing to consider using a career development program.

1. The structure and general design for such a program should be locally developed to reflect the needs and environment of the particular institution. While staff work and outside consultation may facilitate this endeavor, local development and a feeling of ownership are essential.
2. If possible, the career development program should involve all faculty members and administrators.
3. A strong commitment by the top executives of the institution is essential. Their active participation in the processes for their own evaluation and career planning will provide a good example for others.
4. Funds must be secured and made available to support individual career development projects.
5. Evaluation should be an integral aspect of the career development program so that it can be as realistic as possible.
6. The institution must sensitively reward leadership, creativity, growth, and personal development as well as excellence in

teaching, research, community service, and administration.
7. A staff member should be given release time for monitoring the program.

Conclusion

Austin College will continue to give emphasis to its Career Development Program for faculty, administrators, and selected staff members. We hope to provide additional training for Career Development Advisors in the skills of active listening, counseling, and advising. We plan to have a more extensive program of management development on campus while still providing support for individual participation in suitable programs of this type held elsewhere. We are strongly convinced that involving administrators in a Career Development Program will do much to help assure that Austin College will have the strong, effective leadership it needs in the years ahead.

Bibliography

Austin College. "Changing Tasks and Roles in Higher Education; A Total Institutional Project at Austin College." Sherman, Texas: Austin College, 1976.

Bedsole, Dan T. and Reddick, Dewitt, C. "An Experiment in Innovation: The Faculty Career Development Program at Austin College." *Liberal Education* (March 1978): 75-83

Dan T. Bedsole is Executive Vice President and Dean of the Faculty, Austin College.

Chapter Ten
State University of New York: Presidential Evaluation

Murray H. Block

On December 19, 1973, the Trustees of State University of New York formally approved a process for the evaluation of their campus presidents. This action was preceded by almost three years of careful planning and discussions by the Chancellor of the University with the presidents in the system. The idea of evaluations for presidents was originated by Chancellor Ernest L. Boyer within a few months after taking office in mid-1970. Dr. Boyer believed completely in the need for accountability on the part of the leadership of SUNY's complex and geographically scattered system. If the leaders were to hold their constituent groups accountable through various forms of evaluation, they—the leaders—must also be evaluated.

This chapter chronicles the evolution of presidential evaluation at SUNY from 1973 to 1977 when twenty of its presidents were evaluated. The lessons learned at SUNY during each phase may provide guidance to others searching for an effective and just way of assessing the performance of their campus leaders.

Presidential Evaluation at SUNY

Administrator evaluation became increasingly important as we moved from the late 1960s to the early 1970s. The college or university president has always been precariously caught between social extremes. But in recent years, the job has become even more difficult because the president faces greatly reduced flexibility of action, while the expectations of accountability have immensely increased.

The tenure period of presidents has decreased. They have become difficult to find and to keep in office. Those presidents who do remain in office often find themselves caught up in changing social conditions. They need to step back periodically and look at how they are adjusting to these changes. Prior to 1970, the surviving president was usually one who could guarantee campus peace. In the mid-1970s, however, the survivor's dominant characteristic was expertise in fiscal management.

The need to reassess the role of the president became more obvious as the shift in authority returned to the office of the presidency. In the 1960s, campus power was dispersed to various constituent groups. These continue to be active and quite potent, but fiscal stringency has brought considerable leverage back to the president. The balance between the president and the constituent groups, and the proper understanding of the former's role by the latter, were most influential in deciding the type of evaluation to be instituted for the SUNY presidents.

SUNY—a complex of twenty-nine state-operated campuses, five contract colleges, and thirty community colleges—had leaders that believed ways had to be found to encourage the best people to assume and retain leadership roles in its units. Although the Chancellor believed strongly in the need for formal evaluation at the top level, he was not as sure, at first, of his presidents' reactions to the idea. The campus president is buffeted by pressures from all sides and has a thankless job. Decisions that satisfy one group will often enrage another. One of the first evaluation reports in SUNY contained student complaints that the president was away from campus too much; it also praised him for spending much time in Albany fighting for the College's needs. Why subject a president to such an evaluation which could be a painful and certainly a time-consuming process?

The SUNY approach to the question of presidential evaluations was to include it as part of a total package of benefits and built-in protections for the top administrators. As early as February 26, 1971, the Chancellor discussed "benefits for presidents" with the Council of Presidents, the sixteen-member body elected by all sixty-four presidents to represent them in monthly advisory meetings with the Chancellor. The minutes of this meeting show that the "benefits" discussed included appointment to professorial rank on a continuing appointment basis with concurrent appointment as president for renewable term periods, periodic study leaves, housing, and other perquisites. The minutes do not mention evaluation, but this was implied in the concept of renewable term appointments.

More than a year elapsed before the Council again discussed benefits for presidents. As its May 19, 1972 meeting, the Council received the draft of a report prepared by one of the presidents on *Conditions for Professional Employment of Presidents*. This report, too, did not mention evaluation as one of the conditions for employment, but did refer to renewable appointments each five years "upon the recommendation of the Chancellor after consultation with the local College Council and approval of the Board of Trustees." The Council is a group of lay citizens appointed by the Governor to serve at each of the twenty-nine campuses. One of their major responsibilities, as defined in the Education Law of the State of New York is to recommend nominees for the campus presidency to the

State Board of Trustees.

With the encouragement of the Council of Presidents, the Chancellor brought before the Trustees, on September 30, 1972, a document entitled "Proposal for Improving Conditions of Professional Employment for College Presidents in State University of New York," developed by a committee of and endorsed by all the presidents. This document was approved in principle by the Trustees, and the Chancellor was instructed to propose the specific policy changes that would be needed to formalize these employment conditions as Board policy. Any resulting conditions of professional employment requiring additional financing would have to be negotiated with the proper state authorities. Again, evaluation, as such, was not mentioned but rather implied as a future Board of Trustees policy.

On January 24, 1973, the Board received two policy recommendations on formalizing conditions of employment for presidents. One set up appointments of presidents and the Chancellor "for a period of five years, during which he shall serve at the pleasure of the Board of Trustees." Unless reappointed, the service of the Chancellor or a president terminates at the end of the appointive period: "Prior to the expiration of any appointive period, the Board of Trustees may formally evaluate the services" of the president and Chancellor. It further provided for their faculty appointments in positions of academic rank with continuing appointment. The second policy recommendation provided, for presidents and the Chancellor, a two-month study leave at full salary during every third year of service and a one semester study leave at full salary after five years of service (both leaves in lieu of accrued vacation for the year in which the leave is taken). The Trustees approved both policy recommendations and directed the Chancellor to recommend to them a set of guidelines to be followed for the evaluation process provided for in the first policy.

At the next meeting of the Council of Presidents, following this action of the Trustees, the Chancellor appointed a committee of five presidents to meet with central staff to develop procedures and guidelines for periodic presidential evaluation. When this committee reported back to the Council on October 3, 1973, and to a gathering of all the presidents the next day, both groups approved the guidelines report and recommended to the Chancellor that he seek the Trustees' approval. On December 19, 1973—almost three years after the Chancellor first raised the issue of presidential evaluation—the Trustees approved the "Guidelines for the Review Process for the Chancellor and Presidents."

Guidelines for Evaluation. The "Guidelines" began with an explanation of the difference between the search process for and the evaluation of a president:

"The presidential review process is entirely different and distinct from the initial search process for a President. In the latter, the various constituents of the campus join to search for, and recommend to the Trustees, the best possible candidate for the position. The search is extensive, and the screening process may be both lengthy and complex. The Chancellor, through his representative, offers guidance and assistance. However, the major work of the screening process remains a campus undertaking and is coordinated by the College Council.

"The presidential review process differs from the preceding in that the broad search element is not a factor, for the President being evaluated is known to all concerned. He already has served under the direction of the Board of Trustees and the Chancellor as the chief administrative officer of the campus. Thus, the review is a Trustee function and process, and will be initiated and conducted by the Chancellor in behalf of the Trustees. Since the President also has interacted during the period of service with various constituent groups on campus, it is both appropriate and desirable that in conducting the review the Chancellor and Trustees consult at appropriate times and by means determined by the Trustees with representative spokesmen of the College Council, the faculty, the administrative staff, and the students."

The 1973 guidelines for evaluation provided for the following procedural steps:

1. In January of the fourth year of service, the Chancellor asks the president if he wishes to be considered for reappointment.

2. If affirmative, the president begins his statement of self-assessment, due February 15. The Chancellor designates a central staff officer to serve as liaison to the campus evaluation committee. If the president's response is not affirmative, he discusses the alternatives with the Chancellor, including the possibility of assuming full-time faculty status.

3. The Chancellor appoints the following four persons to an ad hoc evaluation committee: the Chairman of the College Council; the elected head of the college faculty governance body; the elected leader of the college student body; and an administrator selected by the president. This committee prepares a written appraisal of the president's performance. Each committee member acts as a representative of a particular constituency and may submit a separate report from his or her constituency. The president's self-assessment statement is made available to the committee, and their report is shared with the president.

4. After the appraisals are in, the Chancellor discusses these with the president. He then makes his recommendation to the Trustees.

5. As the final step in the process, and before acting upon reappointment, the Trustees meet with the president being evaluated.

The ad hoc evaluation committees were charged by the Trustees to develop their own procedure to be followed on their campuses, subject to approval by the Chancellor. This flexibility was deemed necessary because the SUNY campuses vary in size and scope. The Trustees specifically ruled out the formation of any additional committees during the process nor would they condone any form of voting mechanism. Most important, "all parties to the process will observe the proprieties appropriate to a dignified and professional administrative procedure."

The guidelines further charged the ad hoc evaluation committees with the responsibility to provide the Chancellor with a substantive and illustrative evaluation report that covers the President's performance regarding:

- Academic leadership and management
- Administrative leadership and management
- The institutional tone set by the President
- Internal relationships
- External relationships
- Sensitivity to the needs of the campus

At the time of the approval of these guidelines, the dates of the incumbent presidents' appointments were set for evaluative convenience at the nearest July 1. A schedule was arranged in multiples of five years. The first group to be evaluated consisted of those presidents approaching five, ten, or fifteen years of service. When an appointment period was due to end on July 1 of a particular year, the review process began in January of the preceding year when the Chancellor inquired of the president's desire to stand for reappointment. The process was to culminate in action by the Trustees at their June meeting, one full year prior to the July 1 expiration of the appointive period.

Presidential Evaluation 1974—Reactions

The first cycle began with the evaluation of the Chancellor in January 1974 and six of the presidents whose appointment anniversaries would fall on July 1, 1975.

At the conclusion of the first cycle of evaluation of campus presidents in June 1974, the Chancellor asked the six presidents who had just been evaluated to submit their comments, reactions, and recommendations about the process they had experienced. Similarly, the members of the campus evaluation committees were asked for their assessments of the process.

All six of the presidents responded. Seven of the twenty-four committee members responded. The consensus assessment of the process then in effect was that it was generally satisfactory. The preponderance of responses was for continuation of some form of presidential evaluation. Most committee members' responses expressed strong approval of constituent involvement in the evaluation of presidents. Most found the evaluation itself beneficial to both campus and president. There were, however, several suggestions for improving the time frame for the evaluation process.

From the Presidents. Some of the comments submitted by the presidents evaluated in 1974 reveal the perceptions of the advantages and disadvantages of the process then in effect:

"Presidents who don't wish to be renewed in office are inhibited from saying so by the prospect of nearly eighteen months of public recognition as lame ducks."

". . . greater clarity should be achieved and maintained regarding whether the evaluation is of the president *per se,* or the status and health of his institution."

". . . I firmly believe that it is not feasible for the process to culminate in nonrenewal of a president! If things are going so badly that those in authority are convinced that the president should not consider another term, he should be counseled to this effect before the formal process unfolds."

". . . fellow presidents should be involved in this process."

"Somehow the evaluation seemed to bring out the worst in many persons and lowered the campus tone."

". . . nearly everyone on this campus . . . believed that the President would be reappointed. Therefore, the Presidential evaluation was observed primarily as an opportunity to express complaints."

"To the best of my ability I am going to try to see that (this campus) is improved as a result of the evaluation."

"How can one tell by this process when a president has lost his *intellectual* edge?"

". . . in the best sense of the word, I have enjoyed and profited by the evaluation procedure. Perhaps I am too mellow because of the outcome in my case, but I think not."

". . . there is much dissatisfaction on the part of Council members that their role in the evaluation is an extremely minor one . . ."

". . . I am not entirely convinced that having one member of the faculty or one member of the student body on a committee will necessarily result in a fair evaluation with respect to the entire faculty or the entire student body."

"The formal evaluation every five years must represent the culmination of some sort of continuous review."

". . . each constituency felt that it had an opportunity to be heard and the materials which resulted from the exercise were helpful for me and probably for the institution as a whole."

From the committee members. Evaluators too noted problems and suggested modifications:

". . . a considerable shortfall in faculty responses to repeated requests for input. . . . suggesting a degree of fatalism . . . may have been reluctance on the part of some to share with me . . . confidential comments."

"The Evaluation Committee might be chaired by a total outsider to whom confidential comments may be addressed . . ."

". . . the procedures were quite adequate for the purposes and gave ample opportunity for everyone to express whatever he or she wished to bring to the Chancellor's and the Board's attention."

". . . I have difficulty accepting this five-year review process as a substitute for yearly performance measurement . . ."

". . . a caution to the future committees to continually emphasize to the faculty and staff that *evaluation* is requested and not *recommendation for reappointment or non-renewal.* I found that no matter how often this was stressed, people wanted to make a recommendation for reappointment."

". . . the Guidelines functioned well and the process served the purpose of bringing to the campus another way of examining our purposes and goals."

". . . the reports from each constituency were hastily written . . ."

". . . the time frame was too short . . ."

"The mechanism should be that an outside team composed of a president from another SUNY campus, a representative of the statewide Faculty Senate and a representative from Central Administration be made an integral part of the review process. This would provide some distance."

". . . the nature of the committee made it extremely suspect on our campus."

"SUNY is to be commended for holding that public officials are to be periodically reviewed and held accountable for their actions."

". . . an on-going (and preferably two-way) flow of information between Albany and the campuses would be more useful . . ."

"While our report was, thus, not viewed as an important part of the decision process, we conceived of it as an opportunity for giving Albany and ourselves a better understanding of the major problems faced by the . . . campus . . ."

"The first set of evaluations were enveloped in an atmosphere of too much ballyhoo and expectation. A problem at State University is that anything it does is often viewed with too much publicity and national acclaim."

Recommended Revisions—1974

Based on these comments and suggestions, and further review by central staff, several modifications were recommended to the Trustees and adopted by them in a revision of the guidelines, approved October 22, 1974. The role of the local College Council was strengthened by having the reports of the evaluation committees submitted to the Chancellor through these College Councils, rather than directly as before. This would give the Councils an opportunity to make any appropriate comments on these reports when they are transmitted to the Chancellor. Also:

- Provision was made for input of other constituent groups by charging the existing four-member committee with this responsibility without expansion of that group.
- The guidelines for evaluation no longer included references to the basic qualifications of presidents as listed in the guidelines for the search process, since not all of these are germane after the president is selected.

- An optional interview between the ad hoc committee and the president was provided for.
- One year after the evaluation, the reappointed president was required to prepare a progress report addressing the matters discussed with the Trustees during the evaluation interview.
- Finally, the schedule for the evaluations was adjusted to provide more time for Trustees' deliberations. Instead of action at its June meeting, the Trustees would interview the presidents in September and take action at their October meeting.

Presidential Evaluation 1975

In January 1975, the second cycle began, with the evaluations of five presidents whose appointment periods ended July 1, 1976. The then recently revised guidelines were used. Fewer participants in the second year chose to submit comments at the end of the process. However, those received were quite similar to the comments submitted after the first cycle.

Recommended Revisions 1975

At this time, the University Faculty Senate's Governance Committee chose to review the Board's policy and guidelines on presidential review. The Committee presented a report to the Senate at its April 1975 meeting, calling upon the Trustees to consider making several changes in the evaluation process:

- Following the action of the Trustees at the end of the evaluation, the Senate wanted substantive feedback from the Trustees to the constituencies involved.
- The Senate suggested the administrative representative on the evaluation committee be elected by the senior administrative staff, instead of being chosen by the president.
- Separate reports would be required from each constituency.
- The Chancellor would invite one person from a comparable institution to serve as consultant.
- The Chancellor's review of the campus procedures for the evaluation would be eliminated.
- The Senate would eliminate the prohibition against additional committees and voting.
- The Senate suggested adding "sensitivity to the concerns of faculty, students, and staff" to the evaluation.

These Senate recommendations were discussed with the Council of Presidents and a revision of the guidelines prepared for submission to the Trustees. The revised guidelines, approved by the Trustees on November 26, 1975, accepted only two of the seven recommendations. First of all, the Council accepted the evaluation item, "sensitivity to the concerns of faculty, students, and staff." Second, they adopted a requirement for separate reports from each constituency. Both revisions were in effect for the 1976 evaluation but the second—separate constituent reports—furthers appreciation for the complexities of administrator evaluation.

Presidential Evaluation 1976—Constituent Reports

Some of the comments made in the 1976 evaluation reports were quite interesting. The five evaluation documents each contained four reports (from faculty, students, administration, and College Council) plus a letter of transmittal from the College Council. Here are selected quotes from the five sets of reports:

From Faculty reports. "The President seems to totally ignore faculty when making decisions about academically related matters. . . . He has an open door policy. . . . He has presented good ideas in the areas of personnel and affirmative action, but the capability of the people selected in the areas are (sic) questionable. . . . If the President really believes in the democratic process, and his record so far belies that commitment, a major reform must take place. . . . The faculty seems to be in the position of reacting to his decisions instead of being involved in the decision-making process."

"Overall a majority of the respondents agreed with the President's perception of his accomplishments. They felt he is visible and is responsive to individuals. . . . matters of concern include: failure to recognize outstanding faculty members and failure to increase the leadership capabilities of other administrators . . . cool-headed, democratic, a realist, approachable, credible and someone you respect. . . . The service the College renders to the community and the impact of the College on the community was also noted as a positive feature. . . . 86% of those who responsed believed (this College) was a good place to be and only 5% responded that (this college) was not the place for me. . ."

"The most striking conclusion to be drawn from the data is the absence of agreement by the Faculty regarding the President's performance. . . . he needs more direct, visible, articulate contact with his faculty."

"The President's efforts toward achieving full, high-quality, student and faculty complements are wholeheartedly supported . . . a priority that so heavily favors external relationships can be disturbing to a faculty viewing internal problems. . . . He has shown insufficient concern for and lack of personal involvement in the areas of broad academic policy . . . willingness to listen to faculty individuals and groups. . . . Our faculty has great respect and confidence in President. . . . We consider his performance far superior to that of his predecessors of recent memory."

". . . even the most critical of all responses still concluded with an approval and endorsement of (his) overall performance. . . . The campus ethos does not give paramount importance to academic matters."

From administration reports. "He is receptive to new academic ideas and programs . . . he should observe a closer relationship with Department Chairpersons, faculty, and technical assistants in order to gain a clearer appreciation of the academic problems. . . . he delegates freely. . . . He is viewed by some as open-minded, anxious and solicitous. . . . Others perceive the President as being somewhat autocratic . . . has a deep and sincere concern for the College at all times and particularly its human components."

"The President has created an institutional climate wherein. . . . programs have been able to flourish. . . . There is often more verbal commitment than that exhibited by action. . . . has maintained an image of grace and poise in the community which befits the role he has here."

"Several positive comments were made about his frankness, honesty, and openness. . . . criticism centered on what was variously described as low-profile, non-involvement, non-visibility, aloofness, detachment, lack of contact. . . . not viewed as a fault in itself but as leading to misunderstandings."

"His tenure in office has been a difficult one both for the President and the staff. His stewardship began with a widely-divided, essentially leaderless, constituency; fences both within and without this academic community were in need of repair. . . . We believe that (this college) would have been closed down had it not been for (the President)."

"The President portrays a calm presence and the effect is generally a quieting one for the campus. . . . makes himself available to all levels of management as well as faculty and staff. . . . The President appears as an optimist, which is a positive factor in his institutional relationships."

From student reports. ". . . does come across sometimes as too much of a boss but I guess that's his job. He might not always agree with the students' decisions or ideas, but he is an excellent listener. . . . It is certainly an injustice when the good Dr. makes a decision about something before the committee who has worked so hard on a proposal even gets a chance to review the proposal with him. . . . I am pleased that I have had the opportunity to have worked with him."

". . . the most common response (was that the president) provided no leadership in any direction, thus giving the impression of a vacant presidency. . . . There are other problems of inefficiency within the college which the President has made no attempt to correct. . . . Decisions either get made on a lower level or they are forever lost in the great bureaucratic maze."

From College Council reports and letters of transmittal. "The Council would like to bring attention to the fact that some of the comments that have been received do not reflect the general feeling of the total constituencies. This is most obvious in the report of the faculty. . . . We feel that if as much amplification had been made of the strong points as were done on the weak points, that the report would have projected a fairer and more accurate evaluation."

"The report has generated such a healthy discussion about matters completely peripheral to (the president's) stewardship, but important nonetheless. . . . His skills as a diplomat are evident from the relative peace on campus and respect in which he is held by the faculty, administration and students alike."

"He has corrected the major problems and has given a purpose to the College, he has provided great dignity, compassion and understanding to the Presidency. . . . the charming personal help his wife has rendered to him is without comparison. . . . They are a great asset to the entire College and the community at large. . . . It is our opinion that this was a most inopportune time for any evaluation to be conducted. The critical situation the SUNY system found itself in, the necessary budget cuts, certainly did not endear him to members of the faculty. He swiftly handled this problem, however distasteful it was for him to perform, and in so doing alienated many people on campus. . . . the Council furthermore believes that the format utilized by SUNY in evaluating his presidency is outmoded and non-productive. This opinion is a result of reviewing the report of the student representative to the Ad Hoc Committee, a report that in our judgment is capricious and personal."

". . . in the Council's view, (the college) now has a faculty and staff second to none in the State University. . . . In the area of internal management, (the President) has successfully rejuvenated both the academic and administrative teams of the College through a combination of personal example and judicious appointments. . . . Under his able leadership, we look forward to continued progress. . . ."

The quotes give some indication of the involvement of the constituent groups, their satisfactions with the process, their frustrations, and naturally their biases.

Recommended Revisions 1976

Late in 1976, the University Faculty Senate Governance Committee reactivated its interest in the presidential review process. The Chairman of the Committee wrote to those who participated directly in the reviews conducted in 1974, 1975, and 1976—(the sixteen Presidents, the members of their respective ad hoc evaluation committees, and the central staff members who served as liaisons to these committees). This study, although not completed at the time, inspired the Senate to pass a resolution at its April 1977 meeting calling upon the Chancellor to recommend to the Trustees several changes in the review guidelines.

The Senate requested the inclusion of a statement of the purposes of the evaluation indicating its use in reappointment consideration. They requested that the President's Statement of Stewardship be made available to the campus constituencies prior to the evaluation. The Senate wanted provision for members of the Ad Hoc Committee to use consultative bodies within their constituencies to develop data collection processes and to assist in interpretation of findings. They would also include the requirement that upon completion of the evaluation report and after submission of the College Council's recommendation to the Chancellor and the Trustees, the Ad Hoc Committee develop a mechanism for reporting to the campus constituencies the findings of the evaluation, and that the summary reports of the College Council, the Chancellor and the Board of Trustees be made available to the President and the campus constituencies.

These recommendations were taken into consideration by the Trustees in the most recent revision of the guidelines for presidential evaluation. However, many of the recommendations could not be accepted when the newest guidelines were approved on October 26, 1977.

The first of these Senate recommendations places great emphasis upon reappointment as the end product of the evaluation. This is not so in the view of the Trustees. They have instituted periodic reviews to assess the leadership of the University's presidents. The tie-in to reappointment was a convenience of calendar, and not an absolute requirement.

Making the Statement of Stewardship available was not controversial. In fact, some presidents have preferred to share their statements with all on campus. This provision was included in the latest revision of the guidelines.

The Trustees have always stood firmly resolved against additional committees being formed. This stance reflects the Trustees' concern that the evaluation process not be reduced to a campus popularity contest.

Similarly, the Trustees have held fast on the principles of confidentiality which make reporting back to campus constituencies, as recommended in several of the resolutions, problematic. The Trustees review directly with the president the reports of the constituencies. Their reactions, and that of the president, are freely discussed in the meeting held a month before the Trustees take action. These discussions have remained private and confidential. The Trustees did not wish to alter what they consider to be a critically important Trustee-President relationship.

Presidential Evaluation 1977

A variation in the process was instituted for the 1977 evaluation, however, which helped give the constituent leaders a feeling of more direct input to the Chancellor and Trustees. After receiving the reports of the evaluation committee, and before making his recommendation to the Trustees, the Chancellor is to meet with the president to review and discuss the nature of the reports. These meetings in the past have been conducted in the Chancellor's Office. For the 1977 group, the Chancellor decided to travel to the campus to meet with the president under review and with the ad hoc evaluation committee. A meeting with the local College Council, while on campus, would remain optional.

It was hoped that personal interaction between the Chancellor and the evaluators on campus, before a recommendation is made to the Trustees, would serve as a substitute for the requested post-action feedback. A requirement for such meeting was incorporated into the revised October 1977 guidelines. Finally, the new revision tightened the schedule. The process now would begin in September of the fifth year of service and concludes with action by the Trustees in June, just prior to the July 1 anniversary date.

Conclusion

With the 1977 group, SUNY has seen the evaluation of its Chancellor and twenty of its presidents in a four-year period. Does the system work? The answer varies according to the person or group being asked. Some presidents believe the experience to be most helpful and gratifying. It helped them to take stock of their accomplishments, to review their own frustrations, and to step aside and see themselves as their campus leaders see them. Other presidents thought the experience was disruptive and ineffective. Comments from evaluation team members have ranged from appreciation for being able to participate in a constructive process, to dismay with the enormity and frustration of the task.

Despite its in-depth experience with presidential evaluations, SUNY does not profess to have a perfected system. Many unresolved questions continue. Can a procedure be developed for effective feedback from Trustees to constituent groups without violating the confidentiality of the Trustees-President relationship? Should the University require more uniformity among its campuses in the conduct of the evaluation process, *e.g.* use of a common evaluation instrument? Can constituent groups separate the need for effective assessment of leadership from the requirement to periodically consider the President for reappointment? Would outside evaluators be more effective, more objective?

These questions may or may not be resolved as subsequent evaluations continue. The danger is the tendency to evaluate presidents one-dimensionally. Despite the dangers, the frustrations, the criticisms, the recommendations for changes in process, there has been widespread support for the overall concept of presidential review. In this age of accountability, evaluation of top leadership in educational institutions is a necessity. State University of New York has been evolving—and continues to evolve—its own unique way of facing this necessity.

Murray H. Block is Deputy to the Chancellor for Campus Liason, State University of New York.

Chapter Eleven
Furman University: Institutional Planning, MBO, and Administrator Evaluation

Philip C. Winstead

In recent years the need for change in many institutions of higher education has become more acute. Colleges and universities are experiencing rising costs and lessening public confidence. Students are challenging the usefulness of what is being taught. Resources are scarce and competition is keen for the educational dollars that are available. Plus, the demands for accountability are such that tremendous pressure is being put on college and university administrators as they wrestle with these constantly changing circumstances.

As a part of the desire for sound planning and management practices, fair administrator evaluation, and effective administrator development, Furman University[1] in 1971 initiated a comprehensive effort to revitalize its management, planning, and evaluation processes and to develop a management planning/management by objectives (MBO) model that could be used by similar institutions. The term management planning was adopted by the President and top administrative staff at Furman to encompass all of the activities involved in effective planning, management, controlling, evaluating, and decision-making for the institution, including administrator evaluation.

The model developed by Furman brings together theories of organization development, management science, management information systems, and institutional research in a decentralized, participative approach to institutional governance. It stresses decision-making based on using appropriate research, allocation of resources and monitoring of programs based on management by objectives, and administrator evaluation based on fair and appropriate appraisal techniques. The following case study describes this institution's approach to institutional planning and management by objectives, discusses the issues, conflicts, and decisions that formed the content of the undertaking, and attempts to show that systematic management planning processes are essential as a context for proper administrator evaluation and development programs.

Project Background

Furman University, like other colleges and universities around the country, was concerned about the mounting management problems being faced by institutions of higher education. The school had an excellent faculty, a student body with well-above-average academic qualifications, and an administration open to change with a belief that all members of the academic community should participate in decision-making. The desire to make changes in the management planning areas was not the result of great dissatisfaction but rather of knowledge that much could be improved. In addition, Furman was not in serious financial or management difficulty when the new management planning/MBO processes were introduced.

Furman's involvement in the institutional planning and management by objectives effort grew out of an association with the National Laboratory for Higher Education (NLHE) and its Administrative and Organizational Systems (AOS) program. NLHE, through its AOS model, was fostering the concept of consolidating basic principles in the fields of organization development, management information systems, and institutional research into a planning and management model for colleges and universities. It involved activities such as goal-setting, management by objectives, participative planning, and institutional research.

Planning Dynamics Incorporated (PDI), a management consultant firm, assisted in the development of the Furman model by encouraging a process of systematic planning as opposed to static planning. With the assistance of NLHE and PDI, Furman University began to conceptualize a management planning/MBO program for small liberal arts colleges.

All of those involved were aware that a piecemeal approach to complex institutional planning and management could very well do more harm than good. Consequently, several basic decisions were made at the outset. First, it was decided a systems approach to change was needed because different parts of the university affect each other and change in one part usually creates change in another. Second, every attempt would be made to minimize surprise. Management planning/MBO would be doomed if those affected by the changes were not aware of them before the changes were introduced. Third, support for the program would be built and maintained throughout the project and several "go" or "no go" decision points would be built into the schedule. Fourth, Furman would provide the support services needed to assure the program of a fair chance for success. Fifth, all of those involved would adhere to a "golden rule of common sense and value." No one would seek change merely for the sake of change. Furman would not move any further or faster than deemed desirable and thorough evaluation would take place as the program moved along as well as at the conclusion of the project.

Project Groundwork

The management planning/MBO project was organized in three phases. Phase I began in February 1971 and was completed in May 1971. It involved the preliminary analysis of the Furman environment for such a program and the orientation of key administrators to the basic concepts of the process. This orientation was to assure that the nature, scope, and purpose were fully understood and subscribed to by the President and chief administrative officers. During Phase I, in-depth meetings and discussions were held with chief administrators and selected faculty, students, and staff. The decision to move into Phase II could not be made without the concurrence of this group. Management planning consultants from PDI assisted NLHE in providing training for Furman personnel for Phase I of the project.

Phase II, initiated in May 1971 and completed in October 1971, included the design of the planning process and a workshop to demonstrate the applicability of this approach to management planning. Furman University, NLHE, and the Edward M. Ryan Foundation, which provided a grant, covered the management consultant cost of Phase II with PDI again providing the consulting service. The working group of Furman administrators, faculty, students, and staff who were involved received instruction in the basic procedures of the process during Phase II and were asked to maintain a healthy skepticism.

After the workshop at the completion of Phase II, the results of Phases I and II were reviewed critically and the decision was made to proceed with the project. Subsequently, the working group was formally constituted as the Committee on Institutional Planning. A task force on management from Furman's Advisory Council was charged at the same time with the responsibility of providing external advice and counsel to the project. Both this task force and the Committee on Institutional Planning recommended that PDI be used as the management consultant firm for Phase III of the project.

In October 1971, proposals were submitted to the Exxon Education Foundation and the Ford Foundation to fund the further development and implementation of the University's management planning/MBO project. Furman received three-year grants from both foundations to support Phase III of the project.

Following guidelines suggested by NLHE and PDI, a search for a person to fill the staff position of Coordinator of Institutional Planning and Research was begun in December 1971. The Coordinator was hired in February 1972.

There was a period between Phases II and III from October 1971 to September 1972 when the negotiations with Ford and Exxon were taking place regarding the continued funding of the project. Furman was so committed to the management planning/MBO project that it was willing to run the risk of proceeding even though there was no firm commitment from the foundations. NLHE made a grant to Furman to sustain the program during this interim period, and Furman also received grants for this purpose from the U.S. Steel Foundation and the Self Foundation through the South Carolina Foundation of Independent Colleges. Phase III began unofficially in February 1972. The Ford and Exxon grants were made available in September of that year.

Project Guidance

The Committee on Institutional Planning (CIP), made up of the original work group, normally met at least once a month during the project. In addition to giving advice and guidance, the committee provided the means by which the work in management planning has been assimilated into the regular operating procedures of the University. Substantively, the committee has provided leadership in the reexamination of the University's purpose and in the clarification of goals for the university as a whole and for each of its major functional units. The committee also has seen that the five university-wide basic policies (governance, organizational relationships, identity, growth, and policies) were developed as the initial entries in the new Policies and Procedures System described later in this chapter.

The CIP also received assistance from members of the Advisory Council who are business and professional leaders throughout the country and work closely with Furman's administration and trustees in matters where their experience and expertise can be valuable. The Management Task Force (MTF) of the Advisory Council has met twice a year. Along with general advice and counsel, the MTF has produced specific reports suggesting ways of improving both effectiveness and efficiency within the institution. It has also been helpful in assisting staff members to assess the environment and to develop assumptions for planning, as well as reacting specifically to plans for evaluation of the project.

Much of the responsibility for management planning/MBO was, and is, with the Office of Institutional Planning and Research, established to coordinate and expedite the management planning activities. Operating as a part of the President's Office, the new office is staffed by the Coordinator, a research associate, and a secretary/research assistant.

The Office is designed to provide the administration, faculty, and students with information, planning services, and other assistance required to facilitate systematic planning and research. Its general responsibilities at Furman are as follows:

1. To maintain an orderly, systematic management planning process within the University
2. To see that the purpose and goals of the University are clearly stated, that measurable objectives are derived from these goals,

and that Furman utilizes, insofar as possible, a management by objectives approach to institutional governance

3. To design and conduct institutional research studies which will provide information for planning and decision-making
4. To establish and maintain close working relationships with others on campus who are doing university-wide research
5. To coordinate with the Furman Computer Center in developing and maintaining a computer-based management information system which will serve adequately the planning and decision-making needs of the University

The concept of the position of Coordinator of Institutional Planning and Research basically is that of a planned change specialist. It is based on several premises:

1. Planned change and the planned change specialist are amenable to the environs of institutions of higher education.
2. Organization development and management science techniques are generally applicable to colleges and universities.
3. Because of the magnitude and diversity of responsibilities of the college president and the senior administrators, these officers need assistance in using the concepts and principles of these management techniques in carrying out their functions.
4. The quality of administrative and educational operations should improve if important institutional decisions are research-based and are supported by knowledge of the results of pertinent experience elsewhere.
5. When new technologies, such as computer-based systems become available and are used, it is essential for someone in the administration to be knowledgeable about the developments.
6. Change, whether initiated from within or from external sources, is most likely to succeed if strongly supported from the top with due concern for understanding among participants at all levels in the organization.

The job description developed for the Coordinator requires knowledge and experience in planning and research, as well as skills as an administrator. Specifically, the Coordinator:

1. Helps develop and maintain a planning and decision-making process on campus which is responsive to the needs of the University
2. Helps the University keep abreast of changing conditions in the field of higher education
3. Serves as an internal catalyst and facilitator of the planning process on campus
4. Helps appropriate individuals and groups in setting goals and measurable objectives, and monitors progress toward these goals
5. Conducts orientation and training sessions in planning, com-

munications, and interpersonal techniques
6. Provides reliable decision-making information at the time and place of decision
7. Conducts and advises on institutional research
8. Assists in maintaining an effective internal communications network
9. Sees that evaluation is part of the planning process

Support Staff. A research associate is responsible to the Coordinator of Institutional Planning and Research. He conducts appropriate institutional research and provides a written report for each study. The secretary/research assistant provides clerical, secretarial, and research assistance for both the Coordinator and associate.

The idea was to design a planning model to introduce a continuous process of institutional development which facilitates normal administrative operations while at the same time encouraging and supporting constructive and orderly change. The basic premise is that the educational process, organizational structures, and administrative operations of colleges and universities are so complex that it is difficult to be responsive to needs without adequate procedures for decision-making. These procedures must be based on systematic planning, setting of institutional goals and objectives, methods for properly allocating human and financial resources, continuous evaluation, and an MBO approach to institutional governance. It was hypothesized that by using this systems approach the University could achieve a higher degree of educational and financial accountability than in the past.

Conceptual Model

The conceptual model has three components: organizational development, information systems, and institutional research. The first of these components, organizational development, is a process of planned change, participatory decision-making, and institutional self-development. Thus, organizational development integrates the needs and goals of individuals in the institution with the institution's goals and objectives. It involves procedures for clarifying goals, deriving measurable objectives from goals, implementing a comprehensive approach to MBO, and systematic planning.

The information systems component is a support service and provides the means for gathering, compiling, storing, retrieving, and analyzing data for planning and decision-making. Generalized computer-based systems are used to increase the information systems' response to the institution's changing requirements.

The institutional research component is another support service and provides the research designs, measurement methods, statistical techniques, and other tools of systematic inquiry needed to make research-based decisions. Institutional research provides both the "why" and the "how" for gathering and analyzing relevant data, formulating alternatives for sound decision-making, and monitoring progress toward the attainment of goals and objectives. Furman's conceptual model and its components can be further clarified by describing the operation of its key elements, organizing vehicle, and support elements.

Key Elements

Clarification of Goals. In initiating the program Furman, along with four other institutions in 1970, participated in an institutional goals study using the Delphi technique to investigate what constituents perceived to be the institution's goals and what they should be. The instrument used in the study was a preliminary version of the Institutional Goals Inventory (IGI) developed by the Educational Testing Service (ETS). The inventory contained a series of possible goal statements covering a broad range of college and university operations. The instrument was administered by mail three times during the study to two hundred and fifty-two of Furman's trustees, administrators, faculty, parents, alumni, and members of the local community. Two hundred and eleven or 83.7 percent responded.

During the first iteration of the Delphi technique, on a five-point scale ranging from "of extremely high importance" to "of no importance," the participants were asked to indicate which of the suggested goals they thought the institution "is" emphasizing and which it "should be" stressing. On the second iteration, the participants were asked to respond to the same set of suggested goals statements using the five-point scale, but with two additions. First they were provided with the modal response to each statement in the first iteration. Second, if their responses did not correspond with the ratings most frequently chosen on the first iteration, they were asked to enter their reasons in a comments section. In the third and final iteration, the participants again were asked to rank "is" and "should be" for the same suggested goal statements. This time, however, in addition to the modal responses to each statement of the second iteration, they received a summary of the reasons given by those who did not agree with the goal ratings chosen most frequently. The results of this IGI study provided the background for development of goals both for the University as a whole and for each of the organizational units within the institution.

Measurable Objectives. Each organizational unit derived measurable objectives from these goals and began an MBO approach to administration. The implementation of MBO began in June 1973, to correspond with the beginning of the fiscal year. To assist in the process, a workshop was held in which selected budget unit heads participated in a series of activities to help them analyze their goals, specify measurable objectives, and reach agreement with their staff in the assignment of responsibilities.

The functional unit heads were reminded that it was not necessary to write objectives for every goal statement. For the regular or routine areas, most work is ongoing and repetitive in nature and takes place whether or not there is a written objective. For these routine tasks, a measurable objective was written only if the subject deals with a task the supervisor wanted to monitor, or it was an area that the staff member wanted his superior to keep abreast of, or it affected someone else's planning. To this set of basic objectives it was suggested that the administrator add problem-solving objectives which respond to a particular need, and innovative objectives which attempt something which has not been done before.

Management by Objectives. Objectives for a given organizational unit at Furman are derived by members of that unit and reviewed by appropriate higher echelons of the University. The individual objectives are checked for consistency with those of the University before they are authorized. Responsibility for each is assigned to the appropriate person and the available resources are made known. Currently Furman is using quarterly review sessions. At the end of the fiscal year the actual results are jointly reviewed by each employee with his or her supervisor against the agreed-upon goals and objectives.

SWOTs Analysis. MBO must relate to the setting of priorities. In fact, good management is defined as the ability of the institution to create, conserve, and use its resources to accomplish the things believed to be most important. Therefore, before an objective is authorized at Furman it is weighed against the criteria defined in the section on measurable objectives in Chapter VII.

The organizational units at Furman take a look at the *strengths, weaknesses, opportunities,* and *threats* within that unit and are asked to do a SWOTs analysis in the form of an annual report. Next, the individual SWOTs serve as the basis for a generalized university-wide analysis. The SWOTs analysis thus provides a framework, along with institutional goals and available resources, for establishing priorites among the proposed objectives. Using this technique, each objective can be weighed against the needs of the particular administrative unit as well as the university as a whole. As a result, objectives can be authorized which maximize strengths, minimize weaknesses, capitalize on opportunities, and eliminate or minimize threats. (See Chapter VII for a complete description.)

Performance Reviews. The conducting of performance reviews provides the primary interface between management planning/MBO and administrator evaluation. Administrators at Furman follow the concept of the review sessions being non-punitive help sessions designed to accomplish optimum results. As mentioned previously, review sessions have been held quarterly with each person responsible for a program or project, meeting for about one hour with his or her administrative supervisor. The frequency of review sessions is based on what seems to be a reasonable number.

The chief aim is to have sessions often enough to allow for early recognition of problems or deviations from expected results. A balance is desired between meeting too frequently, which might place too much of a time burden on the process, and not meeting often enough, which might not allow enough time for corrective action to be taken. The concept of optimum results stresses "the best possible results with due regard for the circumstances which prevail." It is better to achieve a changed expectation than to be locked into a course of action for which there is little chance of success.

The review sessions at Furman are organized around five questions. The first is, "What progress is being made toward the accomplishment of the objective?" A measurable objective should be quantified to the extent that one should be able to tell if the course of action designed to accomplish the objective is on target or if one is ahead or behind schedule. The second question is, "What can be done to help?" Too often objectives are not achieved because the person primarily responsible for accomplishing the objective does not seek or accept assistance from others in the organization who could possibly turn a potential failure situation into a success. The third question is, "Are additional policies needed in order to accomplish the objective?" Many times successful accomplishment of an objective depends upon the adoption of a new institutional policy or procedure which will help facilitate success. Conversely, the fourth question asks, "Are there policies in existence that are hindering the accomplishment of the objective?" An existing policy may need to be rescinded or changed if the objective is to be successfully accomplished. Finally, the question is asked, "Does the objective need to be changed?" An objective should not be changed just for the sake of change, but in light of changing circumstances it is better to adjust one's expectations rather than fail because of changing conditions.

At Furman the performance review process is initiated by a memorandum from the President to each of the individuals reporting to him. The content of the message is for each person to arrange an appointment with him to review objectives after similar sessions have been held with those program managers who report to them. In the Furman management planning/MBO system this formal process covers three administrative echelons—President, Vice Presidents, program heads. The only span of control problem is with the Academic Dean who has twenty-two department chairpersons reporting to him.

While all administrators at Furman have received the same guidelines concerning review sessions, there is variation in how the guidelines are applied. Some administrators rely entirely on oral discussion and marginal notes written on the pages containing their approved objectives. Others rely on written progress reports and statistical summaries concerning objectives accomplishment. In all cases, the participants have been instructed to stress the positive aspects of accomplishment of optimum results rather than the negative side of failure to meet agreed-upon objectives. The results of the process are stressed rather than the structure of the process.

The question of the relationship between the quarterly review sessions and the university evaluation/reward structure came up early in the management planning/MBO project at Furman. In order to use MBO as an effective decentralized, participative, management planning technique aimed at the accomplishment of the best possible results, the non-punitive, group-help aspects of the concept were stressed. In fact, it was clearly stated from the very beginning of the project that there would not be a direct relationship between the number of approved objectives an individual accomplished and the individual's year-end appraisal and subsequent university rewards. Yet, the administrators involved were not so naive as to recognize that the reviews of objectives could not be separated completely from the evaluation/reward structure.

The dilemma was solved by stressing that the number of objectives accomplished was just one of several inputs into a person's annual evaluation. The extent to which a person accomplished the assigned objectives would be added to criteria such as interpersonal relationships, communication skills, resourcefulness, initiative, leadership ability, and overall administrative effectiveness. Taken together these factors would determine a person's yearly performance level. This decision allowed for the protection of the non-punitive value of the management planning/MBO system while at the same time recognizing the critical role of administrator evaluation.

Organizing Vehicle—the Planning Book

A planning book concept has been the chief organizing vehicle for the entire management planning/MBO model. Purpose, goals, objectives, MBO basic data, and other elements of systematic planning are integrated into the ongoing administrative process by this planning book. The system is represented by a looseleaf notebook with color-coded pages keyed to distribution on a need-to-know basis. Each page can be updated individually depending on the nature of the material. The planning book contents are organized around data categories needed to provide information for decision-making based on the trip analogy shown in Figure 1:

- Present Location—Where are You?
- Destination—Where do you want to go?
- Method of Change—How do you get there?
- Timing—When do you want to go?
- Personnel—Who is going with you?
- Associated Costs—How much will it take?
- Arrival—How will you know when you get there?

Figure 1

Planning Book Data Categories

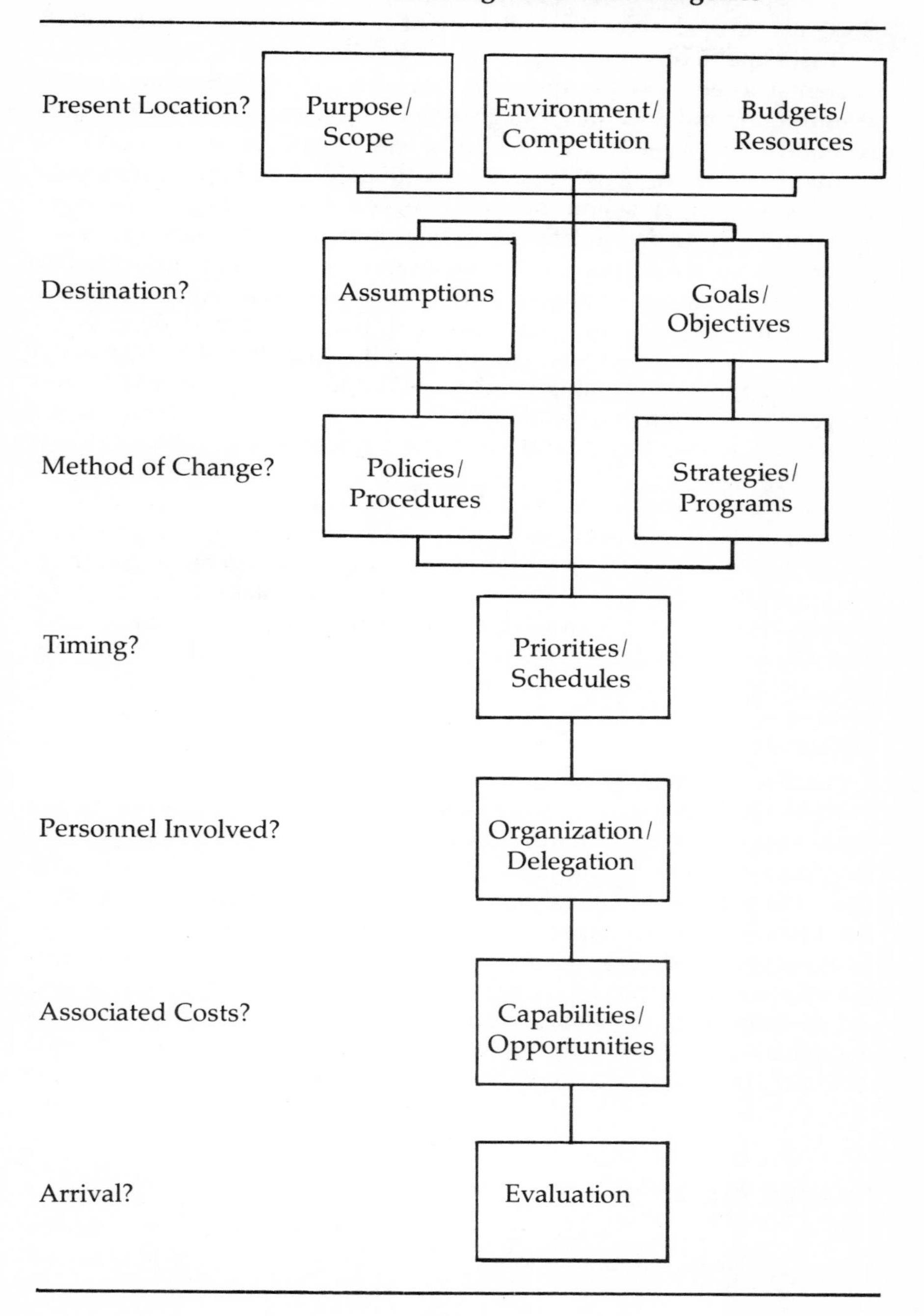

These questions lead to the selection of the information to be included in each of the twelve sections of the planning book.

More specifically, Section 1 contains a statement of purpose or mission; Section 2, an analysis of the environment and competition; and Section 3, an assessment of capabilities and opportunities. This information is designed to address the question, "Where are we?" Section 4 states assumptions and Section 5 lists goals and objectives. These two sections respond to the question, "Where do we want to go?" Sections 6 and 7 tell, "How we want to go," with 6 dealing with policies and procedures and 7 describing programs and projects. Section 8 outlines priorities and schedules. These data relate to, "When do you want to go?" Section 9 covers human resources and the staffing of programs or projects. This information addresses the question, "Who is going with you?" Section 10 projects financial and physical resources, that is, the budgeting of the programs and answers the question, "What will it cost?" Section 11 contains appraisal or evaluation data and addresses the question, "How do you know when you get there?" Section 12 is for miscellaneous. If it does not fit anywhere else and it is important for planning, the material is filed here.

Policies and Procedures System. A major task was rethinking Furman's policies and procedures system. This system was expanded and reorganized into a process that complements the management planning/MBO process. The basic premise is that an individual responsible for a department, function, or activity is responsible for seeing that appropriate policies, procedures, and guidelines are formulated, distributed, revised, and maintained. No individual, however, issues policies and procedures that contravene or conflict with those issued by a higher authority.

In order to initiate the policies and procedures system, five special task forces were appointed to recommend university-wide policies in the areas of governance, organizational relationships, growth, institutional identity, and policies. The Faculty Status Committee was asked to revise the *Faculty Handbook* consistent with the new format and the Vice President for Business Affairs was asked to oversee the conversion of the *Business Office Procedures Manual.* All policies and procedures are maintained in loose-leaf binders, color-coded, have specific file numbers, and are distributed on a need-to-know basis. The eleven sections of the manual are as follows: General/Administration; Academic Affairs; Student Affairs; Business Affairs; Development and Alumni Affairs; Communications; Denominational Relations; Intercollegiate Athletics; Auxiliary Operations; Personnel; and Miscellaneous.

Support Elements

Research Activities. Institutional research activities continuously address special problems. All institutional research at Furman is action-oriented and designed to provide administrators and faculty with alternatives for decision-making. For distribution purposes, two types of institutional research documents are being used. A planning report series deals with topics that are of general interest and have university-wide applicability. A planning memo series responds to specific requests by administrators or faculty members who have need for special information for decision-making. For example, among the topics have been reports and memos on the success of academic prediction at Furman, student attrition rates, summer session enrollment patterns, the need for a special education major, classroom utilization, the effect of the current academic probation rule on undergraduate students, the postgraduation plans of Furman graduates, departmental grade distributions, and freshmen characteristics.

Priorities Task Force. The Priorities Task Force resulted from the need to make still better decisions concerning budgets and other resource allocations among major units of the University. Even with more objective data for decision-making, there presisted the problem of how to decide which worthwhile activities to support across major units of the University as well as within major units. For example, questions could not be answered to the satisfaction of all involved concerning relative merits of certain athletic programs versus certain academic programs and the importance of certain activities in the business area as opposed to ongoing programs in the humanities. The President felt the need for impartial, rationally developed advice. The Priorities Task Force was created as a subcommittee of the Committee on Institutional Planning and includes the four vice presidents, the academic dean, four faculty members, the athletic director, and the president of the Association of Furman Students. The Business Manager and Treasurer and the Coordinator of Institutional Planning and Research serve as resource persons to the Task Force which is charged with examining all aspects of Furman's operations and making recommendations to the President as to (1) the expenditures making the greatest contributions towards achieving Furman's primary goals, and (2) appropriate ways of balancing expenditures with income. The Task Force is to take a university-wide view of things and is to look at the budget allocation across the major units of the University.

Retreats, Workshops, and Seminars. In addition to the initial retreats and workshops to consider the advisability of moving to Phase II and then to Phase III, there were workshops with all of the administrators to discuss the conceptual base for the project and the techniques for its implementation. There were two-day sessions with the Committee on Institutional Planning, the executive officers of the University, the department heads, and other academic administrators. Separate one-day sessions included the business office staff, the development office staff, the physical plant management staff, the Advisory Council, and the Board of Trustees. Staff of PDI and NLHE were used as consultants for these work sessions.

The President has continued to have a three-day administrative retreat off campus each summer where he and his chief administrative officers discuss in depth the major issues facing the University. It is at this meeting that the university-wide SWOTs statement is revised annually.

In-Process Decisions and Issues

Change is seldom easy whether planned or by impulse. Problems did arise with the introduction of the management planning/MBO program at Furman University, and they were handled with varying degrees of success. Following are discussions of issues which surfaced and decisions which, in our view, were significant to the overall conduct of the program. These decisions and issues are examined in hopes that others in similar situations may learn from the experiences at Furman.

Decisions. There was a natural resistance among some, as might be expected, to any type of change. The University, however, relied on what it believed to be a reasonable and open approach to change and consequently there was not any organized opposition to the management planning program or to the management by objectives approach being fostered. Rather, the resistance to change took the form of conceptual disagreements and debate as to the success, failure, or value of various aspects of the program. A key decision was the strategy of a series of workshops, held off campus in most cases, to discuss the need for the program, the conceptual base for the management planning/MBO project, and the various techniques for program implementation. These sessions emphasized the building and maintaining of the support necessary for success. Throughout the discussions the participants kept before them the "golden rule of common sense and value," or if the procedures did not make sense or prove to be of value, they would not be retained just for the sake of change. The intention of these discussion/team-building sessions was not to indoctrinate, but to make certain that all of those involved were thoroughly familiar with the project and would give it a fair chance to succeed.

A second important operational decision was the phasing of the project and the inclusion of the two go/no go decision points in the implementation strategy. The realization by the on-campus participants that formative evaluation was taking place and that the program would be aborted or altered if the evaluations were not positive gave a great deal of credibility to the program. People realized that there was a serious emphasis at Furman on meeting the needs of the institution rather than pursuing a program just because outside money was available.

A third decision which proved to be a distinct asset to the success of the program was the use of well-respected off-campus persons to serve as the primary evaluators of the program.[2] The evaluators were well-known in their fields and recognized by Furman personnel as unbiased observers. This fact contributed significantly to the openness with which the project was pursued.

Finally, the decision by the President to actively back the project and to give visible leadership to the program was a key. He let it be known by words and action that Furman indeed was faced with the problems which led to the undertaking of the management planning/MBO program and that he, as chief officer of the University, saw the management planning program and management by objectives as viable ways to deal with many of the issues before the institution. Consequently he took a leadership role by chairing the Committee on Institutional Planning, adhering to the MBO procedures and schedules adopted, and *by seeing that administrator evaluation resulting from the project did influence the reward structure of the university.*

Issues. Although a number of issues came to the forefront during the implementation years of the management planning/MBO project, six stood out and have import for other colleges or universities undertaking systematic management planning programs or installing MBO procedures. The six issues were: (1) Terminology or jargon; (2) Amount of time involved; (3) Amount of paperwork necessary; (4) Writing measurable objectives; (5) Measurement problems; and (6) Links to the budget process

Terminology or jargon became a controversy on campus during the early stages of the project. In spite of warnings to the contrary, the project leadership did not really appreciate the opposition many educators have to business terms and words associated with fields other than higher education. At first there was an attempt by the project leadership to purge from the conversation and written materials terms such as "manager," "management," "management by objectives," "competition," "environment," "strategies," etc., which were deemed to be troublesome to some persons on campus. In fact, during the first year of the project (1971-72), the term administration by objectives (ABO) was used rather than MBO.

But the attempt to stay away from certain words or phrases created more problems than it solved. For example, there was difficulty in communicating exactly who was supposed to be involved in the program and in what ways. The intent was to have every person with "responsibility for a program" to participate in the management planning activities and in the MBO system. At Furman, however, as with other colleges or universities, there are people with different titles, many at the same level of the organization, all with "program responsibility," *e.g.* president, vice president, provost, dean, director, coordinator, manager, etc. It was decided, after discussion, to use the term "manager" as the generic term for any person with responsibility for a program. This decision provided a common definition and improved communication. It also resulted in a general term which was not prevalent in existing titles as only two administrators on campus (Business Manager and Bookstore Manager) had the term in their official title. Once the decision was made to use the term manager and not apologize for it, the next move was to abandon the term ABO and go back to MBO and other terminology which had agreed-upon definitions. From that point on there was no serious difficulty with the language.

Time involved was a common concern. During Phase I of the project, the statement was made, "It was possible at Furman to undertake this project and to do better planning and management without an appreciable increase in the amount of time normally involved in administrative activities." The truthfulness of this statement was questioned as participants began to total the time they were spending in group meetings, preparation of goals and objectives, developing written programs of action, and periodic reviews of objectives. Looking back one must acknowledge that at the beginning of the project it did require considerable administrative time.

Two things began to ameliorate the problem as the project progressed. One is the fact that while initially it takes more time, it does not take as much time to keep the process going. Second is the realization that different "managers" spend different amounts of time on management planning and management by objectives depending on the nature of their administrative position. For example, a dean spends more time than a department chairperson and a department chairperson spends more time on management planning/MBO than an individual faculty member. Near the end of the implementation period at Furman a computer analogy began to be used in discussing the issue of the amount of administrative time required. The computer analogy is that when a new computer program is introduced the Computer Center usually runs the new program parallel with the old program. Then, when the new program is "debugged" and fully tested, the old program is abandoned and the new program is used with confidence. During the parallel operation more time is required, but when the new program is online, the amount of time decreases. Keeping the amount of time required for a management planning/MBO system reasonable and still getting the desired results is a constant struggle. If viewed as a reallocation of time, however, the management planning activities including MBO do not require substantially more administrative time than other ways of pursuing the same results.

Paperwork required during the implementation of the project raised the question of whether or not the amount of paper required was a help or hindrance. A favorite cliché at Furman became, "Nothing will choke a management planning/MBO system to death any quicker than paper." With written goals and objectives, the SWOTs analysis form, the planning book data, the various institutional research reports, etc., the appearance of a paper overload became an issue. Again the question of too much or too little became a matter of judgment. It was pointed out to those who raised the question that the paper required was not more than necessary and probably not more than in the past. The paper, however, in the management planning/MBO system is more visible. Rather than having numerous memoranda and scattered position papers and reports, the data are contained in planning books, compilations of goals and objectives, program descriptions, and official planning reports—in most cases highly visible documents. A result of the organized data distribution methods is a decrease in duplication and an emphasis on having certain key planning information readily available rather than the uncoordinated collection of general information which is, at times, hard to locate when needed. The amount of paper is a constant battle, but one that is essential to win.

Writing measurable objectives continued to be a difficulty for many administrators in spite of the guidance given through written materials and periodic workshops. Those having trouble felt awkward constructing statements of intent in such a way as to make sure the objective specified the time, outcome, actor, action, performance level, and measurement. Some of those who experienced difficulty began to talk about the inappropriateness of management by objectives to their particular work area rather than to increase their effort toward preparing "good" objectives for their area of responsibility. It was easier in their view to say MBO would not work in their area than to wrestle with exactly which results they wanted to accomplish and how to communicate them in measurable terms.

The strategy in dealing with the administrators who were having trouble was to provide a great deal of individual help and to stress refinement rather than perfection. One of the realities of college administration is that you do not mark a vice president's or dean's objectives wrong in regard to format and send them back with a note to do over. Rather you accept what is submitted if the ideas are clear, and you strive toward improving the format and writing style the next time around. Another cliché for the management planning/MBO project became, "Progressive accomplishment versus postponed perfection."

Measurement problems continued to persist. Although the concept that measurement in a management by objectives program is agreement between the superior and the subordinate was stressed, and that agreement could be reached at any one of three levels—hard data, performance indicators, or effort toward—there were still occasions when misunderstanding resulted as a consequence of not really being sure what result was desired and how success or failure was to be determined. Again, much individual counseling took place, and some objectives were authorized which did not meet fully the stated criteria for acceptable measurement. This area is another one where we had to fall back on the maxim, "Progressive accomplishment versus postponed perfection."

Links to the budget process were mandatory and difficult. Very early in the management planning/MBO project at Furman the involved administrators realized that if the MBO procedures were not tied directly to the institution's budgeting process, the program was doomed to failure. The truth of the maxim that "one is managing by delusions rather than by objectives if programs of action are not developed to accomplish objectives and if sufficient resources are not allocated to these programs of action," became evident as administrators became more deeply involved in the project. If budgeting is not an integral part of management planning/MBO, then the system is incomplete and will very quickly fall into the trap of "busywork" and "too much time and paper."

The chief factor in making the linkage of the MBO system and the budgeting process difficult is the time sequence. Most budget cycles, including preparation time, are approximately eighteen months. Therefore financial commitments in many cases must be made prior to the completion of the ideal sequence of needs leading to objectives and objectives leading to programs of action with budget allocations representing price tags on priority programs of action. It is a dilemma of not being able to delay certain budget decisions and, if setting objectives is moved up to coincide with the budget decisions, then one is operating in many cases too far in the future.

Another problem with MBO and budgeting is that the "purse strings" have traditionally been a source of power in organizational life. Systematic management planning/MBO with its emphasis on goals, needs, objectives, priorities, etc., involves a new way of looking at budgets and their role for many colleges or universities. It requires the planned allocation of available resources to the agreed-upon objectives of the institution. Although administrators still make decisions, they have less discretion because the "rules of the game" are cleaier. This philosophical approach to budgeting becomes a problem for many administrators.

At Furman doubts were expressed about how serious the institution was in adopting the budgeting process fully to the management planning/MBO system. Without a doubt the relationship of the institutional budget to the management planning/MBO system has been the most difficult to deal with at Furman. The President and other top administrators worked very diligently to see that resources were allocated consistent with objectives and agreed-upon priorities. Movement was not as steady in this area at Furman as in the other areas of the project. On several occasions, the time factor was a problem. On other occasions, the personalities of administrators caused budget decisions which were inconsistent with the results of the systematic planning procedures. Overall, however, progress was made, and the recognition of the need for effectively linking the management planning/MBO system to the budget process has not diminished.

Conclusions

Furman University at the time of the writing of this case study is six years into its systematic institutional planning and management by objectives program. What can similar institutions learn from the Furman experience? How does management planning/MBO relate to administrator evaluation and development? What should other colleges or universities be particularly concerned about if they decide to introduce such a program? What mistakes did Furman make that other institutions might avoid? How can the Furman case study contribute to improving the state of the art of planned change, systematic institutional planning, and administrator evaluation and development?

Several suggestions resulting from these questions emerge from the case study of the management planning/MBO efforts at Furman. One is the importance of presidential support. For the best possible results such a program must include all aspects of the institution's operations. It cannot produce optimum results if the program is just for the business area or just for the academic area. Systems theory implies the total integration of the organization. Systematic management planning/MBO implies the allocation of all resources to the agreed-upon goals, objectives, and priorities of the institution. Because all parts of the college or university are involved, the president, as the person with total institutional responsibility, must be closely and actively involved. He or she must assume a visible leadership role.

The same leadership responsibilities are true also for the institution's top leadership team. As the value of academics versus athletics or the merits of buildings and grounds versus student affairs programs are being discussed, there must be a sense of teamwork and of making decisions which are best for the entire institution rather than just one particular part of the organization.

Third, provide the staff support necessary to give the program a chance to succeed. There are numerous logistical problems which will arise that busy administrators will not and should not take the time to deal with. Basic information must be available in usable form, objectives have to be examined for internal consistency, objectives review sessions must be scheduled, and any number of administrative details must be attended to. Someone must be responsible for the management planning/MBO process. This person should not do the work of the individual administrators, but must keep the process going. The importance of the role of a coordinator cannot be overstated.

Fourth, do not hesitate to use qualified outside consultants when they can be of help. There are a number of one-time tasks associated with an effective management planning/MBO system which can be done better by specialists. These tasks include orientations, writing measurable objectives, instructing in how best to conduct review of objective sessions, identifying needed policies and procedures, etc. Make sure, however, that after you use the services of outside consultants that someone on campus retains the skills needed to continue the activities.

Fifth, avoid the unnecessary use of jargon and unfamiliar terminology. The case has been made to use words or phrases which communicate and not to be afraid of language from another field. But do not overdo it. Be sensitive to your colleagues and do not use offensive or easily misunderstood words or phrases if others will do just as well.

Finally, do not use a management planning/MBO system as overly punitive, but do include it as a part of the overall administrator evaluation process. At the same time administrator evaluation and administrator development should not be separated. Systematic management planning/MBO represents a total system designed to accomplish the best possible results for the institution. Administrator evaluation procedures should distinguish among those administrators who are contributing toward this end. Administrator development activities should be available for those where the need for improvement is indicated.

The Furman University management planning/MBO process described in this case study might not be appropriate for all institutions of higher education. Yet it is believed that the potential is great and that the risks are less than the other major options available at the present time.

Notes

[1]Furman University, founded in 1826, is a Baptist, co-educational institution of higher education located in Greenville, South Carolina. It has a student body of approximately 2300 and a faculty of 145. Although steeped in tradition, innovation and change are not new to Furman. The ability to take major steps when necessary has been characteristic of the administration and faculty. Within the past 20 years Furman has moved from a congested location in downtown Greenville to a spacious campus on the outskirts of town. The curriculum has been completely reorganized. A three-term calendar provides for an academic program that permits independent study, foreign study opportunities, off-campus internships and research, interdisciplinary courses, and integrative seminars in the student's major field. In addition to the undergraduate curriculum, Furman maintains graduate programs in education, chemistry, and business administration.

[2]At the time of the external evaluation, Ralph W. Tyler was with Science Research Associates and teaching at Harvard, Peggy Heim was with NCHEMS, and Dale D. McConkey was with the University of Wisconsin.

Philip C. Winstead is Coordinator of Institutional Planning and Associate Professor of Education, Furman University.

Section IV
Planning a Program of Administrator Evaluation

This section moves in two directions. First it looks back over previous chapters to review and emphasize concepts, methods, and the practical wisdom contained in the case studies. Second, the perspective turns from the past to the future as new directions are charted for administrator evaluation and sources are listed to aide in beginning new programs.

In Chapter Twelve Charles H. Farmer summarizes the *why, how,* and *who* decisions to be made initially and culls out a series of recommendations from all of the authors to keep in mind while getting underway. He proposes an implementation schedule which shows it should not be an overnight effort. In the future administrator evaluation will incorporate individual and organizational evaluation and development in an integrated on-going manner.

Twenty-eight administrator evaluation programs are outlined in the *Appendix* so that readers will have an opportunity to gain additional practical insights. The programs come from a variety of institutions in sixteen states. Most readers are likely to find some institutional kinship. The name and address of a contact person is listed if more information is desired.

More than twenty sources for additional reading are described in the *Selected Bibliography*. Although the list does not presume to be complete, it should provide ample information for an institution to move ahead with administrator evaluation.

Chapter Twelve
Administrator Evaluation: Building on the State of the Art

Charles H. Farmer

In the final chapter the *why, how,* and *who* decisions of administrator evaluation are summarized from Section I, "Issue and Perspectives." Also a series of recommendations are drawn from all the authors which will help new programs build on the strengths and experience of their forerunners. For institutions planning to implement administrator evaluation in the near future a hypothetical event chart is offered which can be used to compare the reader's sense of appropriate procedures and realistic milestones with the author's. Finally, conceptual models are proposed for the future which integrate administrator and institutional evaluation and development.

Why, How, and Who Revisited

Figure I presents the flow of the questions and answers related to the basic issues of administrator evaluation discussed in the opening three chapters. The answers outlined for *Why* and *Who* are essentially those given earlier. As discussed in Chapter One, there are legitimate caveats related to evaluating administrators, but they are outweighed by the potential benefits for administrative performance, personnel decision-making, and organizational effectiveness. Chapter Three noted that many individuals at all levels could provide potentially useful information, but decisions on appropriate actions are usually left to one person.

Chapter II stressed the need for role specific criteria and individualized norms, but it did not go so far as to recommend specific approaches. After the detailed descriptions of the four approaches in the second section and the third section's case studies of institutions which have used each approach, several selection guidelines are recommended.

Use growth contracts when the function of evaluation is formative. As Berte and O'Neil presented conceptually and Bedsole described in practice, this approach focuses on the individual and puts growth and development under his or her control. The assumption here is that administrators, like

Why Evaluate Administrators?

Yes, there are problems to be solved—

- program, leader role, and evaluation participant diversity
- lack of technique
- politics

But evaluation can contribute through—

- formative functions leading to improved performance
- summative functions leading to improved personnel and program decisions
- institutional functions leading to improved organizational effectiveness

How Can Administrators be Evaluated?

First, identify criteria and skills related to effective performance for one administrator during a specific time period.

Second, select norms against which performance will be measured, preferably past performance, personal goals, and constituent expectations.

Third, select the approach which fits the function—

- growth contracts for formative functions
- ad hoc committees for summative functions
- MBO for institutional functions
- rating scales for supplementing each function

Who Should Evaluate Administrators?

Depending on the criteria and how closely they work with an administrator, all of these could provide useful data—

- faculty
- peer and superior administrators
- trustees
- students
- alumni
- secretaries

Everyone makes judgments while evaluating administrators, but usually the decision is one person's—

- the administrator being evaluated decides what to do in formative evaluation
- the administrator's direct superior decides what to do in summative evaluation
- the individual who commissioned the assessment decides what to do in institutional evaluation

all healthy people, want and need to grow on the job and should be in charge of their own professional destiny. If the administrator chooses, data gathered in formative evaluation may enter the summative evaluation process.

Use ad hoc committees when the function of evaluation is summative. Anderson's ad hoc committee process, further described in Block's chapter on presidential evaluation, is sufficiently comprehensive and in-depth to arrive at important decisions about an administrator's career. It adheres to the democratic process valued in academe and allows for the opinions of various constituencies. Just as growth contract data can contribute to summative evaluation, data gathered by an ad hoc committee can help plan for future improvement as well as judge past performance. In summative evaluation, whether the conclusion is positive or negative, the discussion should move beyond the bottom line in pursuit of an answer to the question, "Now what?"

Use MBO when the function of evaluation is institutional. Given the questionable utility of most institutions' mission statements and their lack of long-range planning skills, this recommendation is admittedly optimistic at this time. As discussed later in this chapter, MBO is a process to strive for in the future rather than a readily available option. Nevertheless, the recommendation is made because it is the only approach that begins with an institution-wide perspective. Ad hoc committees may contribute data to serve several institutional functions, such as defining roles or re-assigning staff, but because the focus is on the individual rather than the institution, the results will be piecemeal at best.

Use rating scales to supplement each approach and function as necessary. Rating scales can be used to supplement or verify data gathered by any of the other approaches but should not be the sole source as Farmer points out in both his chapters. Numerical ratings provide for widespread direct input and almost total anonymity but have a major drawback—numbers do not talk. Low scores may pinpoint a problem area, but seldom are they descriptive enough to indicate what an administrator should do differently. The best rating scales are tailored to individual administrators and serve as a springboard for candid dialogue.

Recommendations

The fifteen recommendations in this section build upon the suggestions and implications of the preceding chapters. Some are still working hypotheses, but all should be considered carefully when planning a program for administrator evaluation.

Do not start until there is enough time and energy. As Ogden Nash wrote about conscience, a college or university should have a good administrator evaluation program or none at all. If time and energy are not given to dealing with the issues of *why, how,* and *who,* the resulting program will be more trouble than it is worth.

Evaluation should be rooted in the traditions and organizational climate of each institution. Evaluation programs cannot be simply lifted from one college and set in place in another just because the schools have the same size and shape. Authority patterns, faculty maturity, and morale are a few of the additional variables that impact on evaluation. "Judicious adaptation" is a wiser approach than "wholesale adoption."

Clarify the institution's mission and goals. An administrator's performance must be viewed in an organizational context. Otherwise an evaluation might show high merit in a particular segment without indicating value to the institution.

Evaluation criteria and norms should be agreed-on in advance. Role and program diversity in higher education require that criteria and norms be situationally dependent. Performance should be compared to role requirements, not to another administrator with the same title. Every administrator has the right to know how he or she will be judged.

Policies and procedures should be the result of participative planning by administrators and faculty. Effective evaluation programs require the kind of commitment that can only come from direct involvement. Consultants may further the design process by raising key questions, but they cannot dictate correct answers—answers that will work.

Presidential backing is essential. The president as the person with total institutional responsibility must assume a visible leadership role. In fact administrator evaluation should start at the top.

Administrators under review should have full knowledge of the procedures, timetable, and results. Lack of communication leads to misunderstanding which in turn leads to defensiveness. Defensiveness precludes growthful evaluation.

Evaluation data should be gathered at least from those one up and one down in the organizational hierarchy. Other personnel may be useful but the most valid information will come from those working most closely with the administrator.

Data should be descriptive rather than judgmental. Questions should be phrased to elicit descriptions of an administrator's performance before passing judgment. In this way he or she can determine how to behave differently and alter perceptions.

Provide consulting assistance. A trusted colleague can be a useful resource for analyzing data and planning appropriate actions. Sharing evaluation data needs to be strongly encouraged because many administrators take a "bite the bullet" stance.

Establish a policy for distributing results. Administrators favor confidentiality but faculty tend to want to know what was said if not who said it. A compromise can be for the administrator to announce an overall improvement plan without divulging evaluation data.

Accept apparent contradictions in evaluation results. An action by an administrator may be in the best interests of one constituency but not another. A fact of administrative life is, "you can please some of the people . . ."

Establish an appeals procedure. Every administrator has the right of due process to check the validity of his or her evaluation. At the same time an evaluator's confidentiality must be maintained.

Link evaluation to the reward system. One assumption about evaluation and development is that individuals are internally motivated. However, external rewards such as praise, pay, and promotion also contribute to high performance. As previously mentioned, the president needs to play a leading role in administrator evaluation especially with rewards since only he or she has the power to make the linkage.

Add a development component. Stressing development makes reward and punishment less prominent. The term "evaluation" should evolve to "diagnosis" which should be followed by planning and development. The faculty development centers already operating on many campuses can be retooled to respond to the imperative for administrator development.

Following these recommendations and strategies will not guarantee a successful administrator evaluation program, but it will help avoid the most common causes of program failure.

Timetable and Activities

Three of the first recommendations in the previous section called for adequate planning time and administrator and faculty involvement in developing an administrator evaluation program to fit each campus. A general strategy for involving administrators and faculty in the design process will be discussed here. Called the task force approach it has been shown to work successfully in faculty evaluation projects. It begins with the formulation of a task force of campus opinion leaders. The task force gathers information on what administrators need in the way of feedback and then designs a program to meet those needs. Three semesters are a reasonable amount of time to design and test a program.

Formulation of the task force. Task force members can be elected, selected, or assigned—whichever procedure works best in the institution. However, it is essential that the members be influential and respected leaders who are willing to give administrator evaluation a try. The membership should be balanced among constituencies. Administrators from all institutional units should feel that their interests are represented. Faculty and other relevant constituencies who hold administrators accountable should also be represented.

Responsibilities. The primary responsibility of the task force is to design a system for administrator evaluation. In some institutions it will be appropriate to ask the group to do the design and build a prototype. Other institutions will feel more comfortable having the task be a think-tank and only produce a blueprint. The responsibility of the task force should be made clear from the start to avoid problems of "overstepping boundaries" or "disappointing efforts."

Task forces function best when they are given responsibility beyond what is given to committees. Task forces should be presented with a practical problem requiring an applied solution that they can develop, test, and recommend for implementation. However, if the charge includes actually doing the implementation then, the solution's ownership stays with the task force, and the task force falls into the therapy trap where the client fails to accept the responsibility for change.

Activities. The task force needs to conceptualize its activities in cycles that start informally and move to more formal cycles. In the early cycles task force members interview individual administrators and faculty to get their personal suggestions about evaluation and share ideas about various evaluation functions. This information is summarized and reported back to stimulate deeper thought and more explicit statements on needs and goals. In middle cycles interviews and surveys are used to converge the needs into consistent patterns. Important questions to guide this activity are:

- Do administrators want mostly formative feedback to guide their individual development like growth contracting?
- Do administrators want a periodic review by peers like the ad hoc committee approach can provide?
- Do administrators need some way to tie their growth to the objectives of the institution as in MBO?
- Do administrators only want to compare themselves to other administrators on rating scales?

In the final cycles the task force designs an approach based on what it hears the needs are and gives it a pilot-test. The test is monitored and the system is fine-tuned until ready for adoption.

Timelines and Target Dates. It is reasonable to expect a task force of good people to carry out their responsibilities through the recommendation stage over two semesters as shown in Figure 2. The task force is formed at the beginning of the year and becomes familiar with materials on administrator evaluation. From October to mid-November the task force interviews all relevant faculty and staff to sharpen their assessment of needs. This process continues in-depth as a series of middle cycles into March. Starting in January the actual development of the system should begin and interface with the middle cycles of information gathering. No later than March the system should be pilot-tested on a small group of administrators who agree to develop criteria, norms, and gather data. Once again periodic interviewing is important for monitoring the development and testing cycles. By May the fine-tuning begins and recommendations are made shortly after.

Implementation. Beginning in the second year the institution can adopt the program on a trial basis and continue monitoring and tuning. During the trial period the purpose of the evaluation should be purely formative.

Until the properties of the evaluation are more fully understood, it should not be used for personnel decision-making. This strategy will reduce anxiety and allow administrators to be thoughtful rather than defensive. After suggested revisions have been incorporated the program can be relied on more heavily to produce valid information.

Figure 2

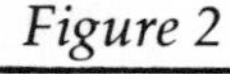

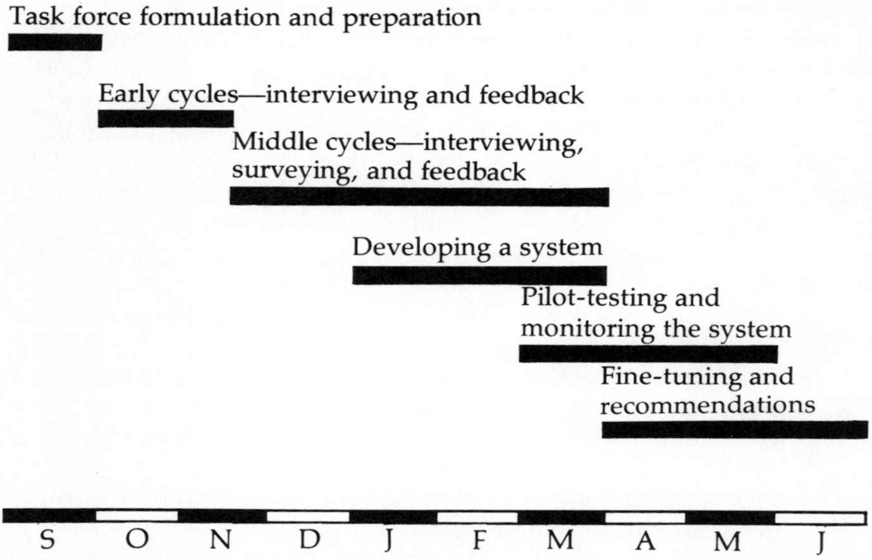

Future Directions

If administrators believe evaluation is little more than a report card, the program will be short-lived. If administrators get good marks, they want to get back to running the institution and not be bothered by further evaluation. If they get bad marks, they also want to get back to running the institution and not be bothered by further evaluation. There are two major causes for administrators to treat their evaluation insignificantly; 1) they believe the evaluation is peripheral to their jobs and the real work of the institution, and 2) they do not believe evaluation can really help them improve performance.

A dominant theme of this volume has been that evaluation should be equated with individual and institutional improvement. Formative, summative, and institutional evaluation functions can be segregated for analysis and planning purposes, but eventually they should be integrated in a single program having the contemporary characteristics shown in Table 1. Such an evaluation program would be in the mainstream of institutional activities rather than peripheral and have a development

Table 1

Characteristics of Traditional and Contemporary Views of Administrator Evaluation

Traditional View	Contemporary View
Organizational Value. Administrator evaluation is of little value to the institution because it is inherently subjective and biased.	Administrator evaluation is an integral feature of institutional evaluation.
Purposes. How do we achieve institutional purposes?	How do we achieve individual and institutional purposes?
Integration. Focus on rating. Relationship of evaluations system to institutional purposes ignored.	Focus on integrating individual needs and institutional goals through evaluation of administrative performance.
Planning. Absence of comprehensive plans for administrator evaluation.	Basis of system for administrator evaluation is comprehensive planning structure, including institutional purposes, policies, position guides, programs, procedures.
Focus on short-range purposes.	Focus on short and long-range purposes of institution.
Administrator evaluation viewed as an isolated activity unrelated to other components of the institution.	Administrator evaluation viewed as an integral component of the institution.
Methodology. Emphasis on task performance.	Emphasis on goal achievement.
Emphasis on symbols of administrative accomplishment.	Emphasis on results.
Emphasis on short-term training programs for administrators.	Emphasis on long-term growth process, self-education, self-development.
Evaluation is trait-oriented.	Evaluation to determine progress toward mutually planned goals; personality of evaluee is not sole focus of evaluation.
Heavy reliance on quantitative approach to evaluation.	Less emphasis on mathematical approach; quality of results stressed.
Methodology. Little institutional interest in instructing evaluators in the evaluation methodology.	Clarifying and promoting understanding of evaluation system is an integral feature of continuing education.
Control. Little institutional interest in feedback relating to evaluation of performance.	Effectiveness of administrator evaluation system in each of its components constantly monitored.
Focus on compensation and retention.	Focus on self-development.

Adapted from Warren G. Bennis' thoughts on organizations.

component which has immediate impact on job satisfaction and performance. It may be some time before such a program is common on campus, but its conceptualization is nearly complete.

In Figure 3, L. James Harvey (1976) presents his vision of a systems approach to accountability in higher education through MBO. He believes that the public has lost so much confidence in higher education that it will no longer tolerate fuzzy goals and a "muddle-through" style of management. The focus must be kept on outcomes and the effectiveness of its services. As shown, administrator evaluation and faculty evaluation as well are parts of a totally integrated organizational system. In this model an administrator could not brush off evaluation as an activity peripheral to his or her job.

In Figure 4, Jack Lindquist (1978) synthesizes the strong points of a dozen administrator development programs into a unified and systematic whole. As he sees it, ". . . development becomes individual problem-solving in the context of program and institutional problem-solving, guided by individual growth plans in the context of program and institutional development plans." In Lindquist's model the starting point is diagnostic evaluation which stresses practical problem-solving with immediate payoffs for the administrator. Here, evaluation would not be taken lightly for obvious reasons of self-interest.

Both the Harvey and Lindquist models share an institution-wide perspective. They differ in orientation as Harvey moves inward from the institution to individual while Lindquist begins with the individual and moves out to the institution. Furthermore, Harvey underplays development, at least in his schematic, while Lindquist does not stress institutional mission and goals as the primary guide for administrator development although they are implied in the institutional development plan.

With a dash of imagination the two models can provide a vision of the future of administrator evaluation and development on college and university campuses. Depending on one's preference, a development component can be added to evaluation in Harvey's model—or institutional and program mission, goals, and objectives can be made more prominent in Lindquist's. The result will be essentially the same—a program that is not simply to be endured and forgotten, but one that leads to healthy institutions and personal job satisfaction.

Epilogue

It is easier to describe an ideal administrator evaluation program than it is to find one. It is difficult, if not impossible, to give out a set of one-two-three rules which will lead to a perfect evaluation system, although it appears the authors have at times unabashedly tried to do so. Let Winstead's maxim of "progressive accomplishment versus postponed perfection" continue to be the guide as we increase our dedication to better-managed and more humane institutions of higher education.

Figure 3
Accountability in Higher Education through MBO

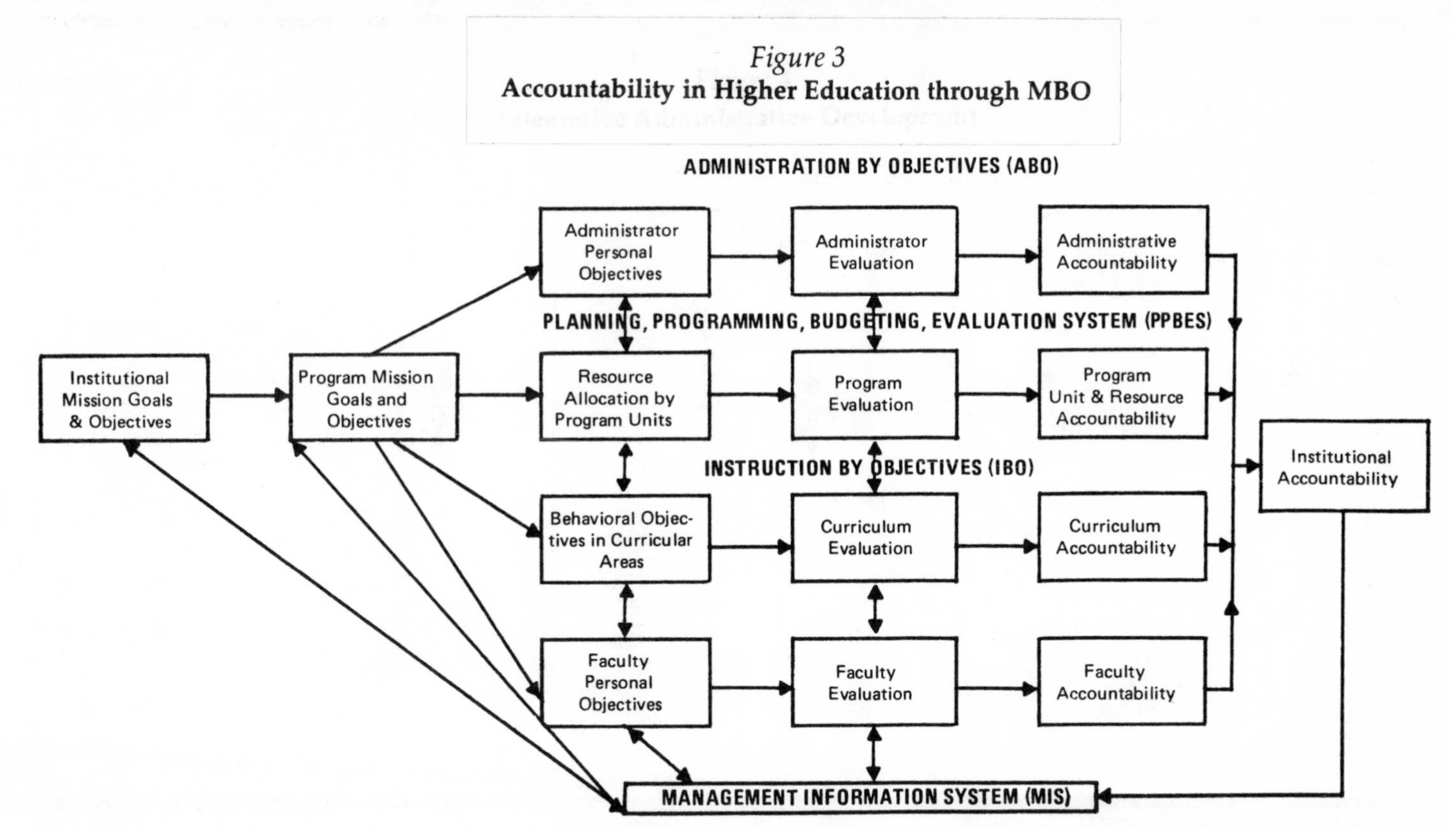

Figure 4

Integrative Administrative Development

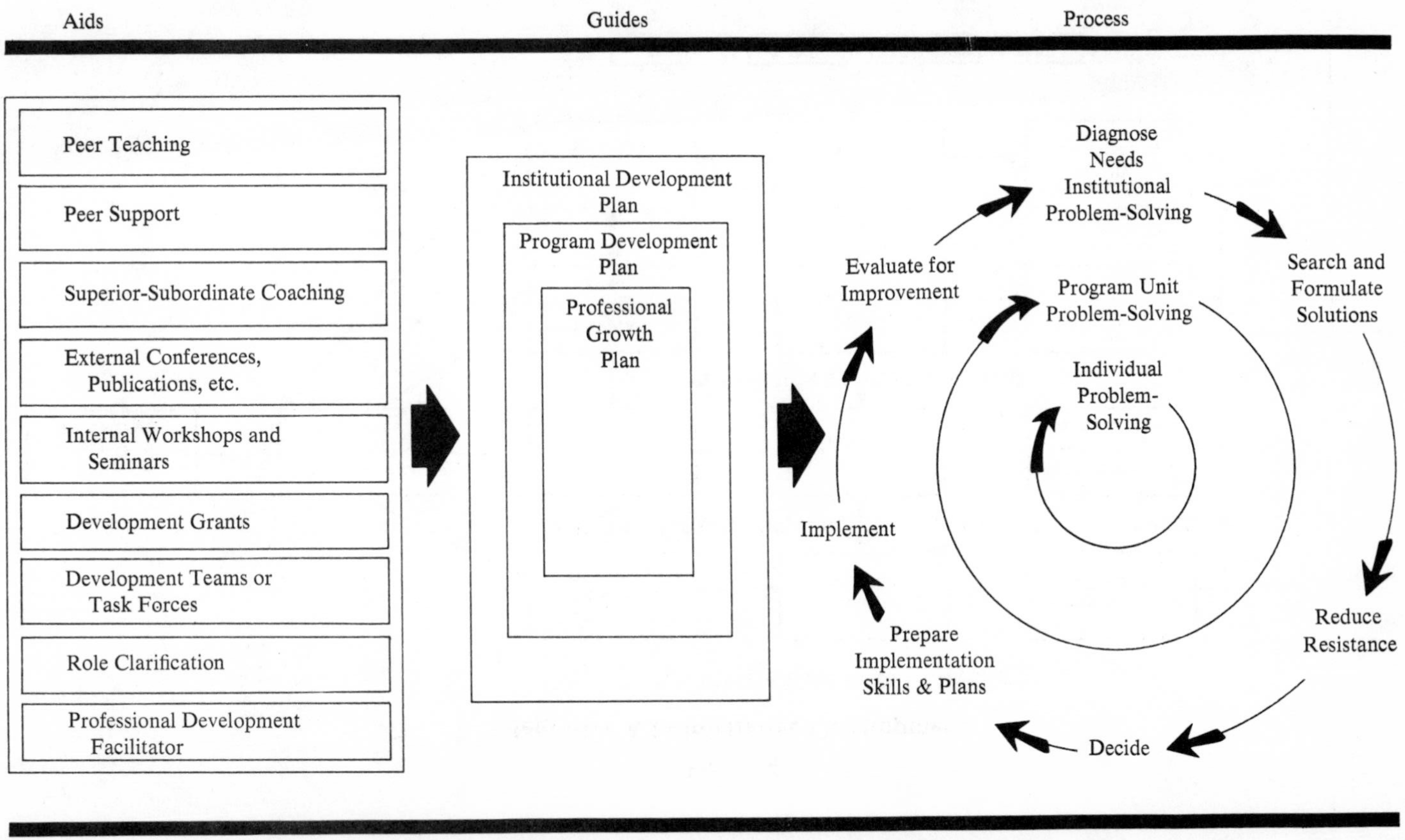

Aids

Guides

Process

Peer Teaching

Peer Support

Superior-Subordinate Coaching

External Conferences, Publications, etc.

Internal Workshops and Seminars

Development Grants

Development Teams or Task Forces

Role Clarification

Professional Development Facilitator

Institutional Development Plan

Program Development Plan

Professional Growth Plan

Diagnose Needs

Institutional Problem-Solving

Program Unit Problem-Solving

Individual Problem-Solving

Search and Formulate Solutions

Reduce Resistance

Decide

Prepare Implementation Skills & Plans

Implement

Evaluate for Improvement

Bibliography

Harvey, L. James. *Managing Colleges and Universities by Objectives*. Wheaton, Illinois: Ireland Educational Corporation, 1975

Lindquist, Jack. "Approaches to Administrative Development: A Synthesis." In John A. Shtogren (Ed.), *Administrative Development in Higher Education, The State of the Art: Volume One*. Richmond, Virginia: Higher Education Leadership and Management Society, 1978.

Charles H. Farmer is Director of Institutional Research, Executive Assistant to the Vice President for Academic Affairs, and Professor of Mathematics, University of Tulsa.

Appendix
Selected Administrator Evaluation Programs

This section describes twenty-eight administrator evaluation programs from the following institutions:

Alabama
University of Alabama

California
North Orange County Community College
University of Redlands
San Jose City College

Colorado
University of Northern Colorado

Illinois
Northwestern University

Indiana
University of Notre Dame

Kansas
Kansas State University

Maryland
Cantonsville Community College
Salisbury State College

Montana
Rocky Mountain College

New Jersey
Gloucester County College

New York
Dowling College
University of Rochester

Ohio
Miami University

Oregon
Oregon State Higher Education System

Pennsylvania
Gettysburg College

Texas
Texas Christian University
Baylor University

Virginia
Central Virginia Community College

Washington
Seattle Pacific University

The programs are divided into four administrator categories: 1) President/Provost, 2) Dean, 3) Chairperson, and 4) Multi-Position where a standard form or procedure is used for various positions. Each program description tells how administrators are evaluated and includes the name and address of an individual who can provide additional information.

President/Provost Evaluation

Source	Dr. Theodore I. Murguia, President San Jose City College 2100 Moorpark Avenue San Jose, California 95114
Form Origin	Moraine Valley Community College
Scale	Qualitative Superior to Poor
Categories	Communications (5), management (5), instructional leadership (4)
Comment Space	Numbered under categories 1 and 2 at the end of the questionnaire and as question 19
Open-ended Questions	What do you think makes this person an effective administrator? How do you feel this administrator could increase his effectiveness? Other—specify
Respondent I.D.	Anonymous
Implementation	This evaluation instrument was used by President Murguia to evaluate his performance after one year in office. It was distributed, collected, and scored by the President with complete results given to all participants. Murguia has not indicated plans as to when evaluation will occur again but, as part of the California system, evaluation is statutory.
Use for	President

Source	Robert S. Palinchak Dean of Academic Service Gloucester County College Deptford Township Sewell P.O., New Jersey 08080
Form Origin	A committee for the evaluation of president
Scale	Qualitative: 1-5 (Strongly Agree to Strongly Disagree)
Categories	34 questions, not by category
Comment Space	None

Open-ended Questions	Essay-type questions concerning the chief strengths and needs for improvement
Respondent I.D.	Anonymous
Implementation	This was the first time for evaluations at Gloucester. The forms are mailed to each full-time faculty member. Two faculty members (one selected by Faculty Council and one by the President) tabulate results of questions 1-33 and summarize responses to question 34. The committee writes a report, discusses it with the president and destroys the original data. Report is given only to the president.
Use for	President

Source	Bruce T. Alton, President Rocky Mountain College Billings, Montana 59102
Form Origin	No information
Scale	Qualitative: 1-5 (Superior to Poor) 0 is Not Applicable
Categories	22 questions, not by category
Comment Space	None
Open-ended Questions	What makes this person an effective administrator? How do you feel this administrator could increase his effectiveness?
Respondent I.D.	Respondents are identified only by characteristics—signature is optional.
Implementation	This is the first time an evaluation has been used at Rocky Mountain College. Others are to be evaluated in the coming academic year.
Use for	President/Provost

Source	Dr. David G. Brown Provost Miami University Oxford, Ohio 45056
Form Origin	No information
Scale	Qualitative+3 to−3 (Excellent to Very Unsatisfactory)

Categories	The form is essentially narrative with one numerical rating provided for each statement and 8 sections for comment on each category. The sections are: vision, leadership, advocacy, communication, fairness in personnel matters, equity in treatment of academic units, fairness in decision-making, appropriate administrative style.
Comment Space	Space is provided for comments on each question. A final comment section appears at the end of the form.
Open-ended Questions	Provide your evaluation of overall performance using the+3 to−3 rating scale. What do you believe are the two most serious weaknesses of the individual?
Respondent I.D.	Respondents indicate only their position as a department chairman, a campus coordinator, dean or director, vice-president, faculty, or student.
Implementation	The form is used every five years. The forms are collected by the president.
Use for	President/Provost

Source	Dr. Miles Romney Vice Chancellor for Academic Affairs Oregon State Higher Education System Office P.O. Box 3175 Eugene, Oregon 97403
Form Origin	New administrative rules were adopted by the state Board of Higher Education governing the conditions of service by faculty in the state system (*e.g.* appointments, promotion, tenure, resignations and terminations.) Among the rules were several that related to the evaluation of faculty. Thus it seemed appropriate that chief administrators also be evaluated regularly and periodically.
Scale	None

Categories	No information as to the number of questions, but the categories are: academic leadership and management, administrative leadership and management, internal relationships, external relationships, physical condition.
Comment Space	None
Open-ended Questions	None
Respondent I.D.	None
Implementation	The Chancellor seeks—largely through personal interview—the views of a cross section of the faculty and staff, community and state leaders, and occasionally administrative peers of the President in state and out, as to the performance of the President being evaluated. The President is also requested to submit a statement of his stewardship as he sees it. The foregoing information, together with the Chancellor's own views of the President's effectiveness, forms the basis of a report made by the Chancellor to the Board as to his assessment of the effectiveness of the President. The Chancellor discusses his evaluation of the President with the President, and the President is offered opportunity to comment as he may wish concerning the Chancellor's evaluation of his stewardship.
Use for	President/Provost

Source	Dr. David McKenna, President Seattle Pacific University 3307 3rd Avenue West Seattle, Washington 98119
Form Origin	A committee established by the President and consultation with Yale were used to form the evaluation instrument.
Scale	The form is narrative.
Categories	There are only 4 questions: How do you rate the President's performance in relation to the needs and goals of the institution? How has the President helped or hindered you in

your job? What do you consider the strong points and weak points of this administration? Do you have major changes to suggest bearing on the policy or the nature of the President?

Comment Space	None
Open-ended Questions	The 4 questions require narrative answers.
Respondent I.D.	Respondents are identified by category: trustees, faculty, alumni, businessmen, Free Methodist Minister, Non-Free Methodist Minister.
Implementation	Conducted by the Board of Trustees at the President's request with a committee appointed by the Board. A report based on the returns is prepared for the Board and the President. A conference with the President is conducted by the Chairman of the Board. A verbal summary is given to the Board of Trustees only.
Use for	President/Provost

Dean Evaluation

Source	Bernard J. Sloan Dean, New College University of Alabama P.O. Box 6211 University, Alabama 35486
Form Origin	Neal Berte
Scale	Qualitative: 1-5 (Very inadequate to superior performance)
Categories	General administration (7), instructional leadership (8), professional leadership (9), personal leadership (8)
Comment Space	Space is provided under each category for respondent to generate and answer his own questions. Additional space is provided for comments or suggestions.
Open-ended Questions	How might the administrator improve his service? What are the major issues facing the college? What are the current and future priorities of

	the college? Should the college retain, replace the Dean? Undecided?
Respondent I.D.	Respondents are identified only as students, faculty, or other.
Implementation	The form was designed, dispersed, and collected by the Dean of New College with an instructional memo. It is used each year.
Use for	Dean

Source	Dr. B.J. Chandler Dean, School of Education Northwestern University Evanston, Illinois 60201
Form Origin	Dean Chandler designed this form.
Scale	Qualitative: 1-5 (Very Inadequate to Superior Performance)
Categories	10 questions in each category: professional leadership, personal leadership, instructional leadership, general administration
Comment Space	Comment space is available after each category and on the summary section.
Open-ended Questions	Respondents were asked for comments and/or suggestions as to how the Dean could more effectively serve the School of Education; the major problems/issues facing the school; opinion regarding retention or selection of a new dean.
Respondent I.D.	Anonymous
Implementation	The instruments were mailed to permanent faculty and returned to a secretary who tabulated the results. The scale developed and used by Dean Chandler illustrates the scope and depth of useful information for an administrator to know. The process provided for permanent faculty to receive a report of their collective responses.
Use for	Dean

Source	Dr. Donald Hoyt, Director Office of Educational Resources Kansas State University Fairchild Hall Manhattan, Kansas 66506
Form Origin	Programs have come from a variety of sources. The standardized instrument for deans represents a sythesis of local opinion devices constructed on other campuses. The structured committee approach was taken from the system used at the State University of New York (SUNY).
Scale	Qualitative: (Definitely True to Definitely False and Too Little Information)
Categories	18 questions scored in 4 categories (communication, administrative leadership, consideration, recruiting)
Comment Space	Comments are requested with an indication that the education resources office will type them for the dean's study.
Open-ended Questions	Asks "on balance, does the dean fulfill his or her responsibilities to your satisfaction" with 4 scaled possible answers.
Respondent I.D.	Respondents are categorized according to length of time on KSU faculty, current academic rank, whether or not respondent is a department head, and how often the respondent has dealings with the dean. Separate analyses are provided if subgroups defined by these variables include at least 5 respondents.
Implementation	Deans have been evaluated on a voluntary basis at Kansas State.
Use for	Dean

Source	Robert S. Palinchak Dean of Academic Service Gloucester County College Deptford Township Sewell P.O., New Jersey 08080
Form Origin	No information

Scale	Part II is qualitative: 1-4 (Strongly Agree to Strongly Disagree)
Categories	Questions not categorized
Comment Space	Part I opens with a frequency of contact question, and 2 other questions are for comments on quality of Dean's performance and other appropriate comments.
Open-ended Questions	Please comment on the quality of performance of the Dean in fulfilling his duties.
Respondent I.D.	Anonymous
Implementation	Department chairmen distribute forms to the faculty. Upon completion, an evaluation committee tabulates the results, reports to the Dean, and a meeting between the committee and the Dean is held. A final report is forwarded to the President.
Use for	Dean

Source	Dr. John X. McConkey Dean, School of General Studies Dowling College Oakdale, Long Island, New York 11769
Form Origin	In accordance with the faculty constitution, a joint committee was designated to evaluate the Dean of the School of General Studies.
Scale	Importance rating: Major, Minor or None Performance in activity: Outstanding, Usually Good, Sometimes Good, Poor, Do Not Know
Categories	Dean's activities (budget responsibilities, recruiting, scheduling courses and teaching loads, long-range planning) 14 questions; behavior (delegation of responsibilities, handling of problems, fairness, flexibility, etc.) 13 questions
Comment Space	Space for comments is provided at the end of the questionnaire.
Open-ended Questions	In your opinion, what are the particular strengths and weaknesses of the administrator? Do you feel he possesses the technical skills and experiences needed for

	the position? Do you feel that he possesses the personal qualities and talents needed for the position?
Respondent I.D.	Respondents are identified either by characteristics (student, faculty, etc.) or by code number.
Implementation	Evaluation at Dowling is conducted by a joint committee of students, faculty, administrators, and members of the Board, and each committee designs a form for the specific individual being evaluated. This is apparently a requirement from the faculty constitution. After the committee has collected the data, they prepare a report. The administrator has the option of challenging any of the information including a request that the respondent appear. The administrator may attach his own report if he wishes.
Use for	Dean

Source	Dr. David G. Brown Provost Miami University Oxford, Ohio 46056
Form Origin	No information
Scale	Qualitative: 0-4 (Unsatisfactory to Outstanding)
Categories	Leadership of the college (15), advocacy for the college (4), communication within the college (7), dean-faculty relations in the college (5), college organization and the dean's administrative style (6), overall evaluation of the dean (2)
Comment Space	Space is provided for comments at the end of each section.
Open-ended Questions	An overall rating, an indication for retention or dismissal, and a page for comments on overall evaluation
Respondent I.D.	The form requests evaluators to indicate academic rank or administrative position.

Implementation	The evaluation is administered every five years. The forms are collected by the Office of the Provost. Lists of questions, respondents, and recipients of results are mutually approved by evaluaee and Provost.
Use for	Dean

Source	Dr. David L. McKenna President Seattle Pacific University 3307 3rd Ave., West Seattle, Washington 98119
Form Origin	President McKenna
Scale	The evaluation is narrative.
Categories	5 questions, not by category
Comment Space	None
Open-ended Questions	5 questions require narrative responses regarding the extent to which the Dean has achieved the following objectives: commitment to the primary task of integrating faith and knowledge in the Christian liberal arts college; leadership stature for the inspiration and confidence of faculties and students; ability to develop lines of communication within the organization; sensitivity to contemporary issues and student needs; perspective for long-range planning.
Implementation	The evaluation is conducted and returned to the President. Participants in the evaluation include members of the Board, President's cabinet, Faculty Council, student body, students on academic committees, the persons who report to the Academic Dean, directors of the schools, and a random selection from the faculty totaling 44 respondents.
Use for	Dean

Chairperson Evaluation

Source	Mr. Bernard R. Flanagan, Vice Chancellor North Orange County Community College District 1000 North Lemon Fullerton, California 92634
Form Origin	Committee designated to include Vice Chancellor, Dean of Instruction, 10 faculty members (5 from each of two campuses in district), 2 division chairpersons (1 from each campus). The committee was established and charged by the Board. Professional personnel evaluation program (Professional & Instructional Effectiveness Study Group—PIE).
Scale	No scale used
Categories	Instructional improvement (7), staff relations (9), selection, supervision, evaluation of division personnel (7), division representation to administration (4), administrative operations (9).
Comment Space	Space is provided for comments in each category.
Open-ended Questions	"Based on specific observations . . . I recommend: congratulate and retain administrator; continue satisfactory performance; retain but improve; change division chairperson."
Respondent I.D.	All scored forms must be signed but are kept in confidence by the Administrative Dean of Instruction and not given to the division chairperson.
Implementation	This is a biennial evaluation which contains a retention question. The Administrative Dean of Instruction distributes, collects, tabulates, and meets with the division chairperson for review. The tabulation is sent to members of the division and to the president. The division chairperson is advised, given formal response time, and then action is taken. All survey forms are

	destroyed; a summary is placed in the file of the division chairperson.
Use for	Division Chairperson

Source	Dr. Donald Hoyt, Director Office of Educational Resources Kansas State University Fairchild Hall Manhattan, Kansas 66506
Form Origin	A number of sources are cited. The department head program originated in a doctoral dissertation and was refined through subsequent empirical findings at four universities.
Scale	The rating form uses two scales: questions 1 through 30 and 61 through 70 use a 5-point qualitative scale; questions 31 through 60 use a frequency scale.
Categories	Items 1-30 are concerned with responsibilities and performance. They are scored on 3 dimensions derived from factor analysis (personnel management; departmental planning and development; building the department's reputation). Items 31-60 are concerned with specific administrative techniques and are scored on four dimensions derived from factor analysis (Democratic Practice; Structuring; Interpersonal Sensitivity; and Vigor).
Comment Space	Comments are invited with the indication that the office collecting the form will type them before returning them to the administrator.
Open-ended Questions	There are four open-ended questions (departmental priorities; policies/procedures needing immediate improvement; administrative effectiveness; administrative style).
Respondent I.D.	Anonymous
Implementation	The procedure has been worked out over a period of 6 years. The first step is to send a form to the department head on which he

	indicates the assigned importance of the various activities on the questionnaire. The form actually given to the faculty for rating the department head includes an importance and a performance answer for these same 15 questions. The results are mailed only to the department head. The department head is given the right to identify people who will evaluate him. The form for this purpose includes blank spaces for 30 names.
Use for	Department Head

Multi-Position Evaluation

Source	Paul W. Brubacher Vice President for Student Affairs University of Redlands Redlands, California 92373
Form Origin	Unknown
Scale	Qualitative: Poorly/Rarely to Effectively/Consistently
Categories	Approachability, Resourcefulness, Communication, and Interpersonal Relationships, Adaptability, Initiative and Effectiveness.
Comment Space	The comment section appears at the conclusion.
Open-ended Questions	The comment section asks for suggestions that reflect overall effectiveness and would assist growth and development.
Respondent I.D.	Asks for signature
Implementation	In the early spring, each staff member identifies students, faculty, and staff (up to a maximum of 15) who would be in a position to evaluate their performance. This list is negotiated with an individual's superior. Then the questionnaire is sent out to these individuals who are informed that a copy of the job description of the person being evaluated is available in my office. An individual's direct superior then discusses all evaluations with the appropriate individual.

	The purpose of our evaluation is professional growth and improvement and information gleaned from these questionnaires is not used directly for salary determination.
Use for	Administrative Staff in Student Affairs.

Source	Eugene D. Koplitz, Ph.D. The University of Northern Colorado Greeley, Colorado 80631
Form Origin	Tyrus Hillway—Eugene D. Koplitz
Scale	Qualitative: 1-5 (Low-Medium-High)
Categories	The form consists of two basic categories: qualities and activities. Hillway and Koplitz indicate that the items on the scale relate to instruction and curriculum, student personnel, staff personnel, school-community, leadership, school facilities, organization and structure, financial and business management.
Comment Space	None
Open-ended Questions	None
Respondent I.D.	Anonymous
Implementation	The instrument is currently being tested by Koplitz at the University of Northern Colorado and can be used according to an institution's needs. A scoring and an analysis print-out, including a profile sheet on each person evaluated, can be obtained through the authors and the University of Northern Colorado Computer Center. Detailed information can be obtained by writing to the National Project for Improving Academic Administration, Box 62, University of Northern Colorado, Greeley, Colorado, 80639.
Use for	Presidents, Deans, and Department Chairmen

Source	(Rev.) James T. Burtchaell, C.S.C. Provost University of Notre Dame Notre Dame, Indiana 46556
Form Origin	A committee performs the evaluation using no standard form.
Scale	None
Categories	None
Comment Space	None
Open-ended Questions	None
Respondent I.D.	An obligation of complete confidentiality is accepted by the evaluating committee. No anonymous correspondence is considered.
Implementation	A committee of 5 faculty members and one student works with and reports to the administrator senior to the person being evaluated. Their report is written, using comments from the evaluee's constituency. When an interview is requested by the evaluee, it is always conducted by at least two members of the committee. Every five years this formal review takes place. All administrators who undergo this type evaluation serve indefinite terms at the pleasure of the President. In the case of administrators at a lower level, they receive renewable term appointments of 3 years. In this case, the process of appointment and review is the same: the Dean consults with all the faculty in the department. As a result of the consultation, the Dean nominates to the Provost his candidate for chairman.
Use for	Administrative Staff

Source	Dr. Cheryl Opacinch Catonsville Community College Catonsville, Maryland 21228
Form Origin	Office of Institutional Research
Scale	Qualitative: 1-4 (Highly Positive to Highly Negative)
Categories	Constituent: Administrative leadership, ad-

	ministrative services Peer: Job preparedness, attitude, personal qualities, nature of peer interaction
Comment Space	Space provided on each question in every category.
Open-ended Questions	None
Respondent I.D.	Respondents are identified only by area of responsibility.
Implementation	The constituency and peer evaluations are administered annually at the end of the fall semester.
Use for	Administrative staff

Source	Ronald A. Phipps Director of Institutional Research Salisbury State College Salisbury, Maryland 21801
Form Origin	Local but source unknown. Modification of survey received from Frostburg State College, Frostburg, Maryland.
Scale	Qualitative: 5-1 (Superior to Inadequate)
Categories	Frequency of contact is one of the 14 questions which cover interpersonal skills including availability, quality of performance, problem-solving abilities, accessability, cooperation.
Comment Space	Space is provided for respondents to indicate why they are satisfied or dissatisfied with particular aspects of an administrator's performance.
Open-ended Questions	None
Respondent I.D.	Anonymous
Implementation	Faculty and administrative input is called for in this evaluation. The results of the entire survey are furnished to the President. Each administrator receives the results pertaining to his respective performance. Supervisors receive the survey results concerning the administrators under their supervision.
Use for	Administrative Staff

Source	James R. Thiry Director of Personnel University of Rochester Rochester, New York 14627
Form Origin	Local (prepared by each staff member's immediate supervisor)
Scale	Qualitative: Consistently Outstanding to Inadequate
Categories	The questions cover quality and quantity of work, meeting expectations, interpersonal relations, initiative, cost awareness, safety, accomplishments, recommendations for continued development, and supervisory effectiveness and affirmative action effort if applicable.
Comment Space	Space for comments is provided after each question.
Open-ended Questions	None
Respondent I.D.	The form is signed by the supervisor, department head, and the staff member reviewed.
Implementation	The evaluation is performed 6 months after appointment, 12 months after appointment, and annually thereafter.
Use for	Administrative Staff

Source	Gaylord Thorne, Director Higher Education Research Program Teaching Research Division Oregon State System of Higher Education Monmouth, Oregon 97361
Form Origin	The form was developed at the Teaching Research Division.
Scale	Qualitative: S= Strength, W= Weakness (Raters are instructed to mark no more than a total of 6 responses—3 S's and 3 W's)
Categories	Administrative Responsibility (19), Planning and Organization (13), Leadership (21), Decision-Making (9), Interpersonal Relationships (11)

Comment Space	Space for comments is provided at the end of the form.
Open-ended Questions	"I believe this administrator could improve his/her performance by doing or considering . . ."
Respondent I.D.	Anonymous
Implementation	This form was used internally for the Teaching Research Division of the Oregon State System of Higher Education.
Use for	Administrative Staff

Source	Gaylord Thorne, Director Higher Education Research Program Teaching Research Division Oregon State System of Higher Education Monmouth, Oregon 97361
Form Origin	Developed at Teaching Research Division
Scale	Qualitative: 1-5 (Outstanding to Unacceptable)
Categories	Questions 1-18 rate the decisiveness, dependability, planning abilities and effectiveness of the administrator. Number 19 is an over-all rating.
Comment Space	None
Open-ended Questions	To which aspect of his/her performance do you respond most favorably? Most critically? What suggestions do you have? What questions do you wish to ask? (Intended to identify areas of faculty concern.)
Respondent I.D.	Respondents are identified only by primary area of responsibility (instructional, research, or administrative).
Implementation	This form, developed for the Oregon College of Education, was used in evaluations by faculty of the college president, academic dean and division heads.
Use for	President, Dean, and Division Heads

Source	Robert C. Nordvall Assistant Dean of the College Gettysburg College Pennsylvania Hall Gettysburg, Pennsylvania 17325
Form Origin	A staff member prepared a review of the literature on the evaluation of administrators. After reading this review, the President's Council appointed an evaluation task force which worked in conjunction with a faculty steering committee to set forth the guidelines for evaluation.
Scale	The evaluation is narrative.
Categories	On the self-evaluation, activities are listed by the evaluee and he identifies, generally and specifically, the constituency served. If the responsibility is shared, the evaluee states whether or not he is satisfied with the interaction and how it could be improved. In this system the constituents (faculty, students, alumni) are the groups whom administrators serve. As indicated under Implementation these groups evaluate (by questionnaire) how well the administrative units serve them. The administrative division heads also evaluate their subordinates (although not as part of this evaluation). The evaluation did not involve evaluation of subordinates by the division heads. The responses on the self-evaluation influenced the decision as to which constituencies should be asked to evaluate the performance of specific administrative programs.
Comment Space	None
Open-ended Questions	Do you have any measure of how well you or your office is performing the activity? If yes, could it be improved and how? If no, what are your suggestions?
Respondent I.D.	Heads of administrative divisions are evaluated anonymously by their constituents.
Implementation	There are two phases of evaluation: 1) self-evaluation, 2) evaluation of programs by

	constituents. Emphasis is on evaluating administrative units and functions, not on individual performance. The division heads do receive copies of the self-evaluations completed by each person in their divisions.
Use for	Administrative Staff

Source	Dr. Richard M. Fenker Texas Christian University Fort Worth, Texas 76129
Form Origin	The instrument was developed by committees within the University.
Scale	Qualitative: 1-5 (1 is low, 5 is high)
Categories	28 questions, not categorized
Comment Space	Space for comments is provided on the back of each page.
Open-ended Questions	The administrator being evaluated is ranked, with five possible responses, in comparison with other administrators at TCU.
Respondent I.D.	Respondents are identified as students, faculty members, administrators, or professional staff and by frequency of contact.
Implementation	The evaluation is performed annually using one instrument which was developed by a committee over a three-year period. For the details of the methods and results of the TCU experience, see "The Evaluation of University Faculty and Administrators: A Case Study," Richard M. Fenker, TCU. This may be ordered by writing Dr. Fenker at: TCU, Psychology Department, Fort Worth, Texas 76129
Use for	Administrative Staff

Source	Herbert H. Reynolds Executive Vice President and Dean Baylor University Waco, Texas 76703
Form Origin	No information
Scale	Qualitative: 1-5 (1 is highest degree of

	satisfaction, 5 is lowest degree of satisfaction)
Categories	No questions are posed in the form. It is simply a list of approximately 50 administrative individuals ranging from the President of the University to the Director of Central Campus Services; the assistant dean of students, director of plant engineering, etc.
Comment Space	18 comment sections are provided at the end of the questionnaire dealing with major areas of university life.
Open-ended Questions	see Comment Space
Respondent I.D.	Anonymous
Implementation	Faculty members are asked to express the extent of satisfaction or dissatisfaction with the capability of listed administrators.
Use for	Administrative Staff

Source	Mr. Ralph W. Brown, Jr. Central Virginia Community College Wards Road South P.O. Box 4098 Ft. Hill Station Lynchburg, Virginia 24502
Form Origin	No information
Scale	Qualitative: 1-4 (Strongly disagree to Strongly agree)
Categories	Administrator's performance (14)
Comment Space	Space for comments is provided at the end of the questionnaire.
Open-ended Questions	None
Respondent I.D.	Respondents are identified by division, administrative or classified staff, length of time in the system, and approximate amount of time spent with the administrator.
Implementation	No information
Use for	Administrative Staff

Source	Dr. David KcKenna, President Seattle Pacific University 3307 3rd Ave., West Seattle, Washington 98119
Form Origin	A committee was established by the President and consultation with Yale was used to form the instrument.
Scale	Qualitative: A 5-point scale (Outstanding to Weak)
Categories	Professional Competency (4), Relationship with Students and Adults (4), Professional Attitudes (4), Personal Qualities (5)
Comment Space:	The director and the staff member are provided space at the bottom of the form for recommendations on continuing assignment and retention.
Open-ended Questions	None
Respondent I.D.	Signed
Implementation	The professional staff members are evaluated by their director. Each first-year staff member is to be evaluated twice during the year; experienced personnel are to be evaluated at least once during the year.
Use for	Administrative Staff

Selected Bibliography

The bibliography is based on the premise that administrator evaluation and development are integral parts of the same process, and the process should be built on a firm understanding of the way colleges and universities function. Therefore, the suggestions for further reading are balanced between sources which are primarily about evaluation and others about development and organizational dynamics in higher education.

Baldridge, J. V. *Power and Conflict in the University*. New York: John Wiley, 1971.

An analysis of decision-making at NYU led to the concept of a political model of college and university functioning. It is a useful model for understanding the dynamics which may underlie evaluation. Scarce resources and diverse goals promote a situation where conflict and power struggles are natural. A leader's formal authority is limited by political pressure and bargaining. Therefore, personal influence is more important than official power. An evaluation based on a political model will be very different from one that looks to a hierarchical or bureaucratic structure.

Brann, James and Emmet, Thomas A., (Eds.). *The Academic Department or Division Chairman: A Complex Role.* Detroit: Balamp Publishing, 1972.

This volume contains chapters from twenty-six authors who participated in an in-service training program for chairmen in the early 1970s. They focus on the role and functions of the division or department chairmen and provide a sound foundation for establishing evaluation criteria. Chapters cover such topics as the chairman as academic planner, the relationship of the chairman to the dean, and what faculty want in a chairman.

Deegan, Arthur X. and Fritz, Roger J. *MBO Goes to College.* Boulder, Colorado: University of Colorado, 1975.

"Higher education needs management even more than money" is the book's motto. Its four objectives are to increase the reader's intellectual appreciation for management, self-awareness of leadership style, MBO skills, and related skills. The workbook format provides hands-on practice for individuals, or it can be used in group settings such as a three-day seminar. The twelve sessions/chapters include institutional needs analysis, developing three kinds of objectives, and results-oriented performance appraisal.

Cohen, Michael D., and March, James C. *Leadership and Ambiguity: The American College President.* New York: McGraw-Hill, 1974.

"Organized anarchy" is the label for their concept of college and university functioning. Its characteristics include ambiguous purpose and goals, vague technology, fluid participation, ambiguity of power, inability to learn from experience, and ill-defined success. Such an environment appears to be almost pathologically chaotic. If the model is accepted for the most part, effective institutional planning is a very questionable process and evaluation criteria need not be specified in advance. Administrator evaluation becomes a matter of what seems to be most important at the moment.

Dressel, Paul L. *Handbook of Academic Evaluation: Assessing Institutional Effectiveness, Student Progress, and Professional Performance for Decision Making in Higher Education.* San Francisco: Jossey Bass, 1976.

This is a complete discussion of the evaluation process in higher education from formulating objectives to determining costs and recommending changes. Evaluation results can lead to reallocating resources, new institutional priorities, and improved learning and teaching. The three major sections cover basic considerations in evaluation, student experience and educational progress, and evaluation of programs and personnel. A chapter on administrator evaluation is included in the last section.

Ehrle, Elwood B. "Selection and Evaluation of Department Chairmen." *Educational Record* 56 (Winter 1975): 29-38.

The selection of a new chairman is organized into five steps from setting ground rules and involving other chairmen and deans to the announcement meeting. At Mankato State College chairmen are evaluated every three years on thirty items. A systematic analysis procedure allows each chairman to quickly identify priorities and areas for improved performance.

Fenker, Richard M. "The Evaluation of University Faculty and Administrators: A Case Study." *Journal of Higher Education* 46 (November/December 1975): 665-86.

Texas Christian University considered which academic personnel should be involved in administrator evaluation. The resulting model is an expanding structure where faculty evaluate the department head, collegiate dean, and vice president for academic affairs; the graduate faculty reviews the graduate dean as well; members of the faculty senate evaluate the director of research, head librarian, etc. Such an extended program offers a unique opportunity for certain insulated staff people to exchange ideas.

Fisher, Charles F. (Ed.). *Developing and Evaluating Administrative Leadership.* San Francisco: Jossey-Bass, 1978.

Twelve authors offer their views on various evaluation topics—strengthening institutional leadership, evaluating the academic dean, and department and chairperson development are a few. The editor describes the volume as a combination "how to" handbook and collection of philosophical essays. Its thesis is that evaluation and development of administrators should be an integral and ongoing process.

Gaff, Jerry G. *Toward Faculty Renewal: Advances in Faculty, Instructional, and Organizational Development.* San Francisco: Jossey-Bass, 1975.

Since administrator evaluation and development may be tied to similar faculty programs, it is instructive to note their organization, implementation, and methods of operation. Among topics covered on internal faculty development programs are financing, staffing, and the politics of improvement centers.

Galloway, Sylvia W., and Fisher, Charles F., (Eds.). *A Guide to Professional Development Opportunities for College and University Administrators.* Washington, D.C.: American Council on Education, 1977.

This annual publication of the American Council on Education assists college and university staff to stay informed about external opportunities for professional development. The 1977 edition listed two hundred and ninety-one programs sponsored by ninety different organizations. These seminars and workshops fell into seven major categories: 1) career planning, 2) administrative role orientation, 3) organization and personnel management, 4) planning, budgeting, and decision-making, 5) financial development, 6) student affairs, and 7) facilities management. Events connected with annual meetings are not included.

Genova, William J.; Madoff, Marjorie K.; Chin, Robert; and Thomas, George B. *Mutual Benefit Evaluation of Faculty and Administrators in Higher Education*. Cambridge, Mass.: Ballinger, 1976.

As the title reflects, the authors are convinced that evaluation can be a positive experience. Their book is a practical guide for developing programs of faculty and administrator evaluation in colleges and universities. It describes operating principles, summarizes research, and displays exemplary practices. The eight recommended steps for presidential evaluation help assess effectiveness in goal formation, goal attainment, resource acquisition, and membership satisfaction. Also appropriateness is gauged in the context of institutional climate, authority patterns, and stage of development. The process can be extended and adapted for evaluating other administrators.

Harvey, L. James. *Managing Colleges and Universities by Objectives*. Wheaton, Illinois: Ireland Educational Corporation, 1976.

The book presents a comprehensive view of management and evaluation in higher education. Its objectives are to assist the reader in: developing a current knowledge of MBO; understanding how to implement MBO; developing a skill in writing objectives; and understanding the linkage of MBO, MIS, PPBS, IBO, and evaluation. The writing is clear, concise, and condensed to provide the busy administrator with the most information in the shortest time. The book presents a comprehensive view of management and evaluation in higher education.

Heaton, C. P. *Management by Objectives in Higher Education: Theory, Cases, and Implementation*. Durham, North Carolina: National Laboratory for Higher Education, 1975.

The main purpose of this volume is to share the early experiences and efforts of those who have used MBO in colleges and universities. Reports come from a community college, a church-related liberal arts college, a major university department, a state university system, and a medical education complex. The high and low points in these cases can help other institutions successfully implement MBO and avoid many of the pitfalls. Most cases include the personnel evaluation issue.

Hillway, T. "Evaluating College and University Administrators." *Intellect* 101 (April 1973): 426-31.

This seminal article emphasizes the parallel between student evaluation of faculty and faculty evaluation of administrators. He proposes a rating scale of fifteen qualities and nine methods. However, his contribution is not with the instrument, but with his vigorous belief that faculty should have structured input in administrator evaluation.

Miller, Richard I. *Developing Programs for Faculty Evaluation.* San Francisco: Jossey-Bass 1974.

The book is designed to help professors and administrators to avoid problems in evaluation such as inadquate planning, inconsistent procedures, and confusion over results. Although primarily concerned with building faculty evaluation programs, there is a brief chapter on evaluating administrators. The need for institutional evaluation is also stressed. However, evaluation is not a panacea nor does it usually deliver all that is expected of it. More than half the book is devoted to an extensive annotated bibliography.

Parlett, Malcom and Dearden, Garry (Eds.). *Introduction to Illumative Evaluation: Studies in Higher Education.* Cardiff-by-the-Sea, California: Pacific Soundings Press, 1977.

Illumative evaluation is suited for educational institutions because of their complex goals, idiosyncratic character, and unique programs. Its approach is flexible and eclectic drawing on techniques which fit the overall situation. The volume is an introduction rather than a how-to or theory piece. Its four parts cover the basic concepts, present a variety of evaluation reports, and raise evaluation issues yet to be pursued in higher education.

Roach, J.H.L. "The Academic Department Chairperson: Functions and Responsibilities." *Educational Record* 57 (Winter 1976): 13-23.

This article stresses the importance of effective chairpersons by pointing out that eighty percent of all administrative decisions that affect a college or university take place at a departmental level. Ironically, chairpersons are selected for reasons other than management competence. The author's insights can help identify performance criteria for evaluation and development.

Scott, Robert A. *Lords, Squires, and Yeomen: Collegiate Middle Managers and Their Organizations.* Washington, D.C.: American Association for Higher Education, 1978.

This is a thorough analysis of nonacademic middle managers—those other than academic deans, chairpersons, and librarians. Such deans and directors of support services are the ones who control the budgets, assign and train support personnel, select the students, and negotiate matters with state and federal offices. Topics include the organizational setting of work on campus, satisfaction and incentives for increased competence and performance, and role conflicts. This is an indispensable resource if evaluation will include nonacademic administrators.

Shtogren, John A., (Ed.). *Administrative Development in Higher Education, The State of the Art: Volume I.* Richmond, Virginia: Higher Education Leadership and Management Society, 1978.

The sixteen authors have been helpful in the making of administrators in two-year and four-year colleges and universities. The sum of their work represents the current state of the art of upgrading the level of campus leadership and management. In addition to reports of what is being done on campuses across the country, the final chapter synthesizes their work and presents more than twenty recommendations and practical tips for establishing administrative development programs.

Smart, John C., and Montgomery, James R., Editors. *Examining Departmental Management.* San Francisco: Jossey-Bass, 1976.

Enhancing the organizational effectiveness of colleges and universities must recognize the importance of academic departments, since they constitute the fundamental organizational unit of these institutions. This collection of essays provides essential knowledge on the roles of chairpersons, functioning of academic departments, underlying bases of departmental diversity, and helps explain why they respond to issues as they do. It is solid background reading for effective and equitable evaluation of chairpersons.

Sprunger, Benjamin E. and Berquist, William H. *Handbook for College Administration.* Washington, D.C.: Council for the Advancement of Small Colleges, 1978.

The handbook is organized around six of the traditional management functions; 1) planning, 2) organizing, 3) staffing, 4) leading, 5) evaluating, and 6) developing. Each topic is covered in a major chapter. A unique feature is the "Documents" section of each chapter which contains real world examples, ready-to-use forms, and exercises which individuals or small groups can use for skill development.

Waltzer, Herbert. "The Job of Academic Department Chairman: Experience and Recommendations from Miami University." Occasional Paper, Office of Leadership Development in Higher Education, American Council on Education, Washington, D.C. (1975).

The paper began as an effort to better understand the facets and problems of the chairman's job in order to make it more manageable and satisfying. The results were gained from interviews with chairmen at Miami University but are worth considering elsewhere. Among the many insights are all the negative effects the chairman's job has on his or her teaching and scholarship. The job's drawbacks and burdens should be considered in a comprehensive evaluation, development, and reward process.

Zion, Carol. "Role Definition: A Focus for Administrative Growth and Evaluation." *The Journal of the College and University Personnel Association* (Summer 1977): 5-12.

The article's premise is that an effective evaluation and development program must be based on an up-to-date understanding of why each administrator's position exists, and how it fits into the organizational framework. From a clear position rationale and role definition, needed skills are inventoried and development plans established. Within this schema performance-based evaluation and development are compatible components of an ongoing process.